The Crowd

The Cloud

The Crowd

British Literature and Public Politics

John Plotz

UNIVERSITY OF CALIFORNIA PRESS
Berkeley · *Los Angeles* · *London*

University of California Press
Berkeley and Los Angeles, California

University of California Press, Ltd.
London, England

© 2000 by the Regents of the
University of California

Library of Congress
Cataloging-in-Publication Data

Plotz, John.

   The crowd : British literature and public
politics / John Plotz.
    p.   cm.
Includes bibliographical references and index.
ISBN 0-520-21916-3 (cloth : alk. paper).—ISBN
0-520-21917-1 (pbk. : alk. paper)
   1. English literature—19th century—History
and criticism. 2. Politics and literature—Great
Britain—History—19th century. 3. Political
fiction, English—History and criticism.
4. Collective behavior in literature. 5. Public
opinion in literature. 6. Crowds in literature.
I. Title.
PR468.P57 P58 2000
820.9'358—dc21   99-051794
                             CIP

Manufactured in the United States of America

09 08 07 06 05 04 03 02 01 00
10 9 8 7 6 5 4 3 2 1

*To my grandmother
Helen Abrams
and my parents,
Judith and Paul Plotz*

*For my grandmother
Helen Plotz (1913–2000)*

I want you to be

Contents

Acknowledgments

A book about crowds ought to begin by saying something about the crowd that created it. This book owes everything to teachers, colleagues, and friends. If I cannot begin at the beginning, let me at least begin where my adult education does: Charles Cave, Barbara Cianelli, and Barbara Lockwood first put me on this road, and the debt I owe them is all the more enjoyable for being unrepayable. John Farrell, Stephen Greenblatt, David Miller, Susan Pedersen, Derek Pearsall, David Perkins, Marc Shell, Jonah Siegel, Helen Vendler, and Chris Waters have shaped the years since, and I thank them for it here, inadequately but with great pleasure. Finally, in ways innumerable, with a sublime (and sometimes sneaky) division of labor, Philip Fisher and Elaine Scarry were the finest advisers imaginable.

At Harvard, at Johns Hopkins, and in the extended net of the academy, I have been exceptionally lucky in colleagues, peers, and students. For various kindnesses ranging from questions to instructions to camaraderie to scrupulous reading, I thank Amanda Anderson, Mark Blyth, Brigid Doherty, Sharon Cameron, Mary Esteve (who suggested the cover photograph), Frances Ferguson, Jonathan Goldberg, Allen Grossman, Neil Hertz, Paul Kramer, Walter Benn Michaels, Michael Moon, Ronald Paulson, Robert Reid-Pharr, Irene Tucker, Sasha Torres, and Judith Walkowitz; as well as Christine Banbury, Theo Davis (whose last-minute copyediting and proofreading was invaluable), Francis Dickey, Mary Hong, Kenny Kuhn, Ruth Mack, Ben Slade, Mel-

issa Sydney, Amit Yahav-Brown, and Minn Yang at Hopkins; Mary
Jean Corbett, Ian Duncan, Geoff Eley, Anne Graziano, Mark Greif,
Jonathan Grossman, Martin Hewitt, Susanna Hines, Jane Reynolds,
Marc Steinberg, Charles Tilly, and Martha Vicinus elsewhere. John
Kucich, Sharon Marcus, and Bruce Robbins are the holy trinity who
read the entire manuscript through, in a professional, collegial, and
amicable way. Jean McAneny, Linda Norton, and others at the Uni-
versity of California Press were terrific from start to finish.

Thanks as well to the true power-brokers: at Johns Hopkins, Tasha
Brown, Susie Hermann, and Peggy Mackenzie, and at Harvard, Shawn
DeHart, Anne Furbush, Betty McNally, Robbie Miller, Kate Tuttle,
and Gwen Urdang-Brown. I should also formally acknowledge the support of the National Endowment for the Humanities for a Dissertation
Grant, the United States government for a Jacob Javits Fellowship, and
the Mellon Foundation for summer support. A modified version of
chapter 5 appeared in *Representations* 70 (Spring 2000), and a modified portion of chapter 2 will appear in *Women's Writing*.

A different form of thanks goes to the crowd fueled not by vocation,
but by something else hard to put a name to—you who mostly know
who you are, you who have forgotten who you are, you who don't
think you are what you are: Mike Alterman, Rachel Bers, George Bou-
lukos, Keith Crudgington and John McCole, Sharon Dolovich, Noah
Heringman, David Hollenberg, Phil Joseph and Gillian Silverman, Rachel Karol-Ablow, Jane Katz and Bill Whelan, Yoon Sun Lee, Natasha
Lifton, Simon Manley and Marie Isabelle Fernandez Utges Manley,
Alen Mattich and Lucy Vinten, Dara Mayers, Chaela Pastore, Sarah
Pearse, Rachel Samuels, Joe Saunders, Linda Schlossberg, Gus Stadler
and Anna McCarthy, Geoff Verter, Abby Wolf, Molly Wyman, and
Rachel Yassky. Jenny Raskin gave years of help, encouragement, ad-
vice, and more. Finally, for the seemingly bottomless friendship that
made writing this seem not only necessary but possible, I thank Liberty
Aldrich, Robert Glick, Lisa Hamilton, Dan Itzkovitz, Ivan Kreilkamp,
Alex Ross, and Alex Star, as well as David Plotz and Hanna Rosin,
the best brother and sister-in-law a boy could want.

I can see no way to thank Lisa Soltani, who is the be-all and end-
all of what I do and am.

Baltimore, Maryland
April 1999

Arguing with the Crowd

In England between 1800 and 1850, crowds materialized in two important new ways. When London became the first postclassical city of one million inhabitants around 1800, quantity changed the quality of the city's life.[1] Because London was paved earlier, people walked the streets in London far earlier, and with far more assurance, than they did in Paris, Vienna, or Naples: Walter Benjamin is right to pick the London dandy as the forerunner of the Paris flâneur.[2] On the one hand, then, the city's random crowds meant that chance encounters on London streets produced a new sort of social life, both a pleasant and a threatening urban anonymity. Mundane outdoor life came to include random encounters with strangers, inexplicable aggregations, sudden eruptions of violence, and permanent sites for encountering others *en masse*.

On the other hand, the percolation of society through the streets in changing congeries took on a hundred guises, with a thousand unexpected effects. Friendly societies, pleasure parks, and what Altick dubs the "shows of London" all ballooned under the pressure of a swelling population. And from the 1819 Peterloo massacre of peaceful working-class demonstrators to Chartism's nationwide simultaneous assemblies in the late 1830s, the working classes showed themselves capable of lodging representative claims in a newly expanded public arena.[3] Used to re- (or mis-)describe radical politics, an old word found a new meaning: both the fledgling radical demonstrations of the teens and

Chartism's mammoth "simultaneous meetings" and petition processions of the1840s came to be called "crowds" by those unwilling to
grant them the status of demonstration, assembly, march, or congregation.[4]

Thus two phenomena were amalgamated by a single word. What it
meant to petition for redress or to claim to "represent" a group, class,
or nation changed profoundly and for good when the crowd ceased to
be a shocking and irregular catastrophe and became pervasive evidence
of both the city's diversity and its uniformity, of both public disorder
and new sorts of claim-making.[5] By 1850, the crowds that allowed the
speeches of Chartist leaders to gesture significantly at the "embodied"
power of the English nation existed alongside the unmasterable crowds
of St. Bartholomew's Fair or the motley Strand, pushing and shoving
without center, purpose, or end. The crowd-formations of the nineteenth century are premonitory of the March on Washington as well
as of midtown Manhattan at 5 P.M.

This book is about the effects of these new crowds, riots, and demonstrations on the period's literature. Both kinds of agglomeration—
directed and chaotic—arrived in Britain as nowhere else in the first half
of the nineteenth century, and both are chronicled in the era's literary
texts in ways completely and surprisingly unlike the records left in
other media. The chapters that follow analyze a series of texts written
between 1805 and 1849: one poem, William Wordsworth's *The Prelude* (1805); two novels, Maria Edgeworth's *Harrington* (1817) and
Charlotte Brontë's *Shirley* (1849); and three texts perhaps best classed
as Romantic essays, Thomas De Quincey's autobiographical *Confessions of an English Opium-Eater* (1821) and "The English Mail-
Coach" (1849), and Thomas Carlyle's *Chartism* (1839). Filtered or focused, bent or scattered by the change, the light that falls on all six is
shaped by the crowds it passes through. These texts mark an altered
social fabric—along with concomitant psychological, formal, even epistemological alterations—in ways that other historical data do not. I
argue that the unprecedented and unparalleled range of observations
about and reflections upon crowds in aesthetic texts comes about because the enormous changes in the rules of public speech and public
behavior between 1800 and 1850 make crowds, variously defined, into
a potent rival to the representational claims of literary texts themselves.
Sometimes the crowd comes to embody all the chaos that a literary
text may revile and yet admire; at other times crowds offer a variety
of new structures that help a writer delineate some future order. But

every text centrally concerned with crowds proves interested in establishing the role of literature itself within a public discursive space at
least partially defined by those very crowds.

In Book 7 of *The Prelude*, "Residence in London," for example, the
challenge of representing the crowd serves as an occasion for Wordsworth both to test the powers of literature against the depersonalizing
effects of the city's crowds, and to reaffirm poetry's ability to offer
controlled chaos in their stead. In *Shirley*, by contrast, an 1812 Luddite
crowd is Brontë's way of exploring the claim-making power of the
1840s' Chartist crowds. If the crowd actually seems to offer a new way
to structure social space, then *Shirley* offers itself as an alternative
source of order, thus producing a justification for textual intimacy
made available only by way of public crowd activity. Between these
two possibilities run a host of others. Each in its own way supplies
evidence of a previously undescribed tussle for the right to define public
speech and action, in a Britain whose public spaces have come to seem
as permeated by crowd action as they are by print media.

HISTORY

This book sets out to show that literature records features of the era's
crowds that no other historical sources can supply. But that claim implies no lack of respect for, still less a lack of attention to, the extensive
and profoundly helpful historical work done on the crowds, demonstrations, riots, and assemblies of the era. As a glance at any page of
the notes will attest, I rely on a wide range of recent work that has
served to make the genealogy of demonstrations as well as the hubbub
of everyday street crowds comprehensible even to an archive-awkward
literary critic. The historical studies that have flourished in the last four
decades—under the care and tutelage of E. P. and Dorothy Thompson,
George Rudé, Eric Hobsbawm, and most recently Charles Tilly—have
established an indispensable basic armature from within which to analyze the "collective repertoire of gestures" used by demonstrators,
marchers, and crowd-members of various stripes. Moreover, changes
in London urban politics, its newspapers, its daily life, as well as its
street-plans have left behind a rich variety of sources, and these too
have been well mined in recent years.[6] Contemporary records of other
sorts—e.g. architectural plans, the institution of the Metropolitan Police as a response to the Gordon Riots, and innumerable parliamentary
Blue Books, as well as newspaper and journal accounts—help fill in

the story of crowds less oriented toward political action than those which Rudé, the Thompsons, Hobsbawm, and Tilly have in mind.[7] I also owe a great debt to recent cultural historians such as Mary Ryan, whose interesting questions about the "syntax and structure" of crowd events have usefully articulated one framework for classifying the actions, intentions, and claim-making of intentional crowds.[8]

A broad range of such historical work will reappear often in the pages that follow, so it seems only fair to mention the work that won't. I hope that the Rudé- and Thompson-led history "from below"— which restored to legibility the claims and intentions of working-class crowds—has proved convincing enough finally to dislodge an obstacle that for many years has discouraged historically minded projects parsing the significance of crowds: Gustave Le Bon's 1895 *Les Foules* (rendered into English, oddly, as *The Crowd*). The methodology and the terminology I deploy are a conscious departure from the various forms of purported empirical precision with which followers of Le Bon have attempted to catalogue crowds. Indeed, I originally conceived of this project as a rebuttal of the ahistorical claims made by the gamut of thinkers influenced by Le Bon's pseudo-science—from the sociological (cf. Robert Park, Neil Smelser, Serge Moscovici, and even to a certain extent Erving Goffman), to the psychological (Boris Sidis, Sigmund Freud), and to what might be called the "socio-philosophical" (Elias Canetti, Hermann Broch, and most recently Bill Buford).

At the heart of Le Bon's legacy is his proposal to institutionalize as scientific dogma a move made by several fascinating early reactionary writers, among them Hippolyte Taine, Gabriel Tarde, and, earliest and most important of all, Thomas Carlyle. All three claimed, in divergent ways, that the crowds that they described had an inarticulable essence. Such claims about the innate and timeless qualities of "the" crowd were made tactically in order to describe and contain the unruly energies of revolutionary or suffrage-minded working-class assemblies— I take up the example of Carlyle's *Chartism* in chapter 5. Le Bon's brilliant insight, however, was to see that these claims might be hypostatized into a set of unchanging models for human psychology and social behavior. The tactic worked brilliantly, to the extent that even works generally praised for their inimitable originality—notably those of Canetti and Broch—are deeply shaped by Le Bon's ability to make the passing appear permanent, and the contingent configuration of working-class protest seem a deep-seated fact of the human psyche.

I still hope, by analyzing the genealogy of both claim-making and

chaotic crowds—and the genealogy of representation of such crowds—
to play some small part in disproving Le Bon's notions. But a sustained
effort at rebuttal seems a futile endeavor, as heartily as I continue to
disagree with the distant echoes of Le Bon that one encounters in writers as otherwise divergent as Clark, Moscovici, Smelser, and Goffman.
The best book in this tradition by far, Elias Canetti's *Crowds and
Power,* has unmistakable genius, but I can no more imagine arguing
with it than I can arguing with De Quincey's vision of "the glory of
motion." Canetti offers no proof for his essentialist claims, and has no
convincing way to link his stirring stories of "male" and "female" or
"living" and "dead" crowds to the psychological truths he claims to
discern below. It is possible to be moved by him (he moves me), but it
is not possible to be educated. For that reason the notion of a rebuttal,
even an engagement, came to seem hopeless. How could anything I
propose to show about the shifts in discursive practices around Chartism's simultaneous meetings count as evidence for those committed to
finding the true lineaments of the crowd below all the trappings of
culture?

ENGLISH

One way to avoid Le Bon's quest for timeless certainties is to start the
investigation of literary crowds down in the building-blocks, by considering the uncertainty that accompanies "crowd" even into the
dictionary. There is no better way to grasp the underlying basis of the
productive uncertainty that pervades each and every literary figuration
of crowds than to reflect on the problems inherent even in arriving at
the core meaning of the word. For "crowd" turns out to be as elusive
as any of Raymond Williams's "keywords."

Imagine the alternative: suppose that "crowd" had a straightforward
definition, not platonic perhaps, but stable enough to be readily comprehensible by readers anywhere without a substantial process of con-
textualization and explanation. One would presumably uncover such
a definition by turning to the 1989 second edition of the OED. There,
one would choose to overlook the possibilities of "crowd" as "crypt"
or as "early form of the fiddle"—meanings that may or may not etymologically cohere—and begin with "a large number of persons gathered so closely together as to press upon or impede each other." Or
would one choose the verbal rather than the nominative form as the
word's true center: "to press, push, thrust, shove"? Here our troubles

begin. After all, the word's first recorded use, around the year 1000, was more or less in the sense in which we now say "crowd on more sail." There seems, that is, to have been a verb that did this long before there was a noun to be this. Refusing to decide if "crowd" is a verb or a noun may seem pedantic. It is hardly unique in having the same form as both verb and noun in English. Hardly unique, true, but not exactly usual either. When one observes, moreover, that almost every synonym in English has the same property—*push, mob, press, riot, throng, group, gang, mass* are all identical in verbal and nominative forms—the gray space between noun and verb begins to seem more clearly the proper home of "crowd" and company. Indeed, a grayness seems hung over the word in all its forms.

Of course, one can admit the importance of this observation and still conclude merely that words like "crowd" are in English a grammatical—and not a philosophical—oddity. But the power of this observation does not stop with the grammatical: the noun/verb, or thing/action confusion also insinuates itself into a longstanding tradition of disputes on the ethical and legal status of behavior in a crowd. That is, there are a great variety of legal and philosophical ways of asking whether actions within a crowd adhere to the individual who performed them: can a person be singled out of the crowd? Are actions "in front of" a crowd more or less morally culpable than solitary ones? Can actions performed within the crowd even be ascribed to any one person, once he or she is no longer within the crowd? Charles Dickens's *Barnaby Rudge* (1841) is in some sense a book-length exploration of the question whether individual culpability can outlast the temporal scope of the crowd itself. Die rioting and you die justly, Dickens suggests, but let none be put to death in non-crowd time for what happened in a crowd.

It might be argued that all that really changes in the semantic fluctuations of "crowd" are metaphorical extensions of the word. Thus De Quincey's "crowd" of phantoms pressing within his brain during opium visions is simply analogy, and the Riot Act's proclamation that twelve makes a crowd, like the common-law reduction of that number to three (as well as the subsequent idiomatic borrowing, "three's a crowd"), may seem nothing more than linguistic gerrymandering. Such elongations and condensations do not, one could argue, absolutely destroy what might be called the essential properties of the (noun substantive) crowd. And even if I do succeed in showing that the word is used in importantly divergent ways by the various poems, novels, and essays under consideration, such differences may still seem to come back to variations on that original "large number of people."

The danger of such coming-back, however, is that it erases a set of distinctions that this book aims to clarify. That to one writer a crowd was a set of bodies collected on the street, while to another it was the dispersed English citizenry of certain social classes, and to yet another it was the English nation, wherever and however arrayed, makes it vital to keep all three meanings open and available.[9] It is such flexibility that needs to be kept in mind when one considers the various paradigms that evolve between 1800 and 1850. This inherent unfixity reminds us how large a role any individual writer may have to play in marking or modifying the ways in which demonstrations, representations, and street mobs are linked to one another though the action or substance of "crowd."

DISCURSIVE COMPETITION IN THE PUBLIC SPHERE

SPEECH ACTS AND ACTS SPEAK

Linguistic fluidity clearly provides one useful way to undermine Le Bon-style ahistorical claims about the essence of crowds. But taken on its own, linguistic fluidity cannot provide a complete account of what is peculiarly interesting and peculiarly mobile about British accounts of crowds crafted between 1800 and 1850. It seems worth setting down at the outset, then, precisely why the texts I have chosen have something worthwhile to tell. Literary representations of crowds in this era are of note not simply because they convey the linguistic and conceptual problems involved in pinning down what a crowd is—virtually any text about crowds will have something to say about the odd gray space between crowd as thing and crowd as action.[10] My claim is more pointed: sustained attention to this place and time is warranted because the ongoing battle to define what a crowd did and was proved central to the representational struggles that define the British public sphere between 1800 and 1850.

The texts of the period provide a rainbow of accounts of crowds in public, a tangle of competing assumptions about public action that may at first glance seem almost impossibly varied. For example, when De Quincey's "The English Mail-Coach" (discussed more fully in chapter 4) proposes a "grand national sympathy" brought to serially aggregated crowds, he does more than praise the power of the national news:

he amalgamates the aesthetic power of his own essay with a powerful crowd whose basis is a self-abnegating patriotic fervor. That model of text as shadow crowd points toward De Quincey's notion of the representational challenge posed even by the simple act of literary publication. In offering an account of how the nation could be made whole by every individual's strictly temporary participation in a triumphal affirmative Englishness, De Quincey offers an account of shared public space that necessarily competes with a great variety of other accounts, each governed by a different sense of how one might make, justify, and substantiate claims in public.

De Quincey's text is of interest, then, not simply for its distinctive conception of a linear national crowd, but because of the relationship that account of the crowd has to other ways of conceptualizing representations of the nation's will in public. Chartist crowds, as I argue in chapter 5, offer quite another way of ascribing meaning to concerted action. As Thomas Attwood puts it in 1839, the Chartist crowds signaled that "the men of Birmingham *were* Britain." Thomas Carlyle memorably and self-servingly proclaims in *On Heroes, Hero Worship and the Heroic in History* (1841) that "Literature is our Parliament" (164); Attwood proposes that one instead see England's true Parliament in Birmingham's signifying crowds. Like De Quincey's vision of a national crowd gathered around a speeding mail coach, Attwood's claim bespeaks a world in which gestures can be made legible, and bodies can operate like language.[11] But if the upshot of De Quincey's claim is that De Quincey's own essay can produce the same glorious feeling that the mail coach crowds had initially enjoyed, Attwood signals something quite different: that only a substantial Birmingham crowd can stand in for the "real" England in the public arena. The two offer profoundly different, in fact rival, interpretations of what counts as speech and action in the public realm, and the disjunction between the terms of the two claims is exactly the point. The most important sort of public debates depend on just such seeming incommensurability, because two claims can be phrased in comparable terms only when there is already agreement about the nature of public speech and action.

The chapters that follow explicate claims for public attention expressed principally in literary texts, but also in newspapers, pamphlets, and other accounts of crowd actions. The range of claims buried in those different sources—but principally in the literary ones—suggests that between 1800 and 1850 there coexisted a huge variety of ways to talk about a crowd, its nature, its extent, its aims, and its actions. Accounting for that variety demands a model of public speech and action capable of showing how various discourses might interact to shape a public sphere within which such phenomena as crowds could be argued over. Constructing such an account seems to me impossible without reference to that hoary bogeyman, the "public sphere." Jurgen Habermas's claim, in his seminal *Structural Transformation of the Public Sphere* (1962), to have described the golden age of a "rational critical bourgeois" realm—in which market news and political debate cohered into a space of "communicative action"—has triggered thirty-five years of productive debate on both the historical credibility and the normative intentions of the phrase. But while most of the important recent work on the question—that of Negt and Kluge, Benhabib, Fraser, Jameson, Warner, and other influential writers whose essays are collected in Robbins (1993) and in Calhoun—has focused on the nature of Habermas's prescriptive or normative claims, an equally pertinent question about Habermas's model is whether it can be successfully modified to describe accurately the circulation and transmission of ideas in early nineteenth-century Britain.

The answer seems to be a qualified yes. As Geoff Eley has convincingly argued, "a wide variety of [social scientific] literatures confirm the usefulness of the core concept of the public sphere" in the nineteenth century (294), but such "literatures" by no means confirm Habermas's later normative claims for communicative rationality. To Habermas, the public sphere is essentially defined by rational interaction without contingent pressure or power exerted from without: "The public sphere comes into being in every conversation in which private individuals assemble to form a public body. . . . Citizens behave as a public body when they confer in an unrestricted fashion about matters of general interest" (1974; 49). But the present historical consensus seems to be that the public sphere through which ideas circulated was so far from approaching such an ideal that—rather than classify the public sphere as either fully and normatively rational or as nonexistent—the time may have come to posit an entirely different set of rules to describe how any given idea, action, or phenomenon ever entered into or came to define the public sphere. I hope that my description of the implicitly contestatory relationship between literary texts and crowds—as evidenced by the twists and gyrations wrought upon literary texts by the task of representing crowds—will prove useful in accounting for the slippage between Habermas's ideal and the actual shape of the public sphere as Eley and others have recently described it.

By my account, the public sphere in early nineteenth-century Britain was not a site where rational-critical conversation either took place or failed to take place, but the arena wherein the disputes between various discursive logics were staged: the space, one might say, in which it was decided what would come to count as public conversation at all. Because there existed no understanding of what success or failure in public conversation might be, every text that circulated, and every social phenomenon that moved into public awareness—crowds being the paramount instance of such a phenomenon—served to shift the terms of debate, to unsettle in a small or a great way the notions of what counted as public speech and action. The proof of that claim lies in the readings that follow: the accounts I give of the day's literary debates suggest that the public sphere of Britain between 1800 and 1850 was the subject of a violent contest to determine what sorts of discourses would count as central to public speech and performance.[12]

The questions that this ongoing debate generates are telling. For example, one important question that shaped the day's debates was whether an organized crowd action—say a Chartist petition presentation—could be counted as a form of speech, and whether counting it as such would change the parameters of what was construed as public conversation, change where the boundaries between private and public fell. In their answers to that question—both explicit and implicit— Thomas Carlyle's *Chartism* and Charlotte Brontë's *Shirley* provide revealing accounts of the ways that aesthetic texts too are imagined to move within a public sphere, in competition with such rival phenomena as working-class crowds. The crowd is an important test-case for the limits of the public sphere because—like the literary text— it is neither vestigial nor merely parasitic on the dominant world of rational newspaper debate, but a vigorous and emergent rival to many of the era's most ingrained assumptions about the segregation of classes and the segmentation of public spaces. To analyze the implicit claim for a changed definition of public space and public action implicit in a Chartist crowd—or in a Thomas De Quincey essay about Napoleonic crowds—is thus to take a useful step toward understanding the public sphere not as a world of lustrated and pure rational conversation, but as always the product of a struggle to order meaning, a struggle at once epistemological and ideological.

Literary texts shaped by the struggle to lodge claims about the nature of crowds signal the existence of a public sphere defined by acknowledged interaction between radically different sorts of claims. In such a public sphere, a text guided by one set of logical assumptions cannot rule any seeming rival's seemingly incompatible claims out of bounds simply by fiat: to the extent that a rival has a public presence, some sort of definitional struggle must take place, and some sort of claim must be lodged. Seemingly rivalrous logic must be parsed, and a response offered. When Maria Edgeworth builds the plot of *Harrington* around a series of violent crowds, she intends both to censure their wild democratic spirit, and to claim that she has found a way to incorporate an attractively attenuated version of that spirit into the novel itself. My analysis aims to document the process whereby the implicit claims of some new social structure such as the crowd enter into the public realm, and precipitate a variety of responses from the discourses already present within that realm.

I do not mean to describe here a pure democracy of linguistic paradigms, a free-for-all of ideas—and may the most logical win. The contestatory public sphere is by no means a tabula rasa within which all claims must be granted equal attention. Latter-day scholarship must remain scrupulously aware of the strong pressures of extant social and political forces that shaped every claim from its onset, and that made certain kinds of public gestures inherently illegible: in chapter 5, for example, I argue that such Chartist practices as growing moustaches to make political statements were doomed to failure, whereas petition marches had a chance of success. A careful study of the era's history is vital to garner a sense of the various pressures that went into shaping conversation and action in public.

Fortunately, recent historiography has very successfully anatomized a wide range of the competing assumptions that underpinned the forms that public debate had to take, and the stakes of that debate. Davidoff and Hall's *Family Fortunes*, for example, has convincingly and influentially explored the ideological pressures that went into shaping the all-pervasive Victorian configuration of public roles and private spaces, and the relentless gendering of work, religion, and family structure. But one important conclusion to be drawn from the model of a contestatory public sphere is that no one ideological structure, no matter how powerful, no matter how seemingly dominant, will supply the overarching and unifying logic of debate in the public realm. Given a public sphere such as existed in the early nineteenth century, an ongoing, always political debate between various ways of defining the public sphere and the private realm was inevitable. One important effect of Linda Colley's recent work demonstrating the importance of patriotism and nationalist fervor in the Napoleonic period—as well as of Adela Pinch's convincing account of how emotions and a wide range of theatricalized gestures attached to sentiment were imagined as "circulating" through the nation—is to signal the need to entertain a very broad sense of the range of competing discourses circulating within the same public sphere.[13]

The divergence between Colley's account of the growth of a consciously British identity and Davidoff and Hall's account of a consciously middle-class and gendered one ought to remind us of the complications inherent in accounting for the conflicting claims of various ideologies.[14] Scholars may even find themselves asking the sort of questions that Wordsworth, Brontë, and De Quincey have in a certain sense already asked: When is a Londoner not a Londoner but a crowd member? When does a novel-reader become a woman? What makes a private citizen into a Briton? Because the era's public sphere was made of interacting contestatory discourses, a swarm of competing assumptions (some class- and nation-based, some gender- and religion-conditioned) circulated through the public realm.[15] The trick, then, is not to find the particular ideology that trumps all others, but to describe the matrix, the shared public space, within which competition among ideologies can take place.

Literary criticism has a great power to shed light on the communicative structures that explain the apparent paradoxes of a society shaped by several ideological matrices not logically reconcilable with one another. One of the abiding merits of literary analysis is that it can uncover not simply a single pervasive ideology, but a buzz of discord within a single text. Given a public sphere not uniformly filled by the privatizing ideology of the bourgeoisie, nor by the patriotic fervor of the Briton, nor even by the generalizing compassion that "humanitarian narratives" create, an author may still simply choose to endorse and inhabit one single intellectual position. But an author may also, within a single work, strive to reconcile, to compare, even adjudicate among a variety of inconsistent ways of conceiving the public realm. That striving leaves the sorts of traces that can allow us an unequalled look at an era's contestatory public sphere. The texts I analyze below reveal an arena defined by perpetually revised arguments not only about what might constitute public speech and action, but even about what might constitute the public within which such speech and action could occur.

PART I

1800–1821

CHAPTER I

The Necessary Veil

Wordsworth's "Residence in London"

What say you then
To time when half the city shall break out
Full of one passion—vengeance, rage, or fear—
To executions, to a street on fire,
Mobs, riots, or rejoicings?

(The Prelude, 7, 645–49)

In the first decade of the great century of crowds, the literary
changes wrought by new forms of social aggregation come nowhere
more vividly to light than in Wordsworth's 1805 *The Prelude*. Wordsworth puts London's crowds to work in Book 7, "Residence in London," by making the unprecedented and striking claim that those
crowds have gone to work on him. Wordsworth underscores his final
mastery of London's self-alienated crowds, that is, by representing the
crowd as an initially successful invasion that requires the mobilization
of a formidable poetic arsenal both in reaction and in a form of imitation. Wordsworth's claim of poetic confusion when faced with the
crowd allows him to claim unique intensity not only for the depicted
crowd, but for the poetry produced in response:

> O friend, one feeling was there which belonged
> To this great city by exclusive right:
> How often in the overflowing streets
> Have I gone forwards with the crowd, and said
> Unto myself, "The face of every one
> That passes by me is a mystery."
> Thus have I looked, nor ceased to look, oppressed
> By thoughts of what, and whither, when and how,
> Until the shapes before my eyes became

A second-sight procession, such as glides
Over still mountains, or appears in dreams,
And all the ballast of familiar life—
The present, and the past, hope, fear, all stays,
All laws of acting, thinking, speaking man—
Went from me, neither knowing me, nor known.
                          (7, 593–608)[1]

The effect of the city's confusion and hubbub here is to throw Wordsworth out of himself. He can feel secure neither as an individual,
nor as a Briton, nor as a "next-door neighbour" (7, 119; used consciously as an urban nonce phrase) to other Londoners. "Neither
knowing me nor known," the world seems to be as ignorant of itself
as the speaker is.

Wordsworth fails to stabilize his perceptions by making this
crowded cityscape provide legible reliable facticity, because the event
has only the solidity of a dream.[2] The despair of "Thus have I looked,
nor ceased to look, oppressed / By thoughts of what, and whither,
when and how" is precipitated by the mere observation—magnified to
a general rule by the pervasive crowds of the city—that the narrator is
passing among people unknown to him. Complaints about their madness, drunkenness, immorality, and so forth are all only secondary to
the fact that in a crowd where Wordsworth knows no one he loses not
only social adhesion, but even himself. What seemed to be no more
than a social problem (I never properly met these people) broadens
outward to a physiological one (is this a phantasm?) and an epistemological one (is it my rules or the world's that have gone awry here?).

The dissolution of sensoria threatens—as it will in De Quincey's
Confessions of an English Opium-Eater (1821)—to undermine the
world's tangibility more generally. Spectacle seems to replace rocky
reality with ephemeral thought. Yet Wordsworth is not simply describing a mental London: the feeling that "belonged / To this great city by
exclusive right" is an actual urban experience, as real as any newspa-
per-chronicled riot. As the useful work on the history of phantasmagoria by both Jonathan Crary and Terry Castle suggests, visual simulations and dissimulations of the camera obscura and "smoke and
mirrors" variety spread so rapidly in the early nineteenth century that
skillful illusioneering was seen as a plausible explanation even for apparent daydreaming: the lines between technical artistry and loss of
mental control came to seem terribly hard to draw. Here, however, the
occasion of loss is not technical but social and political: the whelming

masses are not a deliberate trompe-l'oeil, but the accidental yet unavoidable product of mundane street life.

This dissolution of the cityscape into a dreamscape marks a fascinating break with the literary texts about urban crowds that preceded Wordsworth. Indeed, it offers an account of the intriguing definitional problems that city crowds will come to pose not only to literary writers later in the century (to De Quincey and Carlyle as well as to Poe and Baudelaire), but to the culture at large—an account that may seem eerily prescient. That is, Wordsworth's account of city crowds may seem proleptic because no other contemporary source in the extant historical record—not its newspapers, nor its journals, nor such indirect sources as records of trials and army deployments—records anything like the profound effects that Wordsworth describes crowds' having on the individuals who moved daily among them.

Wordsworth has not, however, prophesied a later form of crowd.[3] Rather, Wordsworth's work reveals certain aspects of the crowds of his own day recorded nowhere else. Not because he mines a deeper stratum of reality, but because aesthetic texts—for reasons I discuss in the Introduction—turn out to be peculiarly responsive to the changing nature of English crowds. In the London of 1800, the crowd's "collective repertoires of gesture" (Tilly's phrase) become legible to Wordsworth— legible as a telling and useful sort of chaos. Wordsworth's poetry belongs to a decade where crowds do not offer, at least to a wide public, any sort of rival organizational principle for what action in public might entail.[4] The London crowds Wordsworth describes offer instead—as an upstart alternative to poetical truth—a way of convoking in public that potently challenges the stable structures of social interaction, a mode of aggregation that might almost be called antipublic. It is the energetic oscillation between order and disorder implied by the fluctuant presence of crowds on London's streets that Wordsworth seizes on, that he figures both as overwhelming and in turn as being contained by his poetry.

Wordsworth's writing, then, does not address many of the issues of greatest interest to writers of the following few decades. Thomas Carlyle and Charlotte Brontë write about an era when aesthetic texts begin to describe crowds as possessing a more rigid organizational structure, and as offering in their own right new forms of publicity. And even Maria Edgeworth's *Harrington* and Thomas De Quincey's *Confessions of an English Opium-Eater* belong to an era where such organizational properties leave at least some cloudy traces on middle- and upper-class writing. Wordsworth, by contrast, is interesting because of the ways in which the ceaselessly repeated yet seemingly unclassifiable crowds of St. Bartholomew's Fair precipitate a sense of permanently muddled boundaries between self and world. In the world of West End sidewalks and East End fairs, of Sadler's Wells and the House of Commons, where being English must be in conflict with being a Londoner, the city under the sway of crowds comes to seem shockingly resistant to the imposition of poetry's "steady outlines."

SALUTARY ALIENATION AND THE FOREIGN CROWD: GOETHE, KLEIST, MORITZ

Nowhere can I be more alone than in a large crowd
through which one pushes one's way.
                                        Goethe, *Italian Journey*, 58

To understand Wordsworth's innovations, one must understand his point of departure. The crowd begins to emerge in late eighteenth-century writing throughout Western Europe as a potentially salubrious force hovering in the urban background, shaping minds without invading them.[5] In the decades just before London became the center of a profound shift in everyday city crowds and their representations, J. W. Goethe's famous *Italian Journey* is only one of a wide range of texts that discovered the advantages of loneliness within the crowd. Though Walter Benjamin claims that "Fear, revulsion, and horror were the emotions which the big-city crowd first aroused in those who observed it" (210), the late eighteenth-century writers who were the first to write about "whirlpool cities" (Fishman's term) would have disagreed. The era's travelogue accounts were quite often filled with wonder and delight, followed in quick succession by bafflement and incomprehension. Indeed, accounts of the undisciplined swarming of crowds from 1780 to 1810—when London was nearing a population of one million, and Paris was about half that size—are often colored largely by a pleasant feeling of sanctioned anonymity. According to the three German travel writers whose works stand as useful prooftexts against Wordsworth's *The Prelude*—Goethe, Carl Philip Moritz, and Heinrich Kleist—to be among such crowds is like being among non-Christians, perhaps even closer to being in a desert. One might usefully compare such texts to Baudelaire's prose poem "Les Foules" (c. 1860), which ends by comparing the "intoxicating mysteries" of the crowd to those felt by "founders of colonies, the pastors of people, missionary priests exiled to the ends of the earth" (355).

Goethe's description of his trip to Naples is exemplary:

> It is a remarkable and salutary experience to walk through the midst of such an immense and restlessly active crowd. What a chaotic stream of people, and yet each of them finds his individual way and goal. Only amid such a multitude and so much activity do I feel really quiet and solitary: the noisier the streets, the calmer I become.[6]

In the tumult of purposeful strangers, one is all the more free to pursue one's own course. Being relieved of the pressure of others' observation frees one's motion. The crowd functions as a virtual emptiness, within which one can escape the bother of talking to people very different from oneself, an escape one could not manage in, for example, a foreign village. Even in the 1780s, the crowd already functions according to a paradox highly useful to the traveler at least: surrounding oneself with an alien presence insures that no particular foreigner ever demands more than a mere physical proximity.[7] A paradoxical distance is established between crowd and writer.[8]

The crowd is useful here as a backdrop against which one can do things that one could not have done outside it: one might call this salutary alienation. Crowds are not horrifying but useful, even delightful, to any self-contained individual thrown back upon his or her own resources (writers fit the bill particularly well). Richard Sennett acutely points to Goethe's remark that he will "*solid werden*" [become solid] in a crowd: only in the presence of other consciousnesses that make no claim on his own consciousness can Goethe feel untroubled by the strangeness of the world round him.[9] One can always, Goethe says, take elements of the world glimpsed in a crowd "one by one," unperturbed by curious gazes. The individual in a foreign crowd, by comparison to that crowd, feels legible and comprehensible to himself. Tumult raised to the highest degree breeds paradoxical silence inside the thinking subject.[10]

Like Goethe's *Italian Journey*, Moritz's travelogue, *Journeys of a German in England in 1782*, extracts deep satisfaction from permissible anonymity. Moritz too encounters overwhelming crowds in London, in which he knows no one. But while he worries incessantly about getting cheated or robbed, the sheer numbers of Londoners entirely delight him. On entering the pleasure garden of Ranelagh, for example, he crows:

> But what a sight I saw as I came from the darkness of that garden into the
> glare of a round building lit with hundreds of lamps, surpassing in splen-
> dour and beauty any I had ever seen before! Everything here was circular.
> . . . Around four high pillars all of fashionable London revolved like a gaily
> coloured distaff, sauntering in a compact throng. (45)

Moritz sees, in effect, a whirlpool within the whirlpool city, a flowing
rotundity that promises innate order so seamless it has no need of him.
His stance above and outside the crowd will go unquestioned. Viewed
as Moritz views it, this is a show for the benefit of the outsider, who
is free to treat the "compact throng" as yet another sight for him to
consume. Indeed, in the remainder of Moritz's book he is ill at ease
only when singled out for attention. He worries when a preacher
speaks Germanized Latin to him on a lonely road at night, or when he
comes across a mast stuck in dry land, which is used to lure travelers
out to "a great plain": the notion that this mast was placed there for
his benefit is the most unsettling element of the whole affair (85, 130).

Generally, the foreign writers who visit Paris and London can be
counted on not to treat the crowd as an invasion of their privacy, nor
to figure the crowd as a pervasive factor in transforming public and
private lives of city residents.[11] Whether they decide that crowds are
"charming" or "frightful," foreign writers who report their encounters
with Paris and London find themselves easily able to turn their attention away from what is most distasteful to them.[12] When Heinrich
Kleist writes letters home from Paris in 1801, for example, his eye for
revealing urban encounters seems as sharp as Wordsworth's. Kleist has
a riveting description of a post office official who refuses to hand Kleist
a letter because he has forgotten to bring his passport with him.

> I swore that I was indeed Kleist and did not deceive him—in vain! The man
> was unappeasable. He demanded to see black on white; he was no judge
> of people's faces. A thousand times betrayed, he no longer believed there
> was one honest man left in Paris. Although I felt such contempt, or rather
> such pity for him, I went for my passport and forgave him as he handed
> me your letter. (123)

Every detail of this encounter suits it for such pathbreaking works of
the early twentieth century as Rainer Maria Rilke's Notebook of Malte
Laurids Brigge. The inability in the city to distinguish pity and contempt, the ever-so-shortlived emotion attached to the postal worker's
office rather than to him as individual, the distinction between faces
and textual evidence: all of these details open up fascinating aspects of
the life of an overfull city.

Yet none of what is most interesting about this encounter ever surfaces in Kleist's published work. He simply moves away from specu-
lating on the implications of what he has seen. The concerns with paper
evidence return in Kleist's obsession with publication in both *Michael
Kohlhaas* and "The Marquise of O." But neither story features the
urban crowds that are the backdrop to textual evidence in Kleist's letter, and neither explores the notion of published or public identity as
it relates to the world of urban anonymity in proximity. As he himself
says, Paris is only an interlude in a German life:

> Of course here in Paris [my heart] is as good as dead. I open my window
> and see nothing but this colorless, flat stale city, with its high grey slate
> roofs, and formless chimneys, something of the top of the Tuileries, and
> mobs of people whom one has forgotten by the time they have turned the
> corner. . . . And therefore I close my eyes from time to time and think of
> Dresden.[13]

As long as there is a Dresden of the mind, the press of the metropolis
can remain safely sequestered in the suburbs of the writer's consciousness. The problem of loneliness abroad is not a trivial one, but it requires little involvement in the patterns of a foreign city to depict it,
and involves the writer in few representational issues of any enduring
interest.

WORDSWORTH AS TOURIST

... to move among them as a bird
Moves through the air
        (*The Prelude*, 6, 697–98)

Wordsworth's representation of foreign crowds in *The Prelude* does not
diverge in any striking way from the patterns already visible in Goethe,
Kleist, or Moritz. In fact, the innovations of "Residence in London"
are all the more startling when one compares London's dizzying "second-sight" appearance to *The Prelude*'s far different descriptions of
French crowds. It is customary for critics to stress in these encounters
abroad the sense of solidarity that Wordsworth felt with French
crowds—or indeed with the world as a whole—when "the whole
earth, / The beauty wore of promise" (10, 701–2). But Wordsworth's
presence as part of rejoicing French youth—like Goethe's visit to Naples or Moritz's to London—is so pleasant because it is both temporary

and honorary, a matter of choice and not of destiny. There remains a fundamental and saving duality about Wordsworth's participation in these crowds: he is completely in them at times, but he is never of them.[14]

One can trace Wordsworth's honorary exclusion from crowd frenzy through its various facets by considering his description of his passage through France in mid-July 1790. It is the first anniversary of the storming of the Bastille, and the event is nothing but joy, stripped of any implication of violence.[15]

> France standing on the top of golden hours,
> And human nature seeming born again.
> Bound, as I said, to the Alps, it was our lot
> To land at Calais on the very eve
> Of that great federal day; and there we saw,
> In a mean city and among a few,
> How bright a face is worn when joy of one
> Is joy of tens of millions.
>
> (6, 353–60)

No writer before Wordsworth had ever made quite that observation: that one can read the effects of a crowd even when only a few of that crowd are present. The crowd he refers to here is dispersed across an entire country, a country riven by war and panic, and with no effective communication system. Yet each person, Wordsworth believes, can be sure that everyone else in the country is celebrating as well: the crowd gathers strength from its invisible mirrors elsewhere. It is a moment repeated with considerably different import in De Quincey's 1849 essay, "The English Mail-Coach." But the insight, however innovative, does not function as it will in De Quincey: it leads to no reflection on the power of poetry itself, it provides no sort of solution for the problems of London's chaotic crowds that emerge so vividly in Book 7. Wordsworth remains as separable from French crowds as Goethe had been from Italian, or Moritz from English ones.

Within fifty lines Wordsworth and Jones are traveling down the Rhône river on July 14 and 15, and they meet crowds celebrating the "spousals" in which Louis XVI swore fidelity to the new constitution:

> A lonely pair
> Of Englishmen we were, and sailed along
> Clustered together with a merry crowd
> Of those emancipated. . . .
>
> . . . .

Like bees they swarmed, gaudy and gay as bees;
. . . .
We landed, took with them our evening meal,
Guests welcome almost as the angels were
To Abraham of old.

(6, 391–404)

Crowds have been described as swarms of bees ever since Homer,[16] and the effect is often, as here, to establish a space between the narrator and the crowd. The distance thus established is to some extent bridged by the narrator's enjoyment of the beauty of the scene—and perhaps by the reader's concurrent enjoyment. But a bridge does not unify; it merely connects. A gap remains between that swarming crowd and a "lonely pair" who resemble that other oxymoronically lonely pair, Milton's Adam and Eve sent packing from God's paradise.[17]

At the end of Book 6, Wordsworth describes crossing France just as the Swiss and the Belgians are preparing to follow the French to freedom. He reads these uprisen armies as yet another marker of his own intimate distance from the energies of the commonalty.

We crossed the Brabant armies on the fret
For battle in the cause of Liberty.
A stripling, scarcely of the household then
Of social life, I looked upon these things
As from a distance—heard, and saw, and felt,
Was touched, but with no intimate concern—
I seemed to move among them as a bird
Moves through the air, or as a fish pursues
Its business in its proper element.
I needed not that joy, I did not need
Such help: The ever-living universe
And independent spirit of pure youth
Were with me at that season, and delight
Was in all places spread around my steps
As constant as the grass upon the fields.

(6, 691–705)

Though he flies or swims within the elements of general rejoicing, he forms no part of the French crowds—crowds who are here annealed into the celebratory emotions so seamlessly that they are clearly meant to be understood as embodying rather than experiencing their country's joy. Such crowds-turned-emotions are in the end superfluous: "I needed not that joy, I did not need / Such help." If the London crowd demands of Wordsworth a perpetual response, the French revolutionary fervor

works on him only during these celebratory moments, brief enthusiasm
dying away eventually into postrevolutionary amnesia.[18]

There is no better proof of the distance that lies between Wordsworth and the French crowds than a passage that at first seems to be
strong evidence of his fascination with them: the discussion of the Carrousel Massacres of August 1792. Coming to Paris in October, Wordsworth looks at the site where both rioters and defenders of the Tuileries
had been killed. The salient feature of Wordsworth's visit is not that
he is moved by the loss of life, but that he is moved by his own failure
to be moved.

> I crossed—a black and empty area then—
> The square of the Carousel, few weeks back
> Heaped up with dead and dying, upon these
> And other sights looking as doth a man
> Upon a volume whose contents he knows
> Are memorable but from him locked up,
> Being written in a tongue he cannot read,
> So that he questions the mute leaves with pain,
> And half upbraids their silence.
>   (10, 46–54)

One might usefully compare this to Emerson's analysis, in his "Experience" (1844), of his own impassivity after the death of his son. He
describes as "this most unhandsome part of our condition" the failure
to be moved to mourn: "In the death of my son, no more than two
years ago, I seem to have lost a beautiful estate,—no more. I cannot
get it nearer to me. . . . Our relations to each other are oblique and
casual" (156). Here in Wordsworth, however, the claim of lost tangibility applies specifically to the sensation of witnessing, alone, the site
of a disaster in a strange country, with no straightforward way to reach
the emotions involved. The relations are made oblique primarily by
national difference.

The "mute leaves" of the Parisian cityscape also offer an interesting
comparison to the "lifeless" book (8, 700–760) that is a figure for
London as it might look without optical illusions—a passage discussed
below at some length. In Paris, the mute book analogy means that the
city is illegible when it lacks the helpful illusion—that is, without a
crowd to animate it. While this suggests the usefulness of the French
crowd—by comparison with the profoundly irritating English one—it
also suggests that the foreign crowd has something of the function of
a tourist's guidebook: it is the necessary accessory that decodes a for-

eign country for an outsider. That Wordsworth chooses to illustrate his sense of loss with a quote from *Macbeth* is a suitable reminder of his declaration of English allegiances at this juncture: "I seemed to hear a voice that cried / To the whole city, 'Sleep no more!'" (10, 76–77). A city's foreign crowds pose arduous tasks of translation. But when the crowd has vanished, the inherent gap between nations is glaringly visible.[19]

In his "On Going a Journey" (1821), William Hazlitt delineates the opportunities and the costs of foreign travel:

> There is undoubtedly a sensation in travelling into foreign parts that is to be had nowhere else: but it is more pleasing at the time than lasting. . . . We are not the same but another and perhaps more enviable individual, all the time we are out of our own country. We are lost to ourselves, as well as to our friends. . . . we can be said only to fulfil our destiny in the place that gave us birth. (147)

The danger in Paris is a relatively simple one. Without the buzz of activity a foreign city shows its alien nature, which promises little in the way of rejoicing, little even in the way of proper mourning. The crowds of "Residence in London," by contrast, throw the whole world into disarray, making what should be decipherable indecipherable, what should be comprehensible incomprehensible. Yet it is precisely for that reason that London's poetical character, its danger and its power, must be mapped and integrated, while Paris's silent streets need not be.[20]

EACH A MYSTERY TO EACH

Here, there, and everywhere, a weary throng,
The comers and the goers face to face—
Face after face—the string of dazzling wares,
Shop after shop, with symbols, blazoned names,
And all the tradesman's honours overhead.
                    (7, 171–75)

The riot . . . is in your head.
                    Jane Austen,
                    Northanger Abbey

In "Residence in London," Wordsworth confronts London in a manner fundamentally different from that in which Goethe confronts the Italian cities in his *Italian Journey*, and fundamentally different from his own encounters with French crowds elsewhere in *The Prelude*. If Goethe appreciates the Neapolitan crowd for its unitary rejection of Goethe, Wordsworth comes to regret in the London crowd its paradoxical unitary rejection of *itself*. Wordsworth describes London's crowds, that is, as an environment where those who should be familiar to him turn out to be far alien not only to Wordsworth, but to each other: "next-door neighbours knowing not each other's names." It is the idea that he is experiencing not simply his own but a general alienation that precipitates the loss of thinking, speaking, and acting in general.

"Residence in London" has a straightforward structure. In the expressive blank verse of *The Prelude*—made distinctive, perhaps, by a few more litotes than elsewhere, a few more adjective-less lists of nouns—Wordsworth describes a post-Cambridge "little space of intermediate time" with which to enter London "if not in calmness, nevertheless / In no disturbance of excessive hope" (7, 65, 67–68). Childhood memories of the glamour of distant London follow, then a catalogue of sights upon entering, most notable among them the reassurance of foreigners amidst the ordinary throng. Wordsworth catalogues his urban pleasures; these include panoramas, and a performance of Jack the Giant Killer ("his garb is black, the word / INVISIBLE flames forth upon his chest" [7, 309–10]). He then tells the story of the Maid of Buttermere (based on a Sadler's Wells melodrama, "Edward and Susan"), allowing him a reminiscence of the Lake Country and occasioning the famous spot of time that features the "London Child," who amidst theater crowds seems "A sort of alien scattered from the clouds" (7, 378). The "painful theme" (7, 436) of prostitution is raised. Finally, with little preparation the various passages of lost control appear: the gliding second-sight procession, the blind beggar who bears round his neck his own story, and the terrible "spectacle" (7, 653–55) of the St. Bartholomew's Fair. Wordsworth then casts his mind's eye up to "The mountain's outline and its steady form" (7, 723) and so recovers serenity enough to end the urban interval.

"Residence in London" is by no means a headlong rush to lose "all laws of acting, thinking, speaking man." Early on, there are passages recording a celebratory joy that in certain ways resembles the pleasure of being English among joyful French crowds. Wordsworth records some easy and pleasant ways out of the threat of mutual incomprehension that London poses to him. Throughout his disheartening encounters with unknown English passersby, a hint of allure flickers faintly in the walks through the "thickening hubbub," whenever foreigners—"The Jew; the stately and slow-moving Turk" (7, 227, 231)—are visible. One mellifluous cataloguing passage reassures the reader that:

> Briefly, we find (if tired of random sights,
> And haply to that search our thoughts should turn)
> Among the crowd, conspicuous less or more
> As we proceed, all specimens of man
> Through all the colors which the sun bestows,
> And every character of form and face:
> The Swede, the Russian; from the genial south,
> The Frenchman and the Spaniard. . . .
>   (7, 233–40)

The list of widely varied nationalities (which continues on a few lines more) is pointedly counterposed to "random sights" that weary the eye. Wordsworth stresses that no threat is posed by the wide variety of characters who are naturally and recognizably different from oneself. Foreigners are a welcome relief because their surface incomprehensibility is comprehensible, their illegibility readily legible.

A brief glance forward to Edgeworth and to De Quincey is useful at this point. In De Quincey's *Confessions of an English Opium-Eater* (1822) too, it is precisely the fact that London is a "nation" unto itself—defined by shared Londonness, rather than Englishness—that sparks unease. And in Edgeworth's *Harrington* (1817) the undifferentiated London mob is an ever-present danger best combated by segregated but peacefully coexisting "nations" (the Irish, the Jews, as well as the Portugese and Russian ambassadors) whose heterogeneity serves to make London great. To all three writers, then, known differences allow asserted continuities, while inescapable difference within a seeming homogeneity poses a real problem.[21]

But the pleasures of the foreign are brief. Wordsworth singles the London populace out as essentially different from any other crowd:

> one feeling there was which belonged
> To this great city by exclusive right. . . .
>   (7, 593–94)

Nowhere else but London can this happen, to none but an Englishman. Wordsworth, it is worth recalling, feels almost as if he has come back home when he enters London.[22] London had always been "A frequent

daydream for my riper mind" (7, 153) and a place that meant more
to the child Wordsworth than "Rome, / Alcairo, Babylon, or Persepo-
lis" (7, 84–85). In this site half-owned and half-strange, the advent of
a spectacle is no diversion à la Moritz or Goethe, but a frightening loss
of control:

> the shapes before my eyes became
> A second-sight procession, such as glides
> Over still mountains, or appears in dreams,
> And all the ballast of familiar life—
> The present, and the past, hope, fear, all stays,
> All laws of acting, thinking, speaking man—
> Went from me, neither knowing me, nor known.
>   (7, 602–8)

This sensation literalizes the loss of "past and present," the free-
floating quality of the "spots of time" returning with a vengeance. Since
the writer has no interaction with this spectacle, it cannot be anchored
in a social present, nor relegated to a historical past. More troubling
still to Wordsworth is the sense that once communication is cut off,
self-understanding vanishes as well.

The Jew or the Turk is legibly different, but the undeciphered, self-
similar crowds of ordinary Londoners present a puzzle that is intractable precisely because of their seeming familiarity. Unlike the purpo-
sive crowds of the French, this aimless perambulation bespeaks a city
lost not to the outside observer but to itself. Wordsworth uses the
rowdy festival of St. Bartholomew's Fair as a figure to explore the idea
of overwhelmingly repetitive mutual incomprehension.

> O, blank confusion, and a type not false
> Of what the mighty city is itself
> To all, except a straggler here and there—
> To the whole swarm of its inhabitants—
> An undistinguishable world to men,
> The slaves unrespited of low pursuits,
> Living amid the same perpetual flow
> Of trivial objects, melted and reduced
> To one identity by differences
> That have no law, no meaning, and no end—
> Oppression under which even highest minds
> Must labour, whence the strongest are not free.
>   (7, 697–708)

London poses the problem of people existing "undistinguished"
from one another, and yet unknown to each other as well. Londoners

are swallowed up in the crowd's homogeneity without even receiving the consolation of coherence. All are homogenized by "differences that have no law," meaning that there is no stable social structure within which differences could be an occasion for communication.

Wordsworth's sense of loss at this juncture differs fundamentally from the pleasurable sensation of immersion and alienation that Goethe and Moritz record. To understand the depth of Wordsworth's puzzlement here, one can turn to the thought Wordsworth describes having had as a child when a schoolmate had actually visited London:

> Above all, one thought
> Baffled my understanding, how men lived
> Even next-door neighbours, as we say, yet still
> Strangers, and knowing not each other's names.
> (7, 117–20)

Wordsworth's insight is that every person who passes in the crowd is a mystery to every other person. The sensation of loss is thus at least theoretically generalizable to describe what not only Wordsworth but what every Londoner ought to be feeling. Indeed, Wordsworth cannot win, for if the feeling is not generalizable—if others do not feel the same loss Wordsworth does—the gap between himself and those seemingly similar Londoners looms yet larger.[23]

In foreign crowds—many nineteenth-century British and French travel books return to this point—the solitary visitor feels excluded from the incomprehensible communication going on around him.[24] But that is not what worries Wordsworth about London. The problem here is that there is no communication going on from which Wordsworth is excluded. He can participate in it all, but it is all like a second-sight. Nothing is true social interaction; all is visual confusion. For all of London to be "reduced / To one identity by differences" means the loss of the commonality of social space implied by the legibility of foreign crowds, or even by that of individual foreigners. All alike in sharing the obligations of physical interaction with none of the differentiated pleasures of social communication, Londoners have given up the world for the whirl.

Finding that he cannot beat London's crowds, Wordsworth next proposes to escape from them. He reaffirms the "unity of man" in encounters with various solitary pedestrians. Yet those encounters too suggest that the crowd's forms of intimate interaction generate not deeper connection but a surface adhesion: deeper voids always lurk beneath. As Walter Benjamin astutely points out in his analysis of Baudelaire, the character who emerges out of the crowd, even someone who seems to serve as a negation of the crowd, turns out to contain various features of that crowd.[25] Out of a vast anonymous backdrop of crowd, filled with staring eyes, figures appear who "took no note" of the crowd passing by, took no note even of Wordsworth himself. There is the London child in Book 7, the brawny "artificer" with his baby in Book 8, and most famously the blind beggar.

The beggar comes at a crucial time—just after the passage in which Wordsworth realizes that "All laws of acting, thinking, speaking man" have gone from him. After gazing without reciprocity at those who can see him, or being gazed at by those whom he cannot acknowledge, it may seem that Wordsworth should feel his encounter with the beggar is a chance to look without pressure, to take a respite from "trivial occupations, and the round / Of ordinary intercourse." When Wordsworth sees the written explanation round the beggar's neck, however, he recoils.

> And once, far travelled in such mood, beyond
> The reach of common indications, lost
> Amid the moving pageant, 'twas my chance
> Abruptly to be smitten with the view
> Of a blind beggar, who, with upright face,
> Stood propped against a wall, upon his chest
> Wearing a written paper, to explain
> The story of the man, and who he was.
> My mind did at this spectacle turn round
> As with the might of waters, and it seemed
> To me that in this label was a type
> Or emblem of the utmost that we know
> Both of ourselves and of the universe,
> And on the shape of this unmoving man,
> His fixèd face and sightless eyes, I looked
> As if admonished from another world.
>   (7, 608–23)[26]

Moved beyond "common indications," Wordsworth is already attuned to supernatural visitations: the crowd has stripped from him the ability to distinguish between reality and spectacle. The signs of mystery come only to one who is already in mystery.[27] This shock is a figure for the lack of fluidity, of responsiveness, in any city communication. All anyone can say to anyone else in this city is like a sign round a blind man's neck.

The exemplarity of the anecdote may take a minute to register on the reader. It is a commonplace of twentieth-century crowd literature to describe passersby oblivious to each other's multiple ways of signaling and opening communication. Kafka and Rilke stage such episodes; so too do T. S. Eliot, Woolf, and Joyce. Here, however, Wordsworth reverses that configuration. The passerby can readily see and readily comprehend the sign, but the one who is initiating the communication himself cannot. This might be compared to the "M" chalked on the murderer's back in Fritz Lang's 1931 film *M*, so that everyone but the murderer himself can read the sign. The narrator can know what the blind beggar is saying only on condition that the beggar does not know what he is saying himself. Even when communication finds avenues through the crowd, each person remains a mystery to himself.

THE NECESSARY VEIL

London's crowds offer Wordsworth a radically strange model for composing poetry. Indeed, he describes them not simply as offering but as actively instituting that new model for composition. Before giving in to the putative force of this obligation, however, Wordsworth slows down the onslaught of crowd upon poetry by offering a mild account of how poetry might be produced by his interaction with the city. This preemptive alternative to the compulsory crowd is what might be called a "small excitements" model of writing about London. Just after the encounter with the blind beggar (7, 608–23), Wordsworth regroups, and proclaims that—despite what he has just described—the most striking experiences to be had in London are ones very similar to the sort of experiences that have struck him with beauty elsewhere in the world. If a scene has what he calls a "finished" quality, he says, it can take possession of the poet with an admirable power that drives the creative mind before it.

In lines 624–45, Wordsworth begins to discuss certain full-formed experiences which do not cause the mind to recoil, but actually replace thought with a penetrating external reality:

> Scenes different there are—
> Full-formed—which take, with small internal help,

Possession of the faculties: the peace
Of night, for instance, the solemnity
Of Nature's intermediate hours of rest
When the great tide of human life stands still,
The business of the day to come unborn,
Of that gone by locked up as in the grave;
The calmness, beauty, of the spectacle,
Sky, stillness, moonshine, empty streets, and sounds
Unfrequent as in desarts; . . .

                              (7, 626–36)

Such scenes are manageable, just as the London glimpsed in "Sonnet composed upon Westminster Bridge" is manageable. The "Ships, towers, domes, theatres and temples" that "lie / Open unto the fields and to the sky" can be granted "still" life, as Cleanth Brooks has famously pointed out, because "all that mighty heart is lying still" (6, 13–14). Indeed, this same trope of a city beautiful because dead recurs in other interesting later Wordsworth poems, most strikingly in "St. Paul's," in which "the huge majestic Temple of St. Paul" is surrounded with "Its own sacred veil of falling snow." It is as if the temple had the power to draw its own veil around itself, a shroud that beautifies it in the hideously living city. It is not surprising that such later poems do not contain the encounters with the city's living crowds that are so assiduously courted in Book 7.

When the city can be compared to "desarts," it allows the poet to become fully involved in the surrounding world (which "take[s] . . . possession of the faculties"), and the invasion is evidently welcome. The orderly external world ought indeed to rule the poet's interior at such moments, so that Wordsworth's own thoughts exactly correspond to the reality of these external occurrences. However, "Residence in London" now proceeds to overrule itself:

              But these I fear
Are falsely catalogued: things that are, are not,
Even as we give them welcome, or assist—
Are prompt, or are remiss.

                              (7, 642–45)

This is puzzling: Wordsworth had said earlier that the experiences he had just listed took possession of him—that recording them was nearly involuntary. So is he now denying that these images came to him involuntarily, deciding instead that he still has control over what he experienced in these instances? "As we give them welcome, or assist" returns to the poet's mind an element of control: after all, the mind is not occupied by peaceful scenes without the mind's own assent. The city, by contrast, must seem to offer another sort of invasion of the mind by the world. Wordsworth thus introduces, seemingly against his own will, another set of experiences that one might have in the city:

> What say you then
> To times when half the city shall break out
> Full of one passion—vengeance, rage, or fear—
> To executions, to a street on fire,
> Mobs, riots, or rejoicings?
>
> (7, 645–49)

The earlier examples of "possession" in the "small pleasures" model are discarded as unsatisfactory examples of the mind's being occupied by phenomena of the city. The sensations about the night street, which seemed to him to come upon him involuntarily, he recognizes in retrospect as a product of his own character—it was fated by who he is, not by what the city is, that these details would strike him. So he tells the reader to reclassify these as the feelings of a Wordsworth, rather than as London sensations.

By contrast, the sights that will follow are included not because he was attuned to them, but because they took possession of him in a quite different way.[28] The possibility of possession has returned, but now it is, we might say, "adverse possession," felt as the loss of personal control to the power of the city's crowds. It is only after this caveat and apology, and with his familiar gesture of prophylaxis by litotes ("a type not false / Of what the mighty city is itself" [7, 696–97]), that he singles out St. Bartholomew's Fair as a vision with true power to stupefy the Imagination:[29]

> there see
> A work that's finished to our hands, that lays,
> If any spectacle on earth can do,
> The whole creative powers of man asleep.
>
> (7, 652–55)

Once Wordsworth has ascribed the power of aesthetic possession not to moonshine or to empty streets, but to a fair or a fairground crowd, its valence is reversed.[30] If the catalogue of foreigners earlier on had an air of utter assurance about it, this one, in its headlong flight, seems deliberately to raise the possibility that the fair is writing itself.

> What a hell
> For eyes and ears, what anarchy and din
> Barbarian and infernal—'tis a dream
> Monstrous in colour, motion, shape, sight, sound.
>   (7, 659–62)

And yet this assertion of mental paralysis does anything but paralyze the poetry:

> All moveables of wonder from all parts
> Are here, albinos, painted Indians, dwarfs,
> The horse of knowledge and the learned pig.
>   (7, 680–82)

The moveables of wonder, like "commissioned spirits," threaten the poet.[31] On the one hand, to the extent that they are contained, they uphold the strength of Wordsworth's new verse form. On the other, to the extent that they push at the bounds of the poet's, and the reader's, consciousness, they bring in the sharpest way possible the sense of a world undiminished elsewhere, one that can come knocking even within the well-crafted poem.

The originality here lies in the discovery that the London crowd, a new sort of social phenomenon, may work in unexpectedly powerful ways to disrupt not only social but physical and psychological laws. Both the possibility of my "knowing" the world and its "knowing me" are under assault in the crowd. Both sorts of loss make their way into the poem, tamed but still ardent.[32] It is little wonder that after detailing the creativity-crushing power of the crowd, Wordsworth asks to ascend above the multitude. But notice how that request is couched:

> For once the Muse's help will we implore,
> And she shall lodge us—wafted on her wings
> Above the press and danger of the crowd—
> Upon some showman's platform.
>   (7, 656–59)

To ascend a showman's platform is at once to seek a refuge by rising above the chaos, and to establish oneself as another sort of showman. Wordsworth's comparative ascension here marks the poet's own status as implicitly responsive to the mutable crowd below (which is potentially an audience as well).

This catalogue of crowd-induced madness ends, after the riot of "Men, women, three-years' children, babes in arms," with a break and the turn to the famous "O, blank confusion, and a type not false" (7, 695–96). But this break is no evidence that Wordsworth is rejecting the catalogue above. Rather, he here invokes the crowd in order to contain it, and contains it in order to invoke it. The confusion now is anything but blank: it has names, numbers, types, and attributes.[33] The tension built into Book 7 results not simply from the fact that Wordsworth feels drawn to the city and yet recoils from losing his identity there. The poem becomes the antithesis of the crowds of the city, yet only does so by borrowing the energy of the crowds of the city. The poem replicates the ephemeral, almost evanescent effect of the bustling crowds moving through that city and animating it by their passage. Walter Benjamin famously argues that in the latter half of the nineteenth century Parisians came to see the crowd as a veil through which the city could be glimpsed. In Wordsworth's account, any poetry that goes beyond the momentary still life of "Westminster Bridge" cannot avoid depicting that moving veil, the shape and drape of which fundamentally shapes "Residence in London."

Wordsworth exits Book 7 by affirming the power of the sense "for the whole" that allows one to suffer such "parts" as London with relative equanimity:

> But though the picture weary out the eye,
> By nature an unmanageable sight,
> It is not wholly so to him who looks
> In steadiness, who hath among the least things
> An under-sense of greatest, sees the parts
> As parts, but with a feeling of the whole.
>   (7, 707–12)

Though the felt whole thus allows one to move into steadiness, it does so by centering the "parts as parts" in the vision. The relationship between the whole and this heretofore umanageable part—the crowd of St. Bartholomew's Fair and of London more generally—remains volatile, precisely because the introduction of the whole depends on the parts' being well seen as parts first. The mountain that makes its appearance at the end of Book 7 promises the requisite stability—"The mountain's outline and its steady form / Gives a pure grandeur" (7, 723–24)—but note that the mountain has never seemed quite so stable, so suitable a picture for all that's "the soul of beauty and enduring life" (7, 737) as when directly juxtaposed to the all-changing countenance of the city. This mountain is bedrock explicitly when invoked as a comparison to Wordsworth's present surroundings, the "second sight" urban reality. Thus in a certain sense the mountain and not the city is the second-sight vision of this moment.[34]

Even beyond the bounds of "Residence in London," the unmasterable London crowd returns intermittently in ways that at once undermine and underline the mastering power of poetry. Toward the end of Book 8, Wordsworth describes his first entry into London. At that moment, with London in view, another set of figures emerges with an exactly analogous significance to the pushiness of the London crowd. Wordsworth recalls that on his first entrance into London:

> A weight of ages did at once descend
> Upon my heart—no thought embodied, no
> Distinct remembrances, but weight and power,
> Power growing with the weight.
>   (8, 703–6)[35]

The danger of that weight is precisely that it indicates the ability of an external phenomenon to penetrate into the mind's own sanctuary. He complains

> That aught *external* to the living mind
> Should have such mighty sway, yet so it was.
>   (8, 701–2, emphasis in original)

Again, as when he had asked to be lifted above the fairground crowds, urban experience has weighed him down with such a multiplicity of images that his mean creative powers no longer predominate. Faced with the seeming destruction of agency, and with no choice of his own as to what images will crowd upon him or into his poetry, he has recourse to the imagery of optical illusion.

> Substance and shadow, light and darkness, all
> Commingled, making up a canopy
> Of shapes, and forms, and tendencies to shape,
> That shift and vanish, change and interchange
> Like spectres—ferment quiet and sublime.
>   (8, 719–23)

Up to this point the description registers the same despair of meaning that the passages at the end of Book 7 do—the loss of sense that accompanies a crowd's ignorance is turned here into synaesthetic turmoil. However, complications ensue. Wordsworth now proposes that such illusions can be overcome. Like the text of a book, something will become (lifelessly) visible:

Which, after a short space, works less and less
Till, every effort, every motion gone,
The scene before him lies in perfect view
Exposed, and lifeless as a written book.
                    (8, 724–27)

This analogy is pleasant enough—if the Parisian book was incomprehensible, this one at least seems to be written in English. But stasis
soon vanishes. If the viewer should "pause awhile and look again" all
the optical confusion will return, "a spectacle to which there is no
end." The pauses for tranquil reverie, then, do not signal closure in the
perception of the city, any more than does the gasping turn to "Composure and ennobling Harmony" (740) in the final line of Book 7.
These are excused absences from the city's power, not an escape.

By the end of this passage, what London has to offer is aligned with
something reliable and permanent in Wordsworth's own character:

        all objects, being
Themselves capacious, also found in me
Capaciousness and amplitude of mind.
                    (8, 757–59)

Yet this new-found connection between the city's capaciousness and
the narrator's inner nature—to pursue the proffered analogy of grotto
and city seriously—exists only within the terms of the renewed spectacle. The spectacle has not vanished; Wordsworth has accustomed
himself to it:

        No otherwise had I at first been moved—
With such a swell of feeling, followed soon
By a blank sense of greatness passed away—
And afterward continued to be moved,
In presence of that vast metropolis.
                    (8, 742–46)

The ability to discover qualities of oneself in the spectacle, or the spectacle in oneself, is thus only a way of continuing onward in the dis-
appointment of illusion, not emerging into truth. This is in no way
inconsistent with the assertion in Book 7 that a continuation of the
spectacle can cause one to lose a sense not only of passersby, but of
one's own interior "Capaciousness and amplitude of mind." Having
lost control over the city's effects, one regains it by accepting the city's
capacity to repeat the experience.

This unexpected side of Wordsworth's poetical principles, this odd

vision of a necessary but also potentially pleasurable antagonism between unmanageable crowd and magisterial poetry, is also sketched in
Book 7, albeit indirectly. It recurs in a childhood reminiscence, the gist
of which is that being reminded of the persistence of the real world
that continues undiminished elsewhere heightens the pleasure of seeing
a play. Wordsworth describes getting from a London play a special
kind of

> Pleasure that had been handed down from times
> When at a country-playhouse, having caught
> In summer, through the fractured wall a glimpse
> Of daylight, at the thought of where I was
> I gladdened more than if I had beheld
> Before me some bright cavern of romance,
> Or than we do when on our beds we lie
> At night, in warmth, when rains are beating hard.
>   (7, 480–87)

For Wordsworth to start talking of an uncontrollable London crowd
within *The Prelude* is exactly like snatching a glimpse of daylight from
inside the theater-tent. Because a glimpse of London with its crowds
seems—but only seems—to shatter the aesthetic spell, it actually provides an enhancement of the power of that spell, a renewed sense of
how pleasant it is to be "on our beds" with a poem.

The urban experience has been set into the world of the poem—the
city crowd has been aestheticized. But not—in the poem's own account
of the uncontrollable powers of St. Bartholomew's Fair—wholly controlled. As the "chink" model suggests, that sense of uncontrolled
power elsewhere is all to the good, because the aesthetic pleasure it is
responsible for providing, like the glint of daylight, would be diminished if the contrast were not vigorous and palpable. There would be
no aesthetic pleasure without the threatening world of the nonaesthetic—both as a continual presence outside the poem, and as an im-
precisely controlled incursion into the poem. If at crucial moments the
poem opens up that chink to make the city visible, then the success of
Wordsworth's poetry depends not merely on a substitutive depiction of
the city crowd, but on an imitation of the crowd's own intermittently
compulsory qualities. The city crowd in "Residence in London" provides much of the poetic pleasure, yet the explicit message of "Residence in London" is that the promiscuity of the city crowd is an exact
antitype to the isolation of poetic contemplation.

Wordsworth has made the city crowd known, then, by figuring it as the intermittently unknown, or even as the force that erases all possibility of knowledge. Because of the peculiar way this urban trace is put into verse, then, the poem tells the latter-day reader a good deal that other contemporary sources on the crowds of London have failed to convey. The city crowd—by a Wordsworthian account that differs substantially from that of any contemporary newspaper report or journal—excites emotions and melts differences—just as poetry itself might. Yet the crowd succeeds precisely by doing something Wordsworth wants poetry to avoid: it erases natural laws, it sends distinctions between theatricality and reality into confusion. The brilliance, but also the perpetual danger, of "Residence in London" is to promise all the tortuous, ribald, mundane tumble of London at the flood, without letting go of the poetic text that has brought the reader there. Like a tightrope walker who throws in mock stumbles to heighten the thrills, or like the "fractured wall" of a summer theater through which "a glimpse / Of daylight" appears, "Residence in London" plays the city crowd's game, but only to establish, in opposition to that crowd, an aesthetic realm—a realm dedicated to the proposition that the educated reader will look for "some sequestered nook" (7, 186), available on the busiest street, and pleasantest perhaps when the roar is busiest outside.

CONCLUSION: CROWD POWER

In *A Tale of Two Cities* (1859), Charles Dickens revisits the problem of urban unknowability that in Wordsworth results in the deeply disturbed cry, " 'the face of every one / That passes by me is a mystery' " (7, 597–98). By 1859, London had already developed the sort of omnipresent social segmentation (between and within neighborhoods, between and within classes) that had so shocked Friedrich Engels and that profoundly shaped the works of Wilkie Collins and James Thomson, as well as later writers in the George Gissing vein. It is a city of neighborhoods whose ignorance of surrounding areas is sanctioned, of clubs for dandies and regions for prostitution,[36] a city that looks forward already to Arthur Morrison's *Child of the Jago* (1896), whose protagonist will commit his juvenile delinquencies only on the few streets bordering the slum of the title.[37] In such a London, Dickens offers a striking exegesis of the problems of knowing one's "next-door neighbours":

> A wonderful fact to reflect on, that every human being is constituted to be that profound secret and mystery to every other. A solemn consideration,

when I enter a great city by night, that every one of those darkly clustered houses incloses its own secrets; that every room in every one of them incloses its own secret; that every beating heart in the hundreds of thousands of breasts there is, in some of its imaginings, a secret to the heart nearest to it! Something of the awfulness, even of death itself, is referable to this: no more can I turn the pages of this dear book I loved, and vainly hope in time to read it all. No more can I look into the depths of this unfathomable water, wherein, as momentary lights glanced into it, I have had glimpses of buried treasure and other things submerged. It was appointed that the water should be locked in an eternal frost, when the light was playing on its surface, and I stood in ignorance on the shore. My friend is dead, my neighbor is dead, my love, the darling of my soul, is dead; it is the inexorable consolation and perpetuation of the secret that is always in that individuality, and which I shall carry in mine to my life's end. In any of the burial places of the city through which I pass, is there a sleeper more inscrutable than its busy inhabitants are, in their inmost personality, to me, or than I am to them? (44)

Dickens generalizes the mystery of London by anchoring it in every sleeping individual, and if he adds the anguish of death as well, he still does not give way to utter confusion about the known boundaries of the physical world. The mystery that in Wordsworth had engendered a dizzied mind and the loss of "All laws of acting, thinking, speaking man" becomes in Dickens the calm explication of the necessary distance of each from each.

This passage is striking not because it proclaims its indebtedness to the social fabric of the heterogeneous city, but because it pointedly refuses to do so. The sense of abiding mystery has spread to the world at large, so that the writer need no longer explain the sensation of loss by proffering fairs, riots, and executions as the occasion for such turns away from legibility. Telling his readers that one will always remain unknown even to the beloved lying right by one's side, Dickens only says what is axiomatic for his story to proceed, with its cavernous mysteries, its sheltered forecourts, its rude public revelations of what ought to have been hidden. The great beauty of this passage notwithstanding, it is unsurprising that it attracted (and attracts now) little attention. What Dickens wrote, his readers already felt they knew, or knew they felt.

But in Wordsworth, the discovery of such befuddling mystery in the daily communication of the crowded streets is newer, odder. Mystery and possession hinge on the descent into tumult and incomprehensibility, aided by the impacted jeering crowd that takes its fun at the fair. The mutual incomprehension of the seemingly compatible—fellow

Londoners, fellow countrymen, fellow feelers—has no saving grace of deeper connection. In Dickens, treasure intermittently gleams in the depths. But in Wordsworth such gleams too are no more than surface phenomena: the blind beggar's eyes have no depths beyond those Wordsworth himself is willing to assign them. Any account of this city's workings will have to come in the contemplation of the crowd's surfaces or nowhere. No wonder, then, that the consolation offered by the Turk and Jew must be so great, for these surfaces are at least definitively legible. Brief glimpses of foreigners and eerily silent moments snatched at dawn when departing the city, or under the "sky, stillness, moonshine" (7, 635), come to bear so much incidental weight in Wordsworth's representation because the complementary task of capturing the city crowd's shimmering motion, its grotto oscillation, produces so many peculiar problems, and abets so little stability.

The approach Wordsworth takes in positioning his poetry both with and against the chaos of a new social situation suggests at least two significant conclusions. First, "Residence in London" is so different from the rest of The Prelude because here the difficulties and possibilities of representing crowds are permanently woven into the fabric of Wordsworth's verse. Wordsworth's own claim that the crowds themselves took possession of both his mind and his poetry is logically impossible, but his undertaking to represent a presumptive invasion reminds us to glean what we can from the space opened up between Book 7 and the rest of Wordsworth's oeuvre. Precisely where representation describes itself as faltering, failing, or begging to be excused, a new strategy of representation becomes visible.

Second—and more important for the discussion of the contestatory politics of the public sphere that is to follow—though Wordsworth represents the London crowd as a dangerous sort of potential chaos, he nonetheless treats it as an important site for proclaiming poetry's own power to define the nature and the boundaries of public discourse. Even in a decade when crowds still seem to writers of the upper and middle classes to be more aligned with pure chaos than with an alternative source of order, those crowds have begun to force changes in the aesthetic writer's claims about the place of aesthetic texts in the public sphere. As I argued in the Introduction, a public sphere shaped both by print media and by sites of open congregation clearly existed in the early nineteenth century. There were a variety of ways in which actions might come to count as part of that public sphere: editorials, parliamentary debates and rulings, protests, and poems could all be construed as circulating speech-acts within a more or less fluidly constituted zone of publicity. But the terms upon which people, words, or even hypostatized entities (the state, the church) took their place in that public resisted—and resist even in retrospect—definitive classification.

Wordsworth's "Residence in London" proves valuable for any effort to understand how the definitional contests about the nature of public speech and public action changed when crowds became a pressing fact of London's social life around 1800. By articulating certain ways in which the crowd's chaos seemed necessarily to dominate the public life of cities without imposing order, seemed to offer an unsteady chaos in place of the rural reassurance of "steady outlines," Wordsworth's "Residence in London" reveals some vital features of the contested nature of the era's ideas of public and publicity. Wordsworth's novel assessment of the city crowd's threat and contribution to literature's potential public power is to imagine that these city crowds pose a threat to poetry, yet also provide a new sort of power that allows poetry to go on.

Public Attention
in a New Direction

Maria Edgeworth's Harrington

Bacon . . . point[s] out as one of the most important subjects
of human inquiry, equally necessary to the science of morals
and of medicine, "The history of the power and influence of
the imagination, not only upon the mind and body of the
imaginant, but upon those of other people. . . ." In this
point of view, if they might possibly tend to turn public attention in a new direction to an important subject, my puer-
ile anecdotes may be permitted. These my experiments, *solitary and in concert, touching fear* and *of and concerning
sympathies and antipathies*, are perhaps as well worth noting for future use, as some of those by which Sir Kenelm
Digby and others astonished their own generation, and
which they bequeathed to ungrateful posterity.

(*Harrington*, 8–9)

The Proust-trained reader who opens a novel and reads "When I was
a little boy of about six years old, I was standing with a maid-servant
in the balcony of one of the upper rooms of my father's house in London" will guess that a productive psychic scar is in the making.[1] True,
Harrington is overjoyed with his first sight of the Jewish ragman,
Simon: as a lamplighter makes "star after star of light appear in quick
succession" he reveals Simon "with a long white beard and a dark
visage, . . . repeating in a low, abrupt, mysterious tone, the cry of 'Old
Clothes!'"(1). Soon enough, however, a vicious nurse's stories of trap-
doors and child-flesh pies instill in Harrington a seemingly immutable
fear of Jews. Quickly becoming the nurse's "slave and her victim,"

Harrington shudders "when I look back to all I suffered during the eighteen months I was under her tyranny" (3). In short, Maria Edgeworth's 1817 novel *Harrington* provides all the requisite building blocks for a Gothic experiment in "solitary" antipathy. The excessive willingness on the part of Harrington to throw himself into a passionate dislike—as well as his cognate willingness, later in the novel, to discover a positive passion as readily—seem to betoken an internal malady that must be overcome if a sensible moral space is to be established in the novel.

Yet for all that, a Proustian model misleads the reader. Edgeworth's real interest lies in the final clause of Bacon's sentence: she cares less for what unchecked imagination can do inside a single mind and body than for its effect "upon those of other people." Immediately, the experiments "solitary" leave off, and those "in concert" begin.[2] Despite an early invitation to spy on psychological unrest in formation, *Harrington* performs its experiments among city crowds. The ongoing effect of "other people's" imagination is constantly summoned as the explanatory matrix within which Harrington's early instilled prejudice can be understood to flower. In that matrix, the London crowds are not simply one problem among many, but the exemplary instance of the imagination Edgeworth ostensibly deplores, a public medium that has become its own message, a vector spreading unease from one mind to another, inflicting damage on bodies as it goes.[3]

Harrington is a congeries of various crowds, centering around the largest violent crowd ever to hit London (a status it still enjoys): the anti-Catholic Gordon Riots of 1780.[4] Prejudice can do little by itself but bring misery (as with Harrington's purely visceral "antipathy" in sight of Jews); trouble begins when such prejudice can be connected to the more palpable physical form of crowd upheaval. Even Harrington's early anti-Semitism is trivial in itself. It becomes significant only when tied to a disturbance in the texture of the fickle London crowd. Real danger begins only when news of his virulent hatred makes him the city's particular prodigy, "Some new wonder," comparable to "Jedediah Buxton, the man of prodigious memory," or "George Psalmanazar . . . with his . . . pounds of raw beef" (7). Such popularity can only be displaced by its like: Harrington is eclipsed as a prodigy only by the waxing of some other site of idiotic amusement.[5]

Harrington is not a novel about the ebb and flow of irrational prejudice inside a single consciousness. It is about the conditions under which such prejudice travels from one body to another, one imagination to another. The "experiments" of solitude and "concert" to which Edgeworth alludes are performed by the novel, with Harrington as their subject: If my imagination can affect other people, through what possible medium can that effect pass? Under what conditions can imagination be curtailed? Could the crowd's dissolving force prove as integral to the novel's appeal as its overt reliance on vigorous rationality? In Wordsworth's *The Prelude* the St. Bartholomew Fair crowd tirelessly denies the possibility of a "platform" above its encompassing pitch and sway. But in *Harrington*, Maria Edgeworth proffers a new sort of novelistic know-how: experiments in the tamed transmissibility of the imagination.[6]

INCESTUOUS CLOSURE IN *THE ABSENTEE*

It is ironic that the beginnings of *Harrington*—a historical novel[7] that was to argue more strongly than any other book of its generation against a unified national body and for the continued presence of resident aliens living unobtrusively in the heart of England—are to be found in Edgeworth's *The Absentee* (1812), a novel that argues persistently for a unified national body, and against any sort of residence anywhere other than one's natal country. In five years, Edgeworth moved from "national tale" to historical novel, from depicting Jews as homeless parasites to depicting them as avatars of bourgeois enclosure. To explore the implications of *Harrington*'s curious mixture of philo-Semitism and antipathy to the English crowd requires a sense of the ideological formation that Edgeworth discarded in order to promulgate *Harrington*'s novel ambitions.

The Absentee is built around those most characteristic aspirations of the national tale: a homeland, a marriage between cousins predicated on national homogeneity, and motion away from the sinkhole of London back to rural Ireland.[8] The plot is easily told: Lord Colambre and his parents, Lord and Lady Colodny, are trapped in London because of Lady Colodny's perverse desire to appear English. Forced to stay in London, the fundamentally goodhearted Lord Colodny gambles and borrows money from the rapacious Jewish coachmaker/usurer Mordecai Lazarus; his debts force him to gouge his own estates through the evil factor, who goes by the aptly diabolical "Old Nick." However, the young Irish patriot Lord Colambre falls in love with his own cousin, the beautiful Grace Nogent, because she has refused to change her name to "Miss de Nogent" on entering society, and because she carries only Irish linen handkerchiefs. On a secret visit to his home estate, Lord Colambre discovers the depredations of Old Nick and the sufferings of his honest beloved peasants. A speedy message resolves all, expels Nick, pays off Mordecai, and cures his mother of her English spirit-possession: a cheering Irish crowd welcomes all the absentees home for good—back to an Ireland where national sameness will ensure permanent, untrammeled, fundamentally unnarratable bliss.

The novel's central idea of national purification depends on the careful purgation of characters who could not be fit neatly into one national type or the other: one must be English or Irish. Mordecai is the force of absenteeship itself, happy only when he can force those of other nationalities to live away from their homelands. His career both as a coachmaker and as a moneylender is, in effect, designed to keep people circulating in spheres where they do not belong. When all is resolved at the novel's end, only the Jew is left unhappy, stranded in London without either his most loyal Irish nouveau riche clientele, or his Irish help—they have returned to Ireland to help bring in the Colambre/Nogent harvest. This is the aspect of Maria Edgeworth that Katie Trumpener has aptly described as almost an incarnation of the ambitions of the national tale, with its paradigmatic "return" to a welcoming provincial existence, out of the dangerous complications of London life and the muddying possibilities of a fully imperial, or global, history (Trumpener, ix *et infra*).

The rules for romantic interanimation in *The Absentee* are reassuringly simple: she whom you have always resembled will you love. And just as straightforwardly, those who have always differed from you will you hate. The novel is all contained within its title: to be an absentee from your eponymous estates in Ireland is to be self-absent as well. The novel's central failing lies entirely inside of Lord Colambre's mother, Lady Colodny. She is the only figure who is in any significant way turned against herself, and the neurotic energy of her self-consumption is the only plot twist that gives any life to what reads in every other way as the stockest of stock national tales. Lady Colodny's infatuation with supercilious social climbers, and the yards of trumpery and insubstantial delusion that they make her buy for spectacularly unsuccessful dress balls are a waste of her substance for the benefit of the London nobility, who delightedly darken her white couches, stain her walls, and rip her woven stuffs. Though the English despise her, knowing she will never be one of them, they pretend to consider the possibility of allowing her to pass. But their attendance at her balls is solely in order to gloat and to do their part in shrinking the Colodny/Colambre estate.[9]

Within Lady Colodny in London, two worlds are warring: Irish affection and English affectation. The result is a Gothic loss of composure: "In Lady Colodny's address there was a mixture of constraint, affectation, and indecision, unusual in a person of her birth, rank, and knowledge of the world. A natural and unnatural manner seemed struggling in all her gestures and in every syllable that she articulated" (87). This is a form of coruscating and delusionary spirit-possession, which most noticeably affects Lady Colodny's voice, as she struggles between her natural Irish syllables and the straitened pinched tones of London that she has begun to affect. Nor is this split merely manifest in a bipartite social world. It is not that Lady Colodny struggles to pass herself off as English in public but returns to her self in private. Though she is marked at every moment as Irish, even in her interactions with those closest to her, she is denied the recourse of a natural default identity: the greatest farce of the novel is that she half-impersonates Englishness even in private. "Half" because the effort is always and everywhere unsuccessful, yet always and everywhere repeated.

On the lowest level of psychic investigation the novel will allow—that of speech—each utterance becomes a contest between what she is (Irish) and what possesses her (affected Englishness). She polices even her vowels—polices especially her vowels. When Lady Colodny thinks of Ireland, or indeed even of affectionate members of her family, a chimeric "true self" temporarily reemerges.

> "There's the truth" cried Lady Colodny, in an undisguised Irish accent, and with her natural warm manner. But, a moment afterwards, her features and whole form resumed their constrained stillness and stiffness, and in her English accent she continued. "Before you put *idears* into my head." (99, emphasis in original)

Out of this slippage in her speech all other wrongs follow. What may seem the salient features of her humiliation all follow simply from this consonantal drift: her attempts to copy English mores, or to mask her own furniture with elaborate foreign trappings—at one point, she even has slipcovers from various Eastern locales blanketing her drawing room, as if a more foreign covering would make her seem more English beneath.[10] The unsuitable hordes of English guests attracted by her doppelganger fetes are in effect projections of her own misguided mis-description of herself as English. The description of Lady Colodny's oxymoronic "successive crowds of select friends" captures the unsuitability of this invention perfectly: those crowds exist only as her attempts to claim an English identity that she can never possess whether her English "friends" be admirable or detestable. Though there are evil English people at her parties, in fact the worst threat of all comes from the pleasant English people, such as the wealthy woman whom Colambre is slated to marry. Such Englishmen and women are dangerous because they offer the mirage of an international union that can never truly occur.

The solution to London's dangerous motility is, in *The Absentee*, straightforward: a Cambridge degree helps teach Lord Colambre that he is better off acting Anglo-Irish among the Irish than he is acting Irish among the English.[11] Once Lady Colodny can be convinced that she is wrong to believe herself "nobody out of Lon'on" (281), she is able to heed Colambre's plea for a return to Ireland: "O mother! . . . restore my father to himself!"(181). Only unnatural mimicry could have crossed the social barriers she had wanted to scale—and the English themselves feel free to unleash a mirror form of that same "mimicry" (of her accent, her furniture, and so forth) when Lady Colodny does dare to cross where she could never possibly be welcome.

Lady Colodny's schizophrenia leaves the novel with only two entirely bad, because entirely liminal, figures: the rapacious agent/middleman Old Nick, and the Jewish moneylender/coachman Mordecai. These two are not independent agents of evil, but they do stand by ready to profit by Lady Colodny's weakness of mind. When she agrees to return to Ireland, they both vanish. There will be no more doppelgangers when the individual is returned to linguistic homogeneity—no more absentees, no more agents, no more Jews. Jews in *The Absentee* facilitate the real evil that lurks within the hearts of those who imagine a dual identity is possible. When Lord Colodny has recourse to Mordecai, the "Jewish" role is simply and entirely to fuel upper-class consumption—the ready cash Mordecai lends out enables the unnatural vagaries of Lady Colodny and the reluctant dissipation of Lord Colodny to continue long past the limits implied by the capacity of their Irish estates to provide sustenance.

Marginal as this may make Mordecai sound, however, the alienation of Mordecai from any true home is in a certain sense central to the dramatic logic and implicit economy of *The Absentee*. Mordecai's very identity lies in the supple deceit he practices in the deceitful city. As a coachmaker *cum* moneylender, he not only greases the wheels of commerce, he actually makes them. At the novel's end, Mordecai's Irish employees return to the Colambre estate, but the Jew has no place. If Disraeli later in the century offered Palestine as a base and grounding for the Jewish nation, no such solution appears here. Being an absentee means defining yourself by an absent ground, while being a Jew means "belonging" in London, yet without a place to revert to anywhere. *The Absentee* ends with two homogenous nations and one Wandering Jew—a figure of fun rather than of emulation.

The Absentee bears an unmistakable resemblance to the dogged pieties of Hannah More, and of such contemporary novelists as Jane Porter (*Thaddeus of Warsaw*, c. 1805) and Mary Brunton, whose *Self Control* (1810) and *Discipline* (1815) neatly frame *The Absentee*. That resemblance is most noticeable in each writer's unwillingness to affiliate the novel with uncontrollable affect. As Brunton's titles suggest, the explicit watchword by which such novels were produced was rational self-possession. Indeed, Edgeworth's *Letters of Julia and Caroline* (1795), part of *Letters for Literary Ladies,* carries the point so far as to create in Caroline a relentlessly reasonable and inescapably boring narrator, and in Julia all the dangers of license, but so bracketed round with moral censure that any sympathy would be unthinkable. We get only one letter from the wastrel Julia; the rest are Caroline's justified rebukes: the good woman has no story, while the bad woman's story can only be told through the salutary filter of her friend's admonitory letters.

The Absentee has moved forward from that representational bind, but—so readers even a few decades later opine, when the star of writers like Brunton wanes and that of Charlotte Brontë waxes—not far enough to move into what might be labeled the world of "portable psychology." In the Victorian novelistic tradition, exemplarity becomes avowedly flexible, so that identification with a surprising range of characters is plausible. Jane Austen remains memorable to later audiences— as Rudyard Kipling's story "The Janeites" acutely shows—because her characters seem detachable from their own social milieu and applicable to the reader's own life far afield (one might also compare Carlyle's 1841 meditations on Shakespeare's transplantability anywhere, or even Evelyn Waugh's 1934 "The Man who Loved Dickens," which denounces just such widespread detachability and applicability of English novels). Emma and Knightley are a readily portable pair, away from *Emma.* By contrast, Lord Colambre and the handkerchief-toting Grace Nogent seem disappointingly rooted.

The solution that is offered by *The Absentee* is, one might say, an accurate representation of the *dis*satisfactions promised by the national tale. Its incestuous closure is a novelistic dead end, perhaps best likened to Hannah More's *Coelebs in Search of a Wife* (1805), another novel that attempts to substitute family (pre)planning for romance. More's two lovers, Charles and Lucilla, are well primed to discover an inner mirror in each other's souls that is precisely a mirror of their parents' wishes. Such a prior disposition to each other, created not by a meeting of minds but by a parental contract, is an awkward compromise between an earlier model of a fully socializable self (one that can be molded by a parent into just the correct shape for a suitable marriage) and the new notion of an unspoken love match—toward which *Harrington* is aimed.

In More's book, as in *The Absentee*'s germane coupling, there lingers a residual, uneasy notion of a familially arranged marriage, grafted onto the idea of a love match that cannot quite be justified by pure attraction. Such a compromise could not have satisfied the readership who a generation later were to clamor for the romantic intensity of a Brontë or a Dickens. More's universe plainly lacks one component that Edgeworth manages to chart in her *Harrington*: a productive passion, a passion that must be disciplined and turned inward to cement a suitably confining bourgeois or genteel marriage. The power of the crowd and unrestrained public circulation open up a new sort of solution in *Harrington*.

MAD CROWDS

Harrington's inception is a good deal more famous than its actual contents. From one country's periphery to another: Maria Edgeworth, resident in Edgeworthton, Ireland, receives a letter from Warrenton, North Carolina, complaining about *The Absentee*. The author, Rachel Mordecai Lazarus, is a member of "the only family of Israelites who reside in, or near" (Lazarus, 7) Warrenton. Starting with professions of her immense admiration for Edgeworth as writer and as educator, Lazarus takes issue with a representation of a Jew that seems to her to reflect received notions rather than realities. It may be true, she admits, that in some places Jews are no better than nefarious coachmakers and moneylenders, but in America at least tolerance breeds a better sort of Jew. In America, it is possible for various sorts to live together, all differences visible but irrelevant: "Each has looked upon the variations of the others as things of course—differences which take place in every society" (Lazarus, 7).[12]

It is from this rebuke—that it is possible in America for every group to preserve its own character, and yet to respect the nature of those around it—that *Harrington* grew.[13] After the eponymous protagonist manages to contain (although not entirely overcome) his emotional sensitivity and his strong childhood antipathy toward Jews, he falls in with a dependable Jewish peddler, Isaac, and then with a wealthy and knowledgeable Spanish/American/Jewish collector, Mr. Montenero, whose daughter Berenice he first glimpses (from behind) when she is struggling to contain her emotion at a performance of *The Merchant of Venice*. Predictable travails, tribulations, and surprise rescues follow on Harrington's decision to pursue Berenice, as he struggles both to repel the overly emotive mobs of Londoners and to cure himself of an overly emotive reaction to Jews—ranging from viscerally negative to alarmingly positive—that verges on madness. The historical content that the subgenre demands takes the form of the Gordon Riots; Berenice is Harrington's reward for conquering both the rioters outside and his own excessive sensibility inside. A Jewish circle at Oxford had first trained his mind, and a Jewish love in London allows that training to take root and flourish. His reward is all the sweeter when it is revealed that Berenice Montenero is not just Christian, but Protestant, and best of all English—her mother, Montenero's wife, having been the daughter of an English ambassador to Spain. Thus he rescues a Jew, applauds Jewish ways and learns from a Jewish store of Christian culture (Montenero's picture gallery), but marries the Jew's daughter as a good Christian.

Each crucial turn in *Harrington* is constellated around the repulse of a crowd that represents the power of prejudice horribly magnified. If in *The Absentee* the central moral problem was Lady Colodny's wish to be two things at once, here the true failure is based on Bacon's proposed object of study: "The history of the power and influence of the imagination, not only upon the mind and body of the imaginant, but upon those of other people." The central failing is decidedly not interior; rather, it is letting others' irrational desires circulate so freely that they end up ruling one's actions or one's thoughts.[14] True, the madness that Montenero suspects is present in Harrington is formally comparable to Lady Colodny's social schizophrenia in *The Absentee*: each occasion of unrest or chaos in the plot clearly tests the nature of Harrington's none-too-stable psyche (see Logan, 109–41). But the Gordon Riots move the question of madness into a larger scale of "ridiculous reports" and "absurd terrors" (148), reminiscent of the "prodigal" metamorphosis of Harrington into a London sideshow in the book's opening chapter.

In *Harrington* the Gordon Riots are said to begin because of rumors that the Pope has somehow come to England,[15] and Edgeworth's account of the riots opens with a man being chased through the streets of Bath because in his nightgown he resembles the Pope—who had been "seen in disguise in a gold-flowered nightgown on *St. James's* parade in Bath. . . . they had pursued him [the putative Pope] with shouts, and hunted him" (148, emphasis in original). The problem is entirely due to the mob's excitability, and it is not at all clear that there is anything wrong with simply instinctively disliking foreigners. The "anti-Gallican antipathy" of the English mob is noted without disapproval, and one of the novel's heroines, the Irish Widow Levy, even believes that some Jews have horns and a "cloven *fut*" (149). It is nothing to have mechanical preconceptions about Jews (or Irish, or what have you): the danger is rising *en masse* against them. That these little peccadilloes of bigotry circulate throughout the novel without consequence works to return the reader's ethical sense to the real enemy, which is not an individual mind perforated with irrationality, but the problem of irrationality as a public phenomenon.[16] When the Gordon Riots begin, Catholics themselves are indeed different from their neighbors—unproblematically so—but they are the harmless irritant that triggers a virulent response. One person's overheated imagination has gone to work on the minds and bodies of others, and the unbounded London mobs are the result.

When madness is not firmly checked (by self-control, or by policing the masses) it balloons:

> The idle joined the idle, and the discontented the discontented, and both were soon drawn in to assist the mischievous; and the cowardly, surprised at their own prowess, when joined with numbers, and when no one opposed them, grew bolder and bolder. (148)

The passion that could have been channeled or controlled through the usual mechanisms of an orderly world finds its like on the streets. In Dickens's *Barnaby Rudge* (1841) the army can be deployed as an answer to this—a reminder that the Metropolitan Police were brought into being in the aftermath of the Gordon Riots, charged specifically with controlling riots. But in *Harrington* the army is itself suspect, and by the time it is deployed the damage has in any case already been done.[17]

The effect of the riot is to trap all who do not conform to a very narrow model of what the "ordinary Englishman" might be. Unsurprisingly, then, Jews are nearly the first casualties.[18] The Monteneros, who conceive of themselves as nothing more than apolitical suburbanites ("preparing to go to a villa in Surrey, which he had just purchased" [149]) find themselves trapped in a city where they are no longer "inoffensive strangers." When the crowd crests in its full force, it does so in a sentence that is itself not quite interpretable, clouded with the undecidability that Edgeworth connects to the inexplicable:

> The very day before Mr. Montenero was to leave town, without any conceivable reason, suddenly a cry was raised against the Jews: unfortunately, Jews rhymed to shoes: these words were hitched into a rhyme, and the cry was, *"No Jews, no wooden shoes!"* (149)

Syntax slips here: the phrase "without any conceivable reason" seems grammatically still connected to Montenero's decision to leave town. Lest that slippage seem trivial, the text then goes on to provide an instance of another sort of slippage: Jews come under assault by the mob because "Jews rhymed to shoes," and even that linkage depends on another equally strained, that wooden shoes sound bad because of "anti-Gallican antipathy." In various ways, then, the effect of a chance combination of words turns out to be at the base of a vast destructive mess. Edgeworth's conceit of the rhyme between "Jews" and "shoes" captures a confluence between verbal play and physical force that can be seen in our own day in Salman Rushdie's *Midnight's Children* (1981), which traces the famous Bombay language riots to a chance-shouted childhood rhyme that triggers a long orgiastic night of violence (chapter 8).

The crowd's irrationality is the substrate upon which all else rests. The challenge faced by Harrington and the prudent Monteneros is not to tame one's own imagination, but rather to establish structures within which all imaginations can be damped down. But how can that be accomplished? Reversing the ideological valences of *The Absentee*, Edgeworth puts ethnic alterity to work not as a threat but as an asset in the task of establishing a properly bounded social space. *Harrington*'s early chapters demonstrate that the power of prejudice in its early internal manifestations can be defeated only by levelheaded family members and loyal retainers, people who would patiently defend one against the "dangerous state of abstraction." Against such eruptions, the novel moves to preach an inward-looking family-based sociality.

STRUCTURES OF DEFENSE

Against the "sympathetic imitation" of the crowd are ranged the powers of bourgeois seclusion, as Davidoff and Hall have so influentially described it.[19] But one abiding historical interest of *Harrington* is that the safe haven of the British middle class is depicted as depending on the adoption of certain Jewish innovations. To treat a diversity of ethnic types living cheek by jowl not as trouble but as a comfortable paradigm for enclosure represents an important shift in Edgeworth's thinking since *The Absentee*. The novel is not so much a plea for reconciliation as it is an exploration of the possibility of vicarious identification and alliance between two dissimilar social groups—an alliance akin to that proposed in Charlotte Brontë's *Shirley* (1849).[20] That is, Edgeworth's attempt to represent and indeed to valorize the social conditions that made *Harrington*'s own production possible includes not only a scrupulous attention to the distinctiveness of various ethnicities, but a willingness to profit by it. The movement from the casual (and effectively nugatory) anti-Semitism of *The Absentee* to this praise of difference by way of far-from-nugatory philo-Semitism reveals something more complicated and interesting than a simple religious change of heart.

Harrington is an extreme example of what both Duncan and Trumpener have suggested is one of the historical novel's underlying ambitions: carving out a new space for cultural nationalism within a larger empire. But it stands apart both from those novels that unhesitatingly preach a geographically separate nationalism (such as *The Absentee* and *Waverly*) and from those that posit the close mixing of two nations as a reason to expel any troubling third presence (such as *Ivanhoe*). *Harrington*, because it chooses to focus not on geographic isolation but on the production of privacy in close quarters, is able to provide a convincing rationale for the domestic insularity that defined Victorian bourgeois ideology, coupled with the strongest possible argument for the toleration of ethnic difference. It argues that only those who have survived the assaults of a homogenous national crowd against the unprotected alien can instruct Britons on survival outside and against that crowd. Jews, that is, are put forward as an indispensable sort of forerunner to the new British identity: cloistered difference is the best instructional site for the cloistered sameness that a full-scale anti-crowd interiorization will produce. It has often been said that Napoleon made the British nation; it has less rarely been argued that the British middle class was made by Jews.

Harrington himself best registers the contribution of Jews in London, then, when he learns finally to cure the temptation to bigotry that had for years made him susceptible to the vagaries of the crowd. The example of the Monteneros has taught him that an alien national identity can come to be valued as an aid to preserving a stable social realm against both mental disquietude and public upheaval.[21] The construction of a palpable Jewish identity within London is a new paradigm for nationality in Edgeworth's work.[22] Laudable domesticity, after all, is the best defense against both madness and crowds. But the kind of domesticity that Montenero and his daughter embody seems only to be possible in a national identity formed outside the mainstream. A sense of possible persecution trains one to weather the possible tragedies of life in a dangerously open public sphere. Heine's 1825 recipe for imitable Jewish insularity resonates interestingly: "The more they were beset with hate from without, the more fond and tender grew the Bacherach Jews' domestic life"(Heine, 6).[23]

Harrington praises a particular contribution Jews have made to the constitution of London as the center of the English empire—and perhaps thus to the structure of Britain overseas (in Gibraltar, in the Peninsular Campaigns, in Canada, in Ireland) as a whole.[24] It is telling, then, that the abilities of other ethnic minorities in London are also depicted as enhancing security and secrecy. The token non-Jewish London minority here is the Irish Widow Levy, whose "credit" with the London mob is in effect a sort of cash that circulates freely in London. Her mastery of London argot, and of the lies best suited to dupe its speakers, enables her to safeguard the Montenero house when the need arises. Her potential mobility too is a stabilizing force: picked out by Montenero as an object of alms, she returns the favor by policing the perimeter of his household. She sends up a quick barrage of subterfuge—taking down a name sign, sending a messenger out to lie to the crowds, and so on.[25] Most revealingly, she rebukes a servant of the house because "when one of the boys went questioning him who he belonged to, and what brought him in it, he got frighted and could think of nothing at all but the truth to tell" (155).

The Widow Levy's trick here, like Montenero's later actions to avert a fiscal panic, showcases a talent that belongs uniquely to the alien within a nation.[26] Moreover, it is a trick that will travel well—something those aliens can teach any law-abiding (Protestant) Englishman faced with the unruly mob. And this in fact is the alien lesson that Harrington eventually learns to use.[27] The Widow Levy herself sets the tone, asserting that she is "what *they* call a *papish*; but I keep it to myself, and nobody's the wiser nor the worse" (150; emphasis in original). That claim of privacy even for a religion as seemingly public in nature as Catholicism (especially in the case of a poor Irishwoman in London) foretells a world in which the full and frank disclosure of the sort that *The Absentee* had favored would only be a concession to the mindless mob. In the Gordon Riots—his final lesson—Harrington is able to prove that Montenero has taught him how to shrug off the madness of his childhood. Sorely tempted in an hour of dire crisis, he does not freeze, like the stupid and stupefied De Brantefield ladies, nor does he rage like the prejudice-inflamed mob.[28] Called into action, Harrington labors with Berenice to hide away the De Brantefields and the most valuable of Montenero's paintings in the collection room that Montenero has just constructed—this they succeed in doing just before the rioters storm the house.

The Gordon Riots establish once and for all—for the reader's as well as Harrington's satisfaction—that it takes not devotion and passion, but prudence and acuity to save Monteneros and De Brantefields alike. Harrington knows that Berenice warms to him here not for his ardent love but because "we were drawn closer together—we *thought* together;—I was allowed to help her in the midst of the general bustle" (158). Against the bustle of the crowd, the affection between them is allowed to grow. Harrington's central triumph is his discovery that he actually possesses the resources to establish a difference between himself and the body most liable to the fits of unchecked imagination: that is, the crowds of London. Jewish mores will train the English to put their faith in well-cloistered spaces and the cash that upholds them.

THE COLLECTION: PRESERVING
WHAT IS "NATURALLY UNNATURAL"

The opinion of the vulgar crowd and the enlightened
individual, the applause of the highest and the lowest
of mankind, cannot be obtained by the same means.

... You will be content with indiscriminate admiration—
nothing will content me but what is *select*.

(Letters for Literary Ladies, 45;
emphasis in original)

The key to success throughout Edgeworth's work is the ability to put
boundaries to use. The invidious distinction that a really useful set of
boundaries necessitates is everywhere in evidence among her heroes,
who know what they want by knowing what they cannot want—and
among her heroines, who know whom they should love and protect
chiefly by knowing whom they should neither protect nor love. "*Select*":
the word implies the inevitability of invidious distinction. The necessity
of eschewing the braying public is the same, whether that public is the
"successive crowds of select friends" at Lady Colodny's party, or the
"fury of the mob" (149) in the streets during the Gordon Riots. One has
to guard, that is, against the mental inflammation that leads to ill-
advised rashness, but also against the magnified public disorder that
leads to violent rioting. The trick of finding stable institutions that check
both at once is not as easy as it may appear. It falls to ingenious Jews to
offer two interlocked solutions—as it falls to the yet more ingenious
novelist finally to overcome those two solutions with a third.

Harrington has recently been described as a conversion novel, as an
attempt to imagine the economic advantages of female text-production,
and as a narrative about curing the nervous body (Ragussis, Gallagher,
Logan, respectively); it ought also to be read as a novel about the
powers and pitfalls of collections. *Harrington* aims to create safe spaces
within which objects, as well as women and harried minorities, are
exempt from both promiscuous reproduction and deformation. The
shape of those spaces runs from a schoolyard that Harrington renders
safe for a poor Jewish peddler, to a plush and opulent apartment that
the Jewish collector Montenero renders safe for his daughter (in which
she can remain Christian) to a Jewish safe house in which Protestant
(indeed, anti-Semitic) nobility are permitted to shelter from a mob that
has with its typically volatile stupidity mistaken them for Catholics.

Always these spaces are meant not to teach readers to love anyone
else who has a safe space, but simply to tolerate what others do in
their own safe spaces: secure boundaries look like the *sine qua non* of
selfhood. From the debate on granting citizenship to English Jews in
the opening pages—the child Harrington demands to know how one

can "naturalize what's naturally unnatural"(17)—to the revelation at the book's end that Montenero has raised and sheltered a Christian daughter, the novel strives not to naturalize the unnatural, but to keep the unnatural naturally present, in a safe space down the street somewhere. The height of collecting is to treat one's own daughter as part of one's collection, a part transferable to another in due course.[29]

The logic of well-sealed collections is exemplified early on when a polite schoolboy asks the Jewish peddler Isaac not whether his father is "good" (how could one expect that of a Jew?) but rather whether he is "good to you" (24). The personalization is a telling one, for it elevates private criteria, and implicitly disallows the notion of objective criteria for the goodness of any sort of familial bonds. Whatever makes familial intercourse good must occur away from the prying, evaluative eyes of any (Christian) outsiders. The novel has already begun to formulate a critique of the Gordon Rioters' inquisitorial zeal for disclosing identities. To ask of a Jew's father only that he be "good to you" allows particularized domesticity to flourish unaltered by public exigencies.[30]

In public, confusion is rampant and potentially deadly. Jew and actor playing Jew are confused for each other (at a performance of *The Merchant of Venice*, it is a Christian actress playing Jessica rather than Berenice Montenero who is praised as the lovely Jewess). That which is hidden by a social alliance between manifestly different ethnic groups is safe (Isaac the Jewish peddler, for instance, is twice sheltered by Harrington from Mowbray's wrath), while that which goes public is always imperiled. When in doubt, button up. It should not come as a surprise then—although it marks a significant shift from the sort of "bardic nationalism" Trumpener finds in Edgeworth's earlier works— that the safeguarding of Montenero's collection is the central event in the novel's depiction of the Gordon Riots. During the Gordon Riots, an unfinished "apartment" within which Montenero's pictures are meant to be both stored and shown is put to use as a riot-proof repository for objects and people alike.[31] The room into which Harrington puts Montenero's "inestimable" pictures—before he has even disposed of the De Brantefield ladies—is a classic collector's interior, worthy of de Sade. It

> had no window opening onto the street: it was lighted by a sky-light; it had no communication with any of the apartments in the house, except with the back drawing-room; . . . there was no access to the picture-gallery but by a concealed door behind the gobelin tapestry. (158)

The power of that room comes from Harrington's willingness to move both pictures and people into it—but it also depends on the Monteneros' ethnic expertise in squirreling things away.

The cash-rich collector is not what the outside world makes him, nor indeed even what the outside world knows him as.[32] Montenero's apparent identity as a "wandering Jew," moving light-footed through an undifferentiated world (he almost goes back to America, the land of perpetual homelessness), conceals his portable homeland: a collection of precious objects. That Mr. Montenero, like the "Jewish" in *Castle Rackrent* with her "diamond cross," is a collector of Christian objects is no cause for opprobrium in this book: he is worthy of esteem partly because he properly esteems those Christian art-works that he did not himself make. The "Murillos" and "Castillos" that he tucks away are an open tribute to the genius that Montenero ungrudgingly attributes to Christian art.[33] What Montenero proclaims as his and as the Jewish contribution is not to be—or even to be related to—a painterly genius. Instead, he styles himself the genius who preserves. He ensures that a legacy, unmistakably Christian, will be transmitted to further Christian generations.

The trope of Jew as collector extends even farther. Montenero's protection of his own daughter, his decision to raise her as Christian in honor of her mother, is the ultimate act of collecting. This ending is not a deus ex machina that allows Harrington to wed Berenice by way of "conversion *manqué*,"[34] for happiness hinges here not on conversion, but rather on a revelation about the stable power of collections. There has to be a meeting of hearts, and yet Berenice's feminine modesty demands the discovery of her enduring constancy. Only within a collection can all remain changeless while everything changes.[35]

Within the context of a novel partially about the virtues of collecting, and of restricting circulation, nothing can be more logical than a father who treats his daughter as the only legacy of his beloved wife. Montenero practices toward Berenice the same loyalty that he practices toward the Christian artworks: they are "representations," just as Berenice is a representation of her English, Christian mother. He keeps her, like those paintings, undamaged for the day when she will be handed off to another.[36] To pass her on to Harrington, then, is not to restore her to the world of circulation, but to teach Harrington the Jewish lesson of collecting: the living legacy of Christianity stored in Berenice is revived precisely insofar as its bearers are willing to disappear back into Jewish-style privacy.[37]

In fact, the novel's final line is a correction to Harrington's father, who attempts to praise Montenero as a "good Christian" for what he has done for his daughter. When Berenice "gently" suggests "and why not a good Jew?" (208), she is not simply equating Jew and Christian, not simply saying that anyone who behaves as a good Christian might just as well behave as a good Jew. Instead, she is instituting a new term of praise. Montenero has been the supremely good Jew in husbanding Berenice-as-legacy until she can be allowed to enter into limited recirculation.[38]

CASH FOR THE CACHE

At the center of *Harrington* is a simple and an intractable question: how to retain national characteristics, in a cosmopolitan city, without treating them as sites for invidious comparison, and for mutual charges of "unnatural" acts? How, that is, to distinguish between a stranger's being "good" and his being "good to" his own family? One answer to that puzzle is the collection. The advantages of a room with no window and only a hidden door are obvious when it comes to evading the overeager "sociality" of a visit from the mob. If the power of the crowd produces as its counterbalance only the need for a public discourse that promotes segregation at all costs, then the collection looks like an exemplary instance of the powers of art to arrest the unsalutary circulation that the "sympathetic imitation" of the crowd best personifies.

Are such barricades enough, however, taken in themselves, to ensure both protection from the truly dangerous and limited intercourse with those who differ? What mechanisms allow talking over the walls? Indeed, this line of questions almost inevitably involves self-reference: if a novelist wishes to position her novel as aligned with strategies of containment that make explicit the distinction between the stable bases of (invisible) social familiarity and the dangerous circulation of potentially classless public space, how can she find a paradigmatic figure for the inevitable circulation that must occur in any society? How does one produce privacy that allows the transaction of social business yet precludes familiarity?

Harrington's answers to these questions all hinge, at least initially, upon the possibility of limited interchange between well-fortified private spaces. The social value of cash in *Harrington* stems from the realization that an instrument which seems to liquefy social institutions can also at times—when deployed by an expert like Montenero—be used to solidify them.[39] The semi-liquid power of cash stands in marked contrast to the most liquid force of all—the magnified power of crowd prejudice, with its free-form emotional motility. One of the central revelations of *Harrington* is that the very fact of solvent mobility (and collecting is oddly a part of that mobility) can sometimes defeat the crowd, that larger, more ominous form of mobility. Cash can provide the Jew with a way of cloaking a true identity that lies buried somewhere within the depths of a capacious house.[40]

Just as linguistic fluency allows the Irish Widow Levy to save the Monteneros from the homogenous and linguistically clumsy mob, the Jews of this novel will turn out to be expert at deploying capital to preserve what they treasure—or what Christian society treasures—in a state of safety and perpetual sameness. That is, they can use cash not to add to society's fluidity, but to arrest it. Montenero's most important boast is that money was invented by the Jews so that "all our property . . . could be carried unseen in a pocket-book" (96). Such perfect portability could certainly seem to threaten disintegration, rather than to promise the preservation of valuables elsewhere. But the Jewish invention will linger precisely because it promotes controlled association among households—or ethnic groups, or nations—that are themselves something very like small collections. For transactions among worlds otherwise detached from one another, the appeal of cash lies in its fungibility: *pecunia non olet* [money has no odor].

The best examples of the protective purposes that cash serves come via Montenero's actions. Montenero's fungible collection itself is a sterling example: it can, when necessary, serve as money to avert a bank riot. The "small but valuable collection of pictures which [Montenero] had been many years in forming" (70) is enhanced in value infinitely by Montenero's intimate knowledge of the financial system. In a threatened bank run Montenero promises "a few of these pictures" (175) as collateral for Harrington's father's deposits. Montenero's paintings are in bank vaults, and the business is accomplished (the paintings effectively transferred to Lord Harrington) with a single letter.

This use of the banking system may be seen as effectively inverting the usual uses of cash. The inherently vulnerable (cash held in a bank) can with a single letter be converted into what will infallibly be convertible, if it is stored as pictures from Montenero's collection. This is, however, also a virtual abstraction of the quality of cash. It suggests that cash really consists of a creditable transfer of goods within a fully dispersed system of banking communication. And this clever dispersal—a compromise between Jewish invention, Jewish money-manipulator, and the world of English banking—is precisely the sort of money that will beat the bank-riot crowd at its own game.[41] Ironically, a riot—symbol of the excessive fluidity and unrestrained circulation of "imagination"—impends precisely because the rioters fear the limits on circulation of money: they fear that all of the cash in the bank will be exhausted. The key infusion of freely flowing cash (in the form of the portable paintings just rescued from another mob!) forestalls the very different extension of promiscuous circulation that would have taken place had the rioters themselves entered the vaults.[42]

It has correctly been argued that in Edgeworth "a creditable character supplants property as the basis for commercial relations" (Michals, 13), but in a bank panic such credit stands to be lost if cash is allowed to return to a merely physical state. Thus the deployment of credit implied in the Jewish proficiency in property transfer is of vital importance (like the "credit" with the crowd that the Widow Levy spends protecting the Montenero house). The acceptance of the Jewish ability to supply credit in this form demonstrates that stability depends (ironically, but not paradoxically) upon freely circulating trust between diverse types within the "upper orders." It depends on an alliance between those whose property, like Lord Harrington's, is in land (he has thirty thousand pounds in the bank only because he just sold an "estate" to get the ready cash for an election[43]) and those whose skill lies in the rapid transfer of capital.

In fact, the novel's most overt foray into self-referentiality exactly depends upon Montenero's application of speedy fiscal power to a problem of excessive artistic power. Montenero's ready wealth allows him to buy at auction an anti-Semitic painting called "The Dentition of the Jews." Had he not done so, it would have been reproduced by an associate of the protean villain Mowbray as a print and circulated throughout London.[44] The ready use of cash to shut down the liquid circulation of bigotry—that is, the magnification of one picture into a thousand prints—suggests that the collector is always, even when laying out cash, committed to the principle of limited circulation.[45]

When Montenero assures Harrington that he can "see this picture to be what it really is, a very poor performance" (103), he is not merely evaluating the quality of the picture. What Montenero's remark registers is the way in which an anti-Semitic print might be deployed—as thousands of copies plastered all over London—so that it could "perform" just as a Shakespearean actor (or a Christian playing the role of a Jewish beggar) might. That is, perform the task of inflaming hatred. What Montenero does when he buys a painting—whether he destroys it or installs it in his windowless room—is to arrest its free circulation. When he destroys this painting, he does so at a dinner party in front of a select group of friends, cutting it to pieces in a remarkably histrionic way.[46]

It is in this light that one should evaluate Montenero's invitation to Harrington and his mother to view his paintings. He intends not indiscreet but limited circulation; not "the fatal desire of universal applause" (*Letters for Literary Ladies*, 13) but the wish to "select" the "admiration" of the "enlightened individual." This is a particularizing act of audience creation, to be directly counterposed to the sort of "fatal" circulation that produces the crowd's anti-Semitism. Buy Murillos to hoard them, buy hate-art to destroy it: in both cases you have used liquidity to reinforce the dry stability of the safely separate household.

Yet this valorization of cash, collections, and their Jewish advocates cannot end on an entirely harmonious note. A problem remains. The production of the safe spaces of the collection, as well as the use of cash to allow "select" communication between collection and outside world, seem in certain ways to be pointedly designed to shut down just the sort of communication upon which the novel itself depends. We seem to be in a world where communication between well-collected households by way of impersonal fiduciary transactions has room neither for the novel's prime selling point, romantic involvement, nor indeed for the novel itself.[47]

Edgeworth may not explicitly figure her own novel as an instance of the circulation of "print" copies all over London: after all, the print in question would have caused prejudice, while her novel (or "moral tale") is intended to dispel it. But there is some reason for Edgeworth to register unease about the power of either cash or collection—in the hands of Montenero—to militate against the sort of unrestrained circulation upon which a novel apparently depends. Cash depersonalizes, yet the novel depends upon vicariously involving the reader in what cannot be other than a personal way: how else could sympathy of any sort be generated? On the one hand, the hermeticization of collections seems to deny emotional intercourse altogether, while cash reinstates circulation in a limited way; on the other hand, the crowd is an emotional firecracker. The question is whether a space can be found for a form of emulation between the prudent restraints offered by collections and cash and the alarming license of an irrational crowd.

"INVERTED SYMPATHY" AND NOVELISTIC TRANSPORT

The triumph of Montenero's rationality seems to be the production of the same in Harrington, who finally learns what it is to be exposed to the powers of irrational "sympathetic imitation," and yet not to succumb to them. If such pure blissful indifference to the emotions of lesser men is to be his goal, there can be no better litmus test for Harrington than his walks among the post-Gordon Riot crowds, in which he demonstrates his ability to refuse to reciprocate uncontrolled emotions.[48] The villain Mowbray has persisted in circulating rumors that Harrington's passion—his "excessive sensibility"—is actually a forerunner of madness. In the Monteneros' eyes the rumors seem plausible: they see Harrington's emotional flightiness—his tendency to prose floridly and to apostrophize great dead Englishmen in the Tower—as a symptom of potential lunacy. To scotch the rumors about his seeming irrationality, Harrington must do something more than Montenero and Berenice (who flee to Surrey on the weekends) are ever required to do. He must face the crowd not over a barricade, but by walking among them.

Harrington's action against the London crowd, which represents that same irrationality that had defined his own childhood, proves invaluable in rescuing him from the "dangerous state of abstraction" into which he had fallen. He knows he has succeeded when he can walk with the feeling of utmost solitude "all day in those streets where I was not likely to meet with anyone who knew me. . . . an individual can never feel more completely alone than in the midst of a crowded metropolis" (178). Overcoming that temptation to meld with the crowd, he can recognize his central accomplishment: to return to a safe space within which he and his allies—Jewish, Catholic, and Protestant alike—can hide from the chaos outside.

Yet these lessons in rational self-collection come to Harrington through an indefensible mimetic attachment to a set of Jews. In a striking instance of the sort of logical inconsistency that makes this book so illuminating of the logic that variously structured many of the novels of the day, Harrington's emotional stoicism actively depends on the very weaknesses that had made him so easily molded by his childhood nurse. It is through emotional imitation that Harrington learns not to fall prey to emotional imitation.

Consider Harrington's first adult experience, his successful Oxford education. Given Edgeworth's interest in replacing Passion with Reason, it would be logical for her to bifurcate the attractions of a college education: on the one hand license and the evils of emulation (falling in with a bad crowd), on the other cerebral illumination and the virtues of self-collection (going your own way). Edgeworth does offer two pedagogical alternatives, but surprising ones:

> There are usually two sets [at the university]: if he should join the dissipated set, it is all over with him, he learns nothing; but if he should get into the set with whom science and literature are in fashion, he acquires knowledge and a taste for knowledge; with all the ardour inspired by sympathy and emulation, with all the facility afforded by public libraries and public lectures. (31)

The publicity of these lectures and libraries, then, turns out to be positively aligned with the "sympathy and emulation" that real enlightenment requires. Walking in the streets so as to prove one's immunity to passions is fine for those who have already avoided the snare of bad companions, but for those to whom bad companions (bad crowds, bad cities, bad Protestantism) remain a living lure, emulating a learned Oxford Jew is the only path. There exists no pure *via contemplativa*.

The pattern thus established resonates importantly through the novel. Harrington may seem to justify a new kind of heterogeneous hermeticism with a surprising space for ethnic alterity: let your father be "good to you" over there, my father will be good to me over here, and we will lend each other money as needed. But one can also see that new logic immediately talking itself into a corner. For the virtues of the new Jewish innovations—collections and cash—turn out to have their attendant vices. And these vices are prominently on display. If the essence of a successful identity is the (Jewish) construction of the secreted selves, selves that meet only in the (Jewish) medium of money (which seems to provide little more than safe communication between one collection and another), what impetus can there be ever to overcome those boundaries, to anneal those of different sorts together?

Reading *Harrington* alongside contemporary novels that seem to share its ideological ambit can make its resolution seem to contain no more than a general affirmation of necessary social boundaries. One might compare it to *Ivanhoe*, for example, where the concluding marriage seems almost explicitly designed to highlight the successful exclusion of a Jewish presence.[49] Thus in *The Absentee*, the only happy solution is separation, and Colambre and Grace represent the extreme of hermeticism. In *Harrington*, too, there may seem to be a tendency toward the sort of inevitable coupling-against-the-odds that seems to act as a dignified stopper to the action, assuring a resolution into silent matrimony. This would appear to be one of the features that marks Edgeworth's as a historical novel in the lineage that Ian Duncan has well described, following Lukacs, as "double representation of individual and collective life" (51).

According to the overt logic of the book, it is precisely Harrington's continued reserve about full union with a Jewish Montenero that eventually wins him Montenero's (Christian) daughter. As Mr. Montenero says, "My daughter was determined never to marry any man who could be induced to sacrifice religion and principle to interest or to passion" (204). When their "true" concordance in religion is revealed, "passion" is seemingly overcome for a prudent union based on homogeneity, a process that should bring to mind the similar short-circuiting of desire in Hanna More's *Coelebs in Search of a Wife* (1805). It may seem almost like the marriage of Grace and Lord Colambre: only those who have already been made similar can reassert their similarity by marriage.

But the new emotional economy *Harrington* establishes itself makes that solution unsatisfying. Between collections and crowds there is indeed a third way, but it is not comparable to an Oxford education acquired without any sympathy and emulation. Nor is it analogous in any way to newspapers, to coffee-shops, to the "rational critical bourgeois" conversation that Habermas argues is inextricably intertwined with the definition of a public sphere.[50] Rather, this middle way has inevitably to traffic in the very form of irrational imitation that the crowd exemplifies throughout the novel. For the end of *Harrington* is a ruse, a perfect seal in a situation that actually suggests anything but. As a resolution, it leaves a vital lacuna. The apparent closure built into the novel cannot fully explain the passions (excoriated but necessary) that brought Harrington to the brink of breaking the barrier upon which all this happy social decorum rests. Harrington was willing to marry Berenice across ethnic lines. To be willing to violate such rules, yet not to have to, may bespeak an unexpectedly happy ending; but it also signals complications lurking just below the surface.

Harrington raises questions about the force of the imagination that cannot be laid to rest easily. The complications left latent in the novel's triumphant trot toward marriage emerge in their most vivid formulation, predictably enough, in the description of Harrington's drift toward desire: the rationale for his attraction to Berenice. *Harrington's* interest in alliance without integration—that is, in a world of collected selves who coexist without undue intimacy in a heterogeneous London—is brought to its most extreme test quite early in the novel. The scene is the performance of *The Merchant of Venice* at which Harrington first catches sight of Berenice Montenero.[51] Harrington's early anti-Semitism, his friendships with poor Jews, his overactive imagination, all find release in this quick juxtaposition of Berenice Montenero and Shakespeare's words. Harrington discovers within himself a power for vicarious identification that the reader last saw in Harrington's childhood, when he grew pale at the sight of the word Jew on a printed page (14). If at that early stage such a strenuous transfer of emotion had no outlet, seemed merely freakish, here under the sign of sexual desire the power of identification takes on a new, and exceedingly odd, sort of power. This power is not the same as the crowd's destructive desires but nonetheless bears uncomfortable resemblances to its emotional motility and indifference to conventional social barriers.

Harrington's identification with Berenice begins, paradoxically (and yet entirely consistently with Edgeworth's strictures on female modesty) with "an indescribable expression in the air of the back of her head and neck" (59). He glimpses that neck when Berenice is embarrassed by being forced unwittingly to witness *The Merchant of Venice*, a play that cannot help but provoke her to emotions that she (as a Jew, as a woman) should have no desire to share with a roomful of strangers. That expressive neck allows her to convey both her awareness of the embarrassment that the public feels about her religion, and her willingness to ignore that embarrassment, to make her own self absent from the public discomforts of others. This is the enactment of Edgeworth's desired "countenance expressive . . . of modest reserve." Even a neck can express that.

Nor could it have been so expressive in private: only public exposure proves a woman's (and a Jew's) true power of privacy-production. This need to produce privacy effects in public—by maintaining strict reserve, or by being seen to maintain strict reserve—is exactly an instance of the gift that Edgeworth's novel credits to the domesticity and intense, laudable privacy of Jews. And yet something more is happening here—something more than the same sort of simple admiration that sparks Harrington's praise of, say, Montenero's collection. Were Edgeworth's logic strictly moral in this case, were we being tutored here in an ethical framework that was simply set to reward reserve while punishing all emotive lability, then Berenice's actions would serve to provoke a similar modesty in Harrington.

However, this is far from being the case. In fact, the very lack of reserve that had brought Harrington into the center of the crowd, that had marked him as nearly mad and a dangerous link to the magnified prejudice of the mob, is of vital use now in pushing forward his attachment to Berenice. If the Jewish character proves capable of freezing herself and so displaying her constancy, Harrington by contrast finds himself opened up to imaginative sympathy, in much the same way as he was opened up to the phobia for Jews that ruined his childhood. Aware that the expressive neck before him is Jewish, Harrington cannot help entering into her sufferings—the more so as they are silent. Successfully enough—in this world of paradoxical morality—it is Berenice's effort not to be looked at that ensures he will look at her.

> I could no longer enjoy Macklin's incomparable acting; I was so apprehensive of the pain which it must give to the young Jewess. At every stroke, characteristic of the skilful actor, or of the master poet, I felt a strange mixture of admiration and regret. I almost wished that Shakspeare had not written, or Macklin had not acted the part so powerfully: my imagination formed such a strong conception of the pain the Jewess was feeling, and my inverted sympathy, if I may so call it, so overpowered my direct and natural feelings, that at every fresh development of the Jew's villany I shrunk as though I had myself been a Jew. . . . I now saw and heard the play solely with reference to her feelings. (60–61)

In this moment, Harrington is given the ability to enter into another's feelings—"inverted sympathy"—precisely because of the work of literature. As a child he had responded to the word "Jew" on a printed page as if he himself were Jewish, because he was not yet rational enough to control his "*antipathy.*" Here his powers of identification return, not simply tolerated but valorized, because critical to the novel's forward progress.

It is of great significance that it is an aesthetic experience—here represented as a weakened form of the dissociative power of the crowd—that liberates him to enter into Berenice's mind. Just as the Jew had entered into his imagination as a figure of terror in the book's opening scene, the Jewess Berenice now returns as a figure of pity. "I anticipated every stroke which could touch her, and became every moment more and more interested and delighted with her, from the perception that my anticipations were just, and that I perfectly knew how to read her soul, and interpret her countenance" (61).[52] This romantic attraction is equally an intrepretive relation, as textual as his reaction to the word *Jew* on a printed page had been.[53]

Paradoxically, the power of the public performance of a play opens up a woman's mild reserve for public inspection, while preserving that reserve. A crowd would seem to threaten to do the same thing, of course, but to a well-trained Jew, or a modest girl of the genteel classes (Berenice is meant to be both), the presence of an actual crowd would simply activate a prudent defensive retreat. In the theater, similar faculties may be activated (we are on Aristotelian ground here) but with the knowledge that no physical harm will be attempted.

Thus far for Berenice's own feelings. But the novel goes even farther. What we see occurring in both Berenice and Harrington is an unwilling identification with another—coupled with a desire to suppress the public acknowledgment of that fact. What we see in the novel itself, however, is something larger: a claim to be documenting, as if from above, just the kind of sympathetic alliance also produced between the text and its reader. And in fact such sympathy is justified already by the imaginative transfer of sympathy involved in watching a play ("I shrunk as though I had myself been a Jew") and the romantic one ("with reference to her feelings"). Berenice's reserved self, we might say, represents the same locus of imaginative sympathy that the Jewish ragman had in Harrington's childhood—both are the site of an intense emotional transfer, one of fear, the other of love. Indeed, Harrington believes Berenice to be the first marriageable Jewish woman he has ever seen, suggesting that "love" already contains within it many of the emotions associated with his lifelong link, as he perceives it, to that "nation." Perhaps the feelings for the ragman were just as intense, and just as useful a model for the transfer of energy associated with reader and text: but because the realist novel is romantically inclined (as I argue above), it can more readily find a way to justify the changed site of his passionate identification.[54]

The theater scene represents a grounding and a justification for the sort of emotional identification that the novel itself is intended to engender. Yet the novel must also make a claim to propriety: it must seem to provide reasons for this attraction to Berenice which are something other than the raw viscerality of Harrington's *ir*rational and *im*prudent eagerness to forge connections with the Jews around him. Justifications are consequent. Harrington's attraction to Berenice is always grounded in understandable appeals: her intelligence, her modesty, her grace, and so on. Despite his parents' certain disapproval of a love-match with a Jewish woman, Harrington is struck, he believes, not by an ineluctable physical charm, but by her "dignified simplicity" and "graceful modesty" (85). An entire rhetoric springs up around this logic. Harrington is not bewitched, but rather the opposite—convinced into love, he would maintain. When Berenice's qualities are compared to the feeble social airs and graces of the Christian young ladies, her refusal to be seen, her "anxious desire not to give trouble, and a great dread of exposing herself to public observation" (62) all prove her as good as a collection—as difficult of access and as rewarding when viewed. So runs the overt logic of the text.

Yet all of the elaborate explanations based on the promotion of modesty are covers for a quite different kind of desire. A subterranean current runs below, a current fed by Harrington's childhood, his excessive sensibility, the chance sight of Berenice's neck and Shylock on the stage. On his first post-theater visit to Berenice, Harrington recalls that "I thought I acted solely from the dictates of pure reason and enlightened philanthropy" (73). As the retrospective narrator is happy to admit, beneath pretended "reason" there runs an admissible ardor.

This shadow motive becomes clearer still if one compares Berenice to her nearest rival (not very near) for Harrington's affections, Mowbray's sister Anne. The reasons that Harrington offers for disliking Anne are on the surface comprehensible. But they soon degenerate into the same sort of paradoxes that explained Harrington's initial attraction to Berenice: Berenice is "so unlike the fashionable forwardness, or the fashionable bashfulness, or any of the various airs of fashionable affectation, that I had seen in Lady Anne Mowbray, and her class of young ladies" (74). Edgeworth helpfully materializes that seeming oxymoron perfectly: when Harrington first meets Anne she is wearing a fabric called "*suppressed sigh*" (46, emphasis in original). That Anne's shoe is provocatively called "*venez-y voir*" spoils the effect of bashfulness slightly, but she is still unmistakably adorned (from the ankles up) by the name of that very bodily marker that ought to denote the absence of performance.[55]

What allows the reader to distinguish the latest Parisian *suppressed sigh* from Berenice's genuinely pleasing "novelty"? When Harrington attempts to catalogue Berenice's appeal, he says finally that she "charmed me perhaps more from contrast and from the novelty of the charm" (64). Novelty, after all, is what fashion itself (Berenice's supposed anti-type) constantly embodies. The desire the reader is meant to perceive below the level of paradox always comes back to Harrington's palpable attraction in that first meeting at *The Merchant of Venice*: his watching Berenice's back and neck is one of the novel's few openly physical moments. The powers of a corporeal, inexplicable, and vicarious attachment are not easily admitted, since they are the very powers granted to Edgeworth's version of London's crowds. Yet those powers are constantly present, and constantly at issue.

"NOTHING AT ALL BUT THE TRUTH TO TELL": THE PERILS AND PROFITS OF FICTION

Harrington's predilection for passionate identification roils the waters. True, his early anti-Semitism and the racially motivated Gordon Riots have set the twin parameters for passions that exceed the realm of common sense. But even when Harrington becomes more likable, the excesses continue. Harrington's "restless imagination" generates numerous embarrassing episodes. For example, in a trip to the Tower of London, as one critic fiercely puts it, "Harrington rants Clarence's dream from Shakespeare" and is thus marked in Montenero's and the reader's eyes as "a contemptible blockhead" (Harden, 200). Even at the time when Harrington has begun to overcome his anti-Semitism, his abiding fascination with the Jewish "nation" leads him to scan every book he reads for the word Jew (12–13).

Whether this reaction be philo- or anti-Semitic, in Edgeworth's economy it is both unbearable and fascinating. One critic even proposes that Harrington has in effect become a Jew in his uncommon obsession with the Jews' welfare (Ragussis, 85). Harrington's fascination seems to me a lingering trace of his inability to control emotions, while the pointed irony is that the object of his attentions, Mr. Montenero, is busy expounding to him the most austere form of anti-emotionality. Harrington is the passionate adherent of a teacher who teaches him to eschew passion. Harrington's connection to the concept of the Jew, even before the appearance of Isaac, or Montenero, or Berenice to ground that attraction, is a vital ingredient in Edgeworth's construction of a protocol of vicarious involvement. Such vicarious involvement is a necessary complement and a corrective to the hermetic separation of collections and the limited circulation of cash.

Harrington is not entirely a novel about turning passion to reason, no matter how chaotic and unattractive the excesses of the Gordon

Riots may seem. At times, it is a novel about putting passion to use. And that observation ought to enable us finally to return to the novel's riots with a fresh sense of Edgeworth's motives in deploying them. The connection is one of excessive exemplarity: the various riots and mad prejudice figure as overt examples of the overdone kind of emotional mobility, and promiscuous emotional connection, that the novel pointedly does not indulge in. By comparison, therefore, the sorts of identification that the novel does happily establish (at the theater, between Harrington and Berenice, between reader and text) can come to seem mild, harmless—perhaps even necessary.[56] The crowd is so useful, therefore, because it allows Edgeworth pointedly to insist that her novel was never intended to do what the crowd does—so strongly. But to do it weakly, or in rigidly controlled spaces such as a theater, or a marriage, or the pages of a book—that, the novel wants us to believe, is a different matter.

Because exemplarity is so flexible, because one can never control what a particular figure will stand for, or how sympathy will be produced, the deliberate deployment of an excessive antitype for the novel is a decidedly dangerous game. Edgeworth accepts both the risks and the stakes, in a way that few novelists of her own time and the decades that followed dared.[57] In Charles Dickens's *Barnaby Rudge*, for instance, the sheer lunacy of the Gordon rioters justifies the deaths of any rioters within the riot itself. But once order has been restored, compassion for those who have rioted is tenable, indeed obligatory. It is taken for granted that a fully comprehensible social realm can be restored, where all pubs are rebuilt, and all publicans restored to their full authority and benevolence.

It is significant, then, that *Harrington* makes no such promise. Though *Harrington* seems a novel less preoccupied with the sheer physical details of riotous damage, it is ultimately a novel far more concerned with the shaky line between the effects of crowds and those of the novel itself, the line between absolute unreason and the sort of checked passion that makes a novel's characters interesting. To establish a matrix within which the accomplishments of the novel seem not only an entertainment, but a compelling representation of the world, Edgeworth has tropologically incorporated the abiding actuality of the crowd and recognized it as a rival sort of social structure, which must be taken into account.[58]

The reader's temptation to sympathize with Harrington in his emotional excess exemplifies a tendency that a retrospective glance will

reveal had been nascently present even in Edgeworth's earlier works—
the tendency to treat life itself as a process of fictional identification.
Thus, for example, even in the seemingly glacial *Letters of Julia and
Caroline,* the virtuous Caroline tells the wastrel Julia to divide herself
into two selves for the purpose of choosing her fate. It is only a thought
experiment, true, but a dangerous one. And in *The Absentee* Lady
Colodny must confront within herself an English and an Irish half at
war. Though Edgeworth openly instructs the reader to attack or to
distrust such doubled selves, nonetheless the doubling sometimes seems
to be what makes the plot go forward. Harrington's ability to sympathize against his own natural intuitions (and across religious lines)
is crucial in rendering possible his turn towards Berenice. Though Harrington never has to marry a Jewish woman, the fictive Harrington
who could envision himself doing so—like the evil Lord Mowbray—
is precisely what enables Harrington to marry Berenice. Had she in fact
been Jewish, he would have been very wrong to love her. But, unethical
or not, he was prepared to do so; indeed, he did so.

It could well be argued that Harrington's passion is weak when compared to the force of the crowd, just as a "moral tale" is simply a
weakened version of a "novel," the genre that Edgeworth explicitly
repudiated (see note 7). Here, however, is the rub: on what grounds
does one prefer a weak passion to a strong one? If the influence of
others' imaginations upon people is the book's central fear, should that
fear not apply to the force of the novel itself?

The apparent answer lies in finding a sensible middle ground for
prudent rational intercourse, the protective heterogeneity of a realm
where Jews and Christians, money-lenders and old property holders,
meet without mingling, each protected by the Jewish innovations of
domesticity, collections, and cash. Yet if the reader has early seen Harrington's inexplicable, undesirable, and in many ways uncontrollable
anti-Semitism initiated by a story that remains deep-rooted in his psyche, and seen moreover the promulgation of rumors spark "other
people's imagination" into violent action, will the reader not ask similar questions about the effect of the novel itself? The power of a novel,
even of this novel, seems to be roughly analogous to the force of a
prejudice that is neither diminished when passed from person to person
nor dislodged by reason.[59]

Edgeworth depends upon the crowd, finally, because her intent is to
suggest that her portrayals of sympathetic attachment are only milder
versions of an aggregative or agglutinative force that exists elsewhere

in far more extreme forms. *Harrington* effectively divides up the world
into terrifyingly effective fictions, and fictions of only limited range and
impact: strong riots versus weak moral tales, "antipathies" versus social bulwarks like collections and cash. Some form of substitutive representation is everywhere: even the crowd's "rhyming" of "Jews to
shoes" is another form of meaning-making.[60] If *Harrrington* is guilty
of publicly trafficking in emotions, therefore, perhaps it is less guilty
than its promiscuity might seem to suggest because it can invoke the
crowd as its complementary antitype, even a scapegoat.

If Edgeworth's solution to the problems of publicly circulating emotion were only to offer the security of the collected household, and the
impersonal meeting site of cash transactions, she would have come up
with a tenable, but not an overwhelmingly compelling justification for
her vision of London. The presence of the theater scene, however, and
of the sexual desire that takes shape between Harrington and Berenice
is proof that Edgeworth needs a crowd both chaotic and ultimately
masterable. Chaotic forces meet in the novel as in the social realm—
all Edgeworth can promise is that those forces now meet within the
known parameters of a book (Wordsworth made the same resolve in
his attempt to master the crowd in Book 7 of *The Prelude*).

The danger of identification—that one must empathize, and yet going too far leads to irrationality—here emerges as a challenge not only
for characters but for readers. Catherine Gallagher argues convincingly
that even Edgeworth's early *Letters for Literary Ladies* "provides short
exercises in the skills of emotional involvement and extrication, thereby
putting fiction to work to teach nonsentimental reading habits, and to
train reasonable, resilient, and agile personalities" (281), and the point
holds true in various ways for much of Edgeworth's work. *Harrington*
goes a great deal farther than the rest, and arrives at a novel way of
cultivating both immersion in and extrication from fictional lives. If the
crowd is the supreme instance of involvement without extrication, then
cash and collection finally represent something like the powers of simple extrication without involvement. It is the novel itself, able to merge
Jewish reserve and Christian (literary, Shakespearean, romantic) emotive mobility, that does both.

It is because Edgeworth is so successful in providing a salutary function for the novel itself, a mastery of disruptive social energies that
does not completely dispel those energies, that I read Edgeworth's omis-
sion of the long months of rural and urban demonstrations that preceded the Gordon Riots as so telling a lacuna. In the age that Mc-

Calman and Prothero have so vividly described, that of Hyde and the
early mass platform, of Benbow's threatened General Strike and early
form of national petition demonstrations, Edgeworth's studious cir-
cumvention of the political crowd's early but unmistakable powers
speaks volumes about the discursive position of her novel. Newspapers
and pamphlets of the day had no such reluctance: the "Bartholomew
Fair Insurrection and The Piebald Pony Plot" (1817), published by
William Hone, is ample proof of that.[61] It is Edgeworth's triumphant
vaunt that Harrington's London has not succumbed to the forces of
lower-class unrest, but the vaunt carries with it a sense of unease. By
telling the story of crowds conquered on the road to an individual's
triumph over irrational antipathy, Edgeworth can make those crowds
loom large, lending power to a novel that nonetheless is represented as
itself transcending them.

We might even say that her Gordon rioters are required to embody
a residual and anachronistic madness in a modern and well-buttoned
London precisely because the increasingly vivid presence of orderly political protest crowds resonates uncomfortably below the audible tumult of the novel's putative period, 1780. The enduring accomplishment of the novel is at once to recognize that fact and to make visible
its struggles to overcome that recognition, to explain its own powers
both by analogy and disanalogy to a crowd it classes as solely irrational. The fascinating struggle this engenders is a confirmation of the
basic structure of the notional "public sphere" I describe in the Introduction. What *Harrington* tells us of its own causes exactly sketches a
picture of contested discursive space where a variety of public perform-
ances—novels and demonstration crowds among them—strive to establish their claims. Is the crowd a social phenomenon or a political
speech-act? Is the novel aesthetic or suasive? These questions cannot
be answered without reference to the contestatory space within which
they were engendered. A discursively contestable public sphere, defined
by crowds as well as newspapers and novels, is the only adequate explanation for *Harrington*'s heterogeneous composition and fascinating
flexibility. *Harrington*'s infatuation with London crowds signals the
existence of a public sphere where legible bodies, like print, can both
represent and speak for the nation.

CHAPTER 3

Crowded Imagination

Thomas De Quincey's Confessions
of an English Opium-Eater

[Toward London] a suction so powerful, felt along radii so
vast, and a consciousness, at the same time, that upon other
radii still more vast, both by land and sea, the same suction
is still operating, night and day, summer and winter, and
hurrying for ever into one centre the infinite means needed
for her infinite purposes, and the endless tributes to the skill
or to the luxury of her endless population, crowds the imagination.

(De Quincey, "The Nation of London")

INTRODUCTION: PERPETUAL FAREWELLS

What goes into Thomas De Quincey's *Confessions of an English
Opium-Eater* (1821) depends on what is left out.[1] Three memories are
lifted "one foot above your ancient level of earth," into the indelible
and irreproducible "literature of power": Ann of Oxford Street, the
London crowds (incarnated as the "tyranny of the human face"), and
the opium-eating Malay (incarnated as a multitude of Asia swarming
De Quincey's brain).[2] When compared to that outstandingly memorable trio, the vast majority of life seems dross. De Quincey dismisses
from his memoir a whole range of events, objects, and characters that
have not passed the requisite threshold of recollection. The question
that has generally seemed the suitable starting-point for comprehending
this text—why are these memories so oppressive in effect, so miserable
in form?—must therefore be preceded by another: why these memories,
and no others?

A seemingly trivial passage at the book's volta, the turn from the pleasures to the pains of opium, delineates very clearly the gap that opens up between the narrative present of the author and the unrecoverable physical facticity of all those other items that never achieve full memorability:

> The years of academic life are now over and gone—almost forgotten:—the student's cap no longer presses my temples; if my cap exist at all, it presses those of some youthful scholar, I trust, as happy as myself, and as passionate a lover of knowledge. My gown is, by this time, I dare to say, in the same condition with many thousands of excellent books in the Bodleian, viz. diligently perused by certain studious moths and worms: or departed, however (which is all that I know of its fate) to that great reservoir of *somewhere*, to which all the tea-cups, tea-pots, tea-caddies, tea-kettles, &c. have departed (not to speak of still frailer vessels, such as glasses, decanters, bed-makers, &c.) which occasional resemblances in the present generation of tea-cups, &c. remind me of having once possessed, but of whose departure and final fate I, in common with most gownsmen of either university, could give, I suspect, but an obscure and conjectural history. (50)[3]

De Quincey establishes a distinction between time as it exists in the empirical world, and time as it exists in his own narrative. He thus carefully distinguishes between events that have passed away for good and the thoughts, dreams, or convictions which yet trouble him mentally, and hence gain a second life within the pages of this text.

The problem raised by this passage and relentlessly explored by the *Confessions* is that the world of physical objects ought to provide entry to the past, but the decay of such objects makes that impossible. The physically extant—such as students' caps—cannot persist unaltered into the present, nor would we necessarily acknowledge their persistent sameness if they did. Though the objective world all around us ought to offer a full and complete account of its own past as well, its "imperfect history" ends up registering a far slighter claim to the reader's attention than do De Quincey's persistent memories. Compared to the sometime and anytime world of opium dreams and the text that captures those dreams, the vanished physical world—"that great reservoir of *somewhere*"—seems greatly diminished.

This decay from objective record to subjective recovery of the past does not, however, imply that De Quincey simply valorizes the power of the enduring mind over the frailty of the external world. If De Quincey were convinced of his own straightforward ability to capture a life that existed as a series of mental traces and no more (a Proust of the Romantic era), paragraphs like the one above might seem a dismissal of the mere physicality of the gown, cup, or cap, when compared to the durable, Bergsonian deep memory stored in the "the palimpsest of the human brain" (13:340). The *Confessions*, however, vehemently abhors the loss of tangible physicality. It circles and recircles the moments that produce both lingering memory and a lingering sense of loss, so that the failure to produce an unmistakable physical trace goes hand in glove with the process of producing a partially satisfying textual one. And it is here that the importance of London crowds begins.

Crowds are so central to the *Confessions* because they are its prime exemplar of objects that are irritatingly evanescent even at their moment of actual presence. It is that state of quasi-presence, and the oddly memorable feeling of quasi-absence that the crowd produces in retrospect, that provides De Quincey a way to understand the vagaries of purely subjective recall. De Quincey has not made a free and enthusiastic choice to forego the world for the pleasures of the mind. Rather, mental traces of the past, those indelible three images around which the *Confessions* centers, are the one substitute available for lost physical traces, but a substitute as potentially infuriating as the text's promise of mimesis itself. De Quincey's dissatisfaction with the unreliability of physical evidence of the past is comparable to the dissatisfaction that Hannah Arendt finds registered in the late works of Schelling: "What this philosophy wants is clearly this world, whose only great failing, however, is that it has lost its reality" (1994, 168). The powerful mental traces that define the remembered life of the *Confessions* are a mediation between a real but unrecoverable world and a recoverable but unreal set of memory-traces.

There are some recent accounts of Romanticism that describe the successful creation of a free-standing self as a way for writers to overcome an obligation to the dead burden of the past. David Bromwich, for example, finds at the core of Romanticism "the imaginative identification of a self with the community of mankind . . . while by contrast the conservative or Burkean idea is that the self . . . can have no authority for asserting an intimate relation to humanity at large, except through the mediating layers of attachment that give reliable texture to this experience" (73).[4] The model suggests that individual identity can become a lens through which all (individuated) human experience can be grasped, and that answerability to social and physical surroundings is thus unproblematically evaded. My account of De Quincey's perceived loss of the world suggests, however, that even the strongest affirmation of one's purely subjective grasp on the world can be shot through with an awareness of the conditions under which the loss of a fully available world takes place. In the *Confessions*, the crowd is situated between reliable physical fact and powerful but intangible mental recall. It is that doubleness that keeps it, and a few phenomena like it, perpetually present in De Quincey's text.

Of course no memoir can contain a complete life: it would be like the Borgesian map that covered the entire nation it represented. But De Quincey has a distinctive and an innovative way of delineating what gets remembered and what forgotten: only the agony of the experience of loss can truly make an indelible memory trace. The sphere of tangible physical reality is trivial because it simply evanesces. The sphere of mental images is unbearable because it retains forever the sensation of loss, a sensation nicely captured in the recurrent phrase, "perpetual farewells!": it is the onset of absence that is perpetual, not the absence itself. Those who drift away, like Ann without a last name or address, like the Malay without language, like the crowds without any individual character, will return as uncontrollable mental horrors. In Edgeworth's *Harrington* (1817) the crowd's disorder betokened irrational chaos, but eventually came to be aligned with certain emotional indulgences practiced by the novel itself. In the *Confessions*, the crowd, like the troubling presence of Ann and of the Malay, baffles certitude even when actually present. It effectively defies the mind's desire to pin definite identities on people and places, to set doubts at rest. Because of that semi-tangibility, it is excruciatingly semi-memorable. That which is glimpsed in the crowd, then lost in the crowd, is cantilevered—against De Quincey's will—into realms of purely mental recollection.

The most beautiful actual school-cap cannot be compared to the slightest incident of the time with Ann. The one gets eaten by moths, the other flourishes inside De Quincey's own mind. Not, however, because memories of Ann attain an immortality that removes them from the taint of the physical world. Rather, the perpetually irritating presence of these memories functions as a representation of the interior problems of tangibility that characterize the dream/memory/opium visions within the narrator's mind, and hence within De Quincey's own text. The traces that linger longest in memory are not images out of childhood.[5] It is those occurrences that already carry within themselves the undecidability, the unapproachability, of a haunting recurrent vision that are the most likely to be recovered, and carried around. The persistence of the partially tangible crowd links London, Malay, Ann, and De Quincey's own crowded imagination.

"SYMPATHISING WITH THEIR PLEASURES"

The *Confessions* earned De Quincey a heroic epithet—"the opium
eater"—and fame he neither lived down nor surpassed with any later
work. The 1821 version of the *Confessions*—generally the preferred
text over the pointlessly expanded 1856 version[6] —is narrated in De
Quincey's own first person, and is, along with "The English Mail-
Coach," the finest example of his periphrastic, excessive, genuinely innovative writing. Its first third tells of a miserable childhood and his
wanderings after escaping from school, and culminates with the famous
"Ann of Oxford Street" episode. While he is subsisting miserably in
London, De Quincey's life is saved by a timely glass of port from Ann,
a streetwalker whose last name he never learns. The middle third of
the book, "The Pleasures of Opium," is generally centered on De Quincey's second extended stay in London—although the whole text is filled
with enough retrospection and sheer meandering to undermine such
straightforward temporal divisions—and describes the joys of drugging
oneself and listening to opera or exploring London crowds at market-
time. Finally "The Pains of Opium" (fully three times as long as the
"Pleasures") describes De Quincey's retreat from the city of London to
a rural freehold, a retreat rendered futile by his persistent dreams,
which carry him back to Ann, to the "tyrannical" faces of the London
crowds through which Ann had moved, and to the figure of an un-
named Malay to whom he had inadvertently given a huge dose of
opium that he fears caused the Malay's death.

London initially bodes well. De Quincey's opium rambles through
crowds of poor Londoners out doing their Friday shopping even seem
to propose a helpful modification to Goethe's, Moritz's, and Kleist's
idea that encounters with a crowd where one has no social obligations
might be a blissful release.[7] In describing opium-fueled passages among
London shoppers, De Quincey suggests that a new sort of casual social
encounter can produce valuably randomized intercourse, saving all that
is good about the social and evading its coercive requirement of later
obligations, long-term interactions. De Quincey contemplates using the
pleasures of the crowd as a way to let go of the duties implicit in
middle-class etiquette and its *longue durée* notion of social intercourse.
If one can train oneself to be satisfied by the transient personalization
of the shopping crowd, great pleasures beckon.

> . . . whereas different men throw their feelings into different channels, and
> most are apt to show their interest in the concerns of the poor, chiefly by

sympathy, expressed in some shape or other, with their distress and sor-
rows, I, at that time, was disposed to express my interest by sympathising
with their pleasures. The pains of poverty I had lately seen too much of;
more than I wished to remember: but the pleasures of the poor, their con-
solations of spirit, and their reposes from bodily toil, can never become
oppressive to contemplate. (46)

This claim to celebrate with the poor when they are happy, rather than
commiserate at their darkest moments, puts De Quincey at odds with
the Wordsworthian account of sympathy toward the poor.[8] In De
Quincey's account, affinity for the poor's suffering is deflected rather
than abetted by the fact that one has suffered oneself: such experience
tends to discourage one from witnessing others going through the same
experience. Poverty's pains, then, serve to keep people apart from those
like them. Poverty's pleasures are what draw the poor together, and
draw the observer after them.

Thus in his effort to engender sympathy with the poor *en masse*, De
Quincey chooses a moment in which the poor have something to celebrate.

I feel always, on a Saturday night, as though I also were released from some
yoke of labour, had some wages to receive, and some luxury of repose to
enjoy. (47)

His solidarity here may appear spurious.[9] He receives no wages himself.
Moreover, ought not the very fact of the poor's receiving wages work
as an occasion for all to be separated from one another, wrapped up
in personal consumption? Yet in De Quincey's account, it is precisely
those wages that bring the crowd together. "Getting and spending"
need not involve competition or selfishness. In a moment seemingly
defined by the competition of the marketplace, De Quincey encounters
solidarity.[10]

The only corresponding spectacle De Quincey enjoys on his opiated
Wednesdays and Saturdays is attending the opera. It is a felicitous and
revealing juxtaposition. Music and crowds both produce in the emotionally malleable observer a vast effect of irresistible sympathy; both
have a rhythm that can compel the observer against his will into unexpected feelings.

For the sake, therefore, of witnessing, upon as large a scale as possible, a
spectacle with which my sympathy was so entire, I used often, on Saturday
nights, after I had taken opium, to wander forth, without much regarding
the direction or the distance, to all the markets, and other parts of London,

to which the poor resort on a Saturday night, for laying out their wages.
(47)

There are various marketplaces where the poor live, and their movements depend on that orderly principle. But it is precisely on account
of the comparative fixity of the poor that De Quincey's movements, by
contrast, can be determined by chance or passing inclination. In De
Quincey's crowd-mandated rambles, specific geography does not matter. Where the poor "resort" is his port of call, and he seems both like
and unlike the crowd at this moment. He can be a man in the crowd
without being a man of the crowd. He can understand—as he understands music—what goes on without himself being either a piece of
music or part of this crowd.

De Quincey seems to regard this simultaneous inclusion and separation not simply as an artist's special privilege, but as a typical human
experience, partaking of a phenomenon that—even as it occurs—com-
prises only a part of one's own identity. It is of abiding interest to De
Quincey that one can be entirely of the crowd, and yet entirely something else as well. Talking about purchases but not making them, De
Quincey manages to immerse himself within this world, even while
standing apart from it. It is not that he has the best of two worlds:
rather, you might say that he has the best of one world in two ways.

> Many a family party, consisting of a man, his wife, and sometimes one or
> two of his children, have I listened to, as they stood consulting on their
> ways and means, or the strength of their exchequer, or the price of house-
> hold articles. Gradually I became familiar with their wishes, their difficul-
> ties, and their opinions. Sometimes there might be heard murmurs of dis-
> content: but far oftener expressions on the countenance, or uttered in
> words, of patience, hope, and tranquillity. And taken generally, I must say,
> that, in this point at least, the poor are far more philosophic than the rich—
> that they show a more ready and cheerful submission to what they consider
> as irremediable evils, or irreparable losses. Whenever I saw occasion, or
> could do it without appearing to be intrusive, I joined their parties; and
> gave my opinion upon the matter in discussion, which, if not always judi-
> cious, was always received indulgently. (47)

These are anonymous strangers, thrown up against each other in the
public sphere in a situation where close contact and shared visual and
aural space are inevitable, but where further knowledge of one another
is not vouchsafed.

At this point, the pleasure De Quincey derives from the crowd seems
to have gone in a very different direction from the anonymity that is

variously and happily practiced by Kleist, by Goethe, or by Moritz. De Quincey's pleasure might be described as personalized anonymity. This is a crowd that coalesces wholesale, segregates into retail transactions, and yet remains homogeneous enough to justify De Quincey's half-participatory overview. Even in his seeming satisfaction, however, there remains a careful marker of De Quincey's need to demarcate a difference. Like Wordsworth among French crowds, De Quincey reports that his drugged delight makes the smallest details of the crowd's own satisfaction (the terms of its pleasure) a matter of comparative indifference to him:

> If wages were a little higher, or expected to be so, or the quartern loaf a little lower, or it was reported that onions and butter were expected to fall, I was glad: yet, if the contrary were true, I drew from opium some means of consoling myself. (47)

This pleasure is akin to the pleasure that J. K. Huysmans reports deriving from the assembled masses of Lourdes, when he can view them from above on a still night: when their candles alone represent their size, it gives him great pleasure to appreciate their appearance, yet great pleasure as well to assert his ability to be as distant from them as he chooses to be (105).

De Quincey is gesturing here at a way of making use of the crowd that does not pin his hopes to them if they should prove unreliable. As long as the myriads remain myriads without differentiation, in the social interchanges of the market, the pleasure of De Quincey's opium is a self-centered one that produces no sense of reciprocated social connection: "For Opium (like the bee, that extracts its material indiscriminately from roses and from the soot of chimneys) can overrule all feelings into a compliance with the master key" (47). This boast ensures that London scenes can be treated the same way that Wordsworth treated the French crowds: all is honey to the bee of opium.

Here, however, De Quincey's troubles begin. True, at this moment the fact that his involvement is voluntary seems to abet the joy. But the paragraphs that follow, still putatively describing the "pleasures of opium," begin to transform De Quincey's ability to move away from the crowd into a source of regret. Left without the crowd to guide his steps and structure his rambles, De Quincey in London moves into a sense of befuddlement as profound as that Wordsworth describes when viewing the Carousel massacres site without the animating presence of French mobs. When the crowds depart, De Quincey is afflicted, within the very city whose mazy turnings he claims to love, with cartographic confusion.

The task of finding one's way home again allegorizes the business of returning to a sole self when a marketing-induced unity abates. The mute streets may aid and abet random movement with a crowd, but try to use those same promising byways to pinpoint a single location, and they turn recalcitrant.

> And sometimes in my attempts to steer homewards, upon nautical principles, by fixing my eye on the pole-star, and seeking ambitiously for a northwest passage, instead of circumnavigating all the capes and head-lands I had doubled in my outward voyage, I came suddenly upon such knotty problems of alleys, such enigmatical entries, and such sphynx's riddles of streets without thoroughfares, as must, I conceive, baffle the audacity of porters, and confound the intellects of hackney-coachmen. I could almost have believed, at times, that I must be the first discoverer of some of these *terrae incognitae*, and doubted, whether they had yet been laid down in the modern charts of London. (47–48)

To be an explorer in the city requires the dead of night, after the shopping is over and the sanctioned voyeurism at an end. The "sphynx's riddles of streets," without opium-reveries or the inducement of crowds, become sterile intellectual problems.

And even the clear temporal separation apparently on offer—first pleasant crowds, then horrible loneliness and loss on the streets—is ruptured by the paragraph's end. The description of markets had at least proposed tranquil "spots of time," where crowd experiences might later be recalled as sheer pleasure, though paid for by pain afterwards. But a retrospect from a time beyond even the "pains of opium" gives the reader the first glimpse of the terrible memory palace that lies in wait to process these memories.

> For all this, however, I paid a heavy price in distant years, when the human face tyrannized over my dreams, and the perplexities of my steps in London came back and haunted my sleep, with the feeling of perplexities moral or intellectual, that brought confusion to the reason, or anguish and remorse to the conscience. (48)

"All this" refers both to seemingly enjoyable crowds and to "knotty" streets. The recombination is an apt one, because the separation itself had been inherently suspect. Does not the initial vagary of motion through the crowd inherently imply the agony of return? Though De Quincey's original experience was divided between pleasant motion through accommodating crowds and unhappy navigation back through mysterious streets, the present of the narrative allows no such luxury of separation. Because both aspects of his experience are present in the process of recollection itself, De Quincey's rambles dislodge certainty and haunt his memories.

THE UNRHETORICAL MYRIAD: ANN OF OXFORD STREET

The underlying danger in the *Confessions* is that (opium) dreams will come to constitute both writer's and reader's reality. Indeed, the work's final thought is that De Quincey's own sleep has fallen prey to inescapably internalized crowds, whose features and attributes retain the hellish vagueness of the half-real: sleep, De Quincey says, "is still (in the tremendous line of Milton)—With dreadful faces throng'd and fiery arms" (79). It is important to grasp, however, the extent that such impending intangibility already manifests itself within the world described. And that impending intangibility is most evident in the dangers that attach to the London practices of partial naming that produce the loss of Ann.

The absence of a direct correlation between people's faces and their full names resonates deeply in the *Confessions*: Ann lacks a last name and the Malay who bolts De Quincey's opium lacks the English to tell his, while the crowds are by definition nameless as long as they remain nothing but crowds. Yet these two feebly named people (is "the Malay" a proper name?) and this antinomical group (perhaps "crowd" too is a sort of improper name) remain peculiarly memorable. Those who get bumped out of the social whirl because no classificatory data attaches to them inevitably return, not in the social, but the phantasmal realm. To lose social stability is to gain textual strength.[11] The process of indelible memory begins with namelessness, that point at which the ordinary methods of correlating past and present fail.

One particular moment of quasi-successful denomination is worth tracing because it marks the moment in the text where the past pleasure of an anonymous encounter ends, and the present pain of lost connections begins. It starts with the question of De Quincey's own identity, which he needs to establish in order to borrow money against his father's will: "one question still remained, which the faces of the Jews pretty significantly suggested,—was *I* that person?" (25). This precipitates a huggermugger trip to Eton to find a wealthy friend willing to vouch for him. But after this conventional story of establishing definite nomination (the trip to the Jews is a familiar enough trope of the day), a decidedly unconventional story on the same theme follows. Because De Quincey must leave town, he must lose touch with his one London friend, the streetwalker Ann. Because he has never known Ann's last name (hence the usual title "Ann of Oxford Street" when the episode is reprinted separately) or street address, she is lost to him. But—and here is the rub that begins to generate the "tyranny of the human face"—because she is lost to him in reality, she returns to him in dreams. What is lost in the crowds of London, in the contingent, temporary identities forged on the streets, is in a certain sense the only thing out of the past that is not lost. The "remorse" engendered in opium visions revolves around the unknowable crowds and the woman who is a figure for all that was lost in London: the unrecoverable Ann.

In fact, this unnaming goes back even earlier. Ann carries with her this curse (or blessing) of partial namelessness from the moment she is introduced.

> Being myself at the time of necessity a peripatetic, or a walker of the streets, I naturally fell in more frequently with those female peripatetics who are technically called Street-walkers.[12] Many of these women had occasionally taken my part against the watchmen who wished to drive me off the steps of houses where I was sitting. But one amongst them, the one on whose account I have at all introduced this subject—yet no! let me not class thee, Oh noble minded Ann——with that order of women; let me find, if it be possible, some gentler name to designate the condition of her to whose bounty and compassion, ministering to my necessities when all the world had forsaken me, I owe it that I am at this time alive.— (20)

Before she is even described, the reader already knows of Ann that she both belongs and does not belong in a category whose very identity is to defy adequate nomination—since all streetwalkers, De Quincey tells us, avoid giving out last names. The double movement of the passage is striking: De Quincey labels her as one of the permanently unknowable, and then thinks better of the label. The effect is not to cancel what he has already said but rather to confuse the reader as to where Ann belongs, a confusion that the three dashes inserted in the text can only increase. Ann does belong with this generic class within the London crowd, but she also belongs somewhere else. Again, the force of a crowd-driven identity is to abet a confusion about classification: people can fit into more than one classificatory category at once or even, as here, both fit and not fit a single order.

It is exactly this duality that is crucial to the unmooring of London crowds, London streets, and Oxford-Street Ann. That De Quincey has recognized and yet refused to recognize Ann's congruence with a larger category of last-nameless people is at the root of her unmooring. Were all streetwalkers always nameless, and unproblematically so, then this particular array of troubling images might be laid to rest. But the form of her introduction serves to create a persistent uncertainty about whether she can emerge from the mass within which her identity is cloaked. If Ann had a last name, a street address, a reputable position in the world, she would not be part of the *Confessions*. And this is the intriguing and enduring problem of the London crowd in De Quincey's work. For if that crowd were namable and simply, straightforwardly knowable, it would have none of its famous sway ("tyranny of the human face") over his dreams.

Ann represents a significant singularity among the crowds. She sets herself at a distance from those other streetwalkers who "had occasionally taken my part" (20) because she has saved De Quincey's life with a glass of port on a cold night: "Then it was, at this crisis of my fate, that my poor orphan companion—who had herself met with little but injuries in this world—stretched out a saving hand to me" (22). But because this connection has been established, Ann must be taken away.

> I agreed with her [when departing for Oxford] that on the fifth night from that, and every night afterwards, she should wait for me at six o'clock, near the bottom of Great Titchfield-street, which had been our customary haven, as it were, of rendezvous, to prevent our missing each other in the great Mediterranean of Oxford-street. This, and other measures of precaution I took: one only I forgot. She had either never told me, or (as a matter of no great interest) I had forgotten, her surname. (27)

Failure or forgetting may seem astonishing and blameworthy. But the absence of certain nomination comports with what might be called a courtesy of the crowd—last names are an impediment to certain kinds of London work, while first names become part and parcel of a living London experience. Thus De Quincey classes the very possession of a last name as the unpleasant attribute of a class of woman who interests him little:

> It is a general practice, indeed, with girls of humble rank in her unhappy condition, not (as novel-reading women of higher pretensions) to style themselves—*Miss Douglass, Miss Montague*, &c., but simply by their Christian names, *Mary, Jane, Frances*, &c. (27)[13]

The sideways slur at novel-reading operates as a class marker, elevating—as suitable for De Quincey's memory vaults—women of a class low enough that they have established virtually no recoverable biographical data. To lack enough of a name to read one sort of aesthetic text is to retain enough of a hold on De Quincey's memory to enter this one.

Within London's semi-social crowds, the absence of information clearly has its positive attributes. In "On Travelling in England in the Old Days" (1834), De Quincey depicts London as a nerve center connected to all the country, a site where information is processed, but that notion of the incipient national nervous system is certainly at odds with De Quincey's willingness to know Anns and Mary Janes without knowing their family names.[14] Ann is lost in the physical universe, but gained in abiding recollection: having a last name and address ("The street where she had lodged I knew, but not the house" [33]) are one way to undergird identity, but entering the sublime heights of the "literature of power" turns out to be quite another, with its own problems.[15]

Ann's loss can be classed—as Walter Benjamin classes Baudelaire's experience in "A Une Passante"—as an instance of the price that is paid for city encounters. In Baudelaire's famous line delivered to a woman seen and passed by on the street, the exquisite sensation and its price occur all at once: "*O toi que j'eusse aimée, ô toi qui le savais*" [O you whom I could have loved, O you who knew it]. All the regret produced by the immediacy of the pleasure is instantly available. In the *Confessions*, De Quincey loves Ann precisely because he met her in the loss-ridden London streets; she is only loved through the lens of loss.[16] Unavoidably bound up with the chosen anonymity of De Quincey's life in and among London's crowds, the loss of Ann echoes and reechoes throughout the book's hundred pages.

The assertion of grief for the loss of Ann is genuine, yet at the same time suspect: this is an emotion that has only come into being at the moment of loss, an emotion that is wrapping itself around Ann as a way of accounting for a feeling that might just as readily be attached to the city at large.[17] De Quincey most strongly articulates that sense of loss by way of a profoundly moving yet deeply unsettling wish for Ann's death. Out of the feeling of beleaguering pressure, of the mixed pleasure and pain of the easy encounters of the street, De Quincey produces this painful cry for any sort of certainty, even certainty of her death.

> But, to this hour, I have never heard a syllable about her. This, amongst such troubles as most men meet with in this life, has been my heaviest affliction.—If she lived, doubtless we must have been sometimes in search of each other, at the very same moment, through the mighty labyrinths of London; perhaps even within a few feet of each other—a barrier no wider in a London street, often amounting in the end to a separation for eternity! (34)

If she has lived, then, the crowd has become his enemy, where it had once been his securest friend. For its anonymity, previously valued, becomes intolerable once Ann—in whom are now personified all the positive features of the crowd—is lost in it. These are the same "labyrinths" through which De Quincey describes wandering at night, miserable because alone. But now the very human forms that could once have been relied on to produce joy only engender more misery.[18]

Out of this sense that the crowds have now become a medium of obstruction, a necessary veil cast over the woman he seeks, a radically new possibility of certainty is engendered—a certainty that is however aligned neither with the crowd nor with the *Confessions* themselves. De Quincey articulates a preference for the forces that bring writing itself to an end: dead certainty. He discards the uncertainty that was only "amounting" to eternal separation in favor of a death sentence that can at least guarantee definite knowledge about that "eternity."

> During some years, I hoped that she *did* live; and I suppose that, in the literal and unrhetorical use of the word *myriad*, I may say that on my different visits to London, I have looked into many, many myriads of female faces, in the hope of meeting her. I should know her again amongst a thousand, if I saw her for a moment; for, though not handsome, she had a sweet expression of countenance, and a peculiar and graceful carriage of the head.—I sought her, I have said, in hope. So it was for years; but now I should fear to see her; and her cough, which grieved me when I parted with her, is now my consolation. I now wish to see her no longer; but think of her, more gladly, as one long since laid in the grave; in the grave, I would hope, of a Magdalen; taken away, before injuries and cruelty had blotted out and transfigured her ingenuous nature, or the brutalities of ruffians had completed the ruin they had begun. (34)

The key words here are "labyrinths" and "myriads." The experience of being overcome by numbers has created the desire for a certainty no longer statistical, but singular and unmediated, even if it is the silent assurance of death. The myriads are meant to stand not for infinity beyond counting, but for what falls within De Quincey's own ken.[19] The juxtaposition of "myriads" and "thousand" is significant in an-

other way as well. He says he would know her among a thousand—
would he know her, though, among the many more than a thousand
whom he has to examine? The casual turn of speech, the assumption
that someone only has to differ from 999 other people in order to be
distinguishable, breaks down in the overpacked city. The rule goes by
myriads here, not thousands.[20]

The "labyrinths," though, suggest that even with such a power of
cognition, or examination, the twists and turns of the crowds will deny
you the information you need about a single person. The crowd that
had turned toward you when you needed to move among anonymous
"myriads" out on the street—the crowd out of which the Situationists
conjured their explicitly De Quinceyan game of the "dérive"[21]—turns
away from you the minute you need to know more of those myriads
than that they are myriad. If De Quincey has rescued Ann from her
peripatetic status by individuating her, he has singled her out not by
making her a permanent part of a known social world, but by making
her into a figure for all that is lost when he experiences the world
through crowds. Because the crowds have already called into existence
the dream-like state of half-responsibility toward those around him,
Ann is fated to return to his dreams as the embodiment of all their
intangible promise.[22]

Might the desire to end all investigations with the certainty of Ann's
death, then, usher in the recurrence of a purely touristic encounter with
the city, an encounter with anonymous faces that no longer have any
claim on De Quincey? This would be a wish for just the kind of city
that Wordsworth would have found intolerable: a city where no one
means anything to anyone else, where you are free to stare and wander
among the crowds, secure in the knowledge that they have nothing to
show you, nothing to share with you. Suppose that Ann is of all London the only human face to him. Will her absence not relieve him of
the burden of feeling connected to the city, thus returning De Quincey
to a conception of London akin to Goethe's vision of Naples, where
the city's crowds are palatable only at a distance, where their alienation
from the writer and from each other provides the only sure wall of
security and where one can "become solid" in response to their very
evanesence? Quite the contrary. Wordsworth finds London intolerable
because in all that city, forcing itself on him with all the insistence of
a vision and a sublime experience, there is no one person with whom
he can establish (as with even such unlikely pastoral characters as the
Cumberland Beggar) an understanding based on something other than

the chaotic tumult of street meetings. De Quincey arrives at the same sense of isolation and conjures from it a singular encounter around which he can warp all his perceptions of the London crowds. De Quincey finds or fabricates, in St. Ann's Parish, along Little St. Anne Street or St. Anne's Court, an Ann who at once stands for and stands against London's crowds. Entering his life during those walks that define his relationship to that city, her relationship with him depends on the chaos and semisocial promiscuity that characterizes his relationship with the city.

Having conjured up a singularity out of multiplicity, De Quincey is able to exert an innovative sort of pressure on his text, able to frame a paradox that Wordsworth never faced. The crowd that gave can also take away, and the very currents that brought Ann to him will waft her away again, all hope of classing and filing her gone. De Quincey's loss is not readily comprehensible, even in his own writings. Ann's loss is not explained in the *Confessions*; it explains them. This is not because the loss is so crushing at the time, but because it remained with him in all the recurring memory-dreams that haunt him and the text.

In one of his last pieces of writing, De Quincey casually remarks that in telling Ann's story he has altered even the most central facts in order to stay true to some imagined "meaning" of his encounter with her.

> The search after the lost features of Ann, which I spoke of as pursued in the crowds of London, was in a more proper sense pursued through many a year in dreams.[23]

The story of the search in the crowds turns out to be true only to the narrator's own experience of his pursuit. Again, this is not a deliberate abandonment of the physical for the mental world, but the only consolation available when that physical world can no longer make its presence vividly felt. The salient fact about Ann's abiding presence is the subjective experience of the search for her: perpetual farewells indeed. If De Quincey is trying to convey the feeling of a pursuit for someone who is not accessible, or no longer accessible, what is the difference between a pursuit in dreams and a pursuit in an unyielding city? The crowds of London are thus at once impediment and solution in De Quincey's memory. If they were only one or the other—only horror, or only delight—they would not be enduring aches. But their central affront is to remain irritatingly not quite there.[24] In effect, De Quincey is pursuing (or pursued by) Ann both outside and inside himself. In both directions, he faces the stuff of dreams or of crowds: vivid, actual, but also ephemeral and unclassifiable.

One figure will never recoalesce out of the stuff of anonymous myriads. But it is only out of and among the myriads that Ann could ever have come into being. Crowds are, one might say, the definitive figuration of a generalizable uncertainty. How can stable definitions of identities, essences, or actions be instituted in a world where objects and persons can simultaneously be classed as part of one phenomenon and another? Can Ann be simply Ann and part of the general class of peripatetics? Can any person be described from two perspectives at once? Along with Ann of Oxford Street, the London crowds—marketing or arguing, in rhythmic motion or lapsed back to individuation—carry with them the tortured aspect of indecision that ensures the "tyranny of the human face" will take on an afterlife in De Quincey's mind and his text.

THE PAINS OF MEMORY

When Shakespeare's Coriolanus leaves Rome, which he hates because its politicking renders all speech a permanent gray-scale of ambiguous meanings, his parting curse is "here remain with your uncertainty" (III, iii, 124). Leaving London, De Quincey by contrast takes with him its uncertainty, stored in the mental landscape of his enduring opium dreams. De Quincey retreats to a rural freehold redolent of Rousseau and ripe for tranquil contemplation ("Let there be a cottage, standing in a valley, 18 miles from any town . . . ; the benefit of which provision is, that all valley families resident within its circuit will compose, as it were, one larger household personally familiar to your eye, and more or less interesting to your affections" [58]). But he is still pursued by memories of London's variety. To make matters worse, De Quincey at this time gives a huge dose of opium to a Malay, whose language he does not speak, then watches in horror as the man eats all the opium at once, and departs.[25] Never hearing any more of him, as he had never heard more of Ann, he can presume neither life nor death: it is the suspension of effect that ensures the Malay too will haunt him.

The "pains of opium" that follow—especially the dreams of uncontrolled movement in a mystical East—represent in part, as Charles Rzepka has argued, De Quincey's worries about publication.[26] In his dreams De Quincey expresses some of the anxiety that he, tucked in a little room somewhere, must feel about the readers who will control his fate. In Rzepka's account, the key distance is between single author and multiple copies of his book. Yet the anguished dream visions of "the pains of opium" have a direct reference to the pleasures that preceded them, especially to the earlier multiplicity of the faceless crowds of London itself. All the opium visions are permeated by notes of limitless presences: "the feeling of a vast march—of infinite cavalcades filing off—and the tread of innumerable armies" (68).

That crowd's presence is all the more striking—be it a crowd of readers or a figure for the intangibility of memory—because it attacks De Quincey with the sensation of multiple unknown personae inside his own mind. Ann was beloved, and met and known in the crowd: yet the crowd is now an impediment to finding her. Crowds and opium engender possibilities, then preclude their fulfillment. The haunting sense of responsibility and of the impossibility of acting—produced by opium and London crowds—power the *Confessions*.[27] The central experience of the opium visions that dominate the "pains of opium" section is one of dissociation and multiplication. De Quincey's terror comes from feeling himself being divided into an entire world of different characters, all coming at him as obstructions to his return to a single true identity. In the crowding-in of the dream, De Quincey best describes the distortions of the sense of the "real" that his heightened attention to idiosyncratic, unreportable sensation brings. First is "sympathy ... between the waking and the dreaming states" (67); then "deep-seated anxiety and gloomy melancholy"; then the "sense of space, and in the end, the sense of time, were both powerfully affected"; and fourth, the "minutest incidents of childhood, or forgotten scenes of later years, were often revived" (68). But such descriptions do not do justice to the repeated, the exemplary figure of all the dreams:

> Perhaps some part of my London life might be answerable for this [tyranny of the human face]. Be that as it may, now it was that upon the rocking waters of the ocean the human face began to appear: the sea appeared paved with innumerable faces, upturned to the heavens: faces, imploring, wrathful, despairing, surged upward by thousands, by myriads, by generations, by centuries:—my agitation was infinite,—my mind tossed—and surged with the ocean. (72)

These figures cohere into a multiheaded leviathan extending out numerically in time, space, and human presence. The social demand is the underlying one, and it is unanswerable because that social demand is inherently no more than the mind itself divided from itself. If "man is a weed" in Asia, the significance is both imperial and psychic: the "sense of infinity and eternity" depends on the sense of division upon division of human consciousness. And all this may be answerable, De Quincey's 1856 revision suggests, not simply to "some part of my life in London," but more explicitly to "the searching for Ann amongst fluctuating crowds" (3:441).

In every passage of the dreams, whether Ann or Malay or other object is the central worry, the crowds resurface, promising the confusion and sense of permanent unresolvability that finally answer satisfactorily the question—What does it take to be memorable? To be lost amidst crowds. The confusion that in the original London scenes had been displaced merely onto empty cartography (getting lost alone on the streets at midnight) has returned with a human component. The "knotty problems of alleys" that made London geography hard on the opium-eater late at night has led into a larger matrix of ongoing losses.

The pains of opium do not involve simply forgetting, or even misremembering the pleasures initially experienced in London crowds. Rather, as those earlier premonitions about the haunting "tyranny of the human face" remind the reader, the hostile elements that have triggered the painful process of uncontrollable recollection were already present in the very aesthetic power of the crowd itself. Though the tyranny of the human face can only be conceived retrospectively, it depends on observations that De Quincey has already made about the absence of cohesive structure to the social encounters of London. Tyranny by the crowd had always lain at the bottom of tyranny by way of dreams, though it takes the long backward look of memory and antinostalgia to uncover it.

The search for tangibility causes De Quincey's retreat from London. But it also causes the attempt, within that retreat, to account for the return of the crowd into De Quincey's own overcrowded mind. So if the central question for the text is why certain things linger in the memory while others disappear, the answer to that question is centrally bound up with the qualities that make the city's crowds and Ann into a nightmare vision, and that make the "tyranny of the human face" memorable when other occurrences fade into oblivion. Those events that were already phantasmagoric when they first occurred will be remembered, because they bring with them the sense of a "second-sight" connection that is at once aesthetically pleasing and ethically troubling.

There is no question that the text aims to make itself part of the "literature of power," and no question that the sublime powers of the London crowd are repeated in the opium dream's sublimity (the loss of space and time, the dissociation of a single identity, and so forth). But there is one crucial difference at least, something that De Quincey's work manifests in establishing the power of text over lived social phenomenon. The crowd is productive of the ongoing pain and confusion that the text's own representation of that pain and confusion will not replicate. To say that De Quincey is doubtful of the crowd's power would be to understate the credit he gives it for the tyrannical hold of his London past over his imagination. But this crowd does not finally provide a positive template for the experience of literature itself. It is a register of a certain sort of excess, of the fluctuation of categories even at the moments when certainty seems most desirable and most plausible. And yet—shades of *Harrington*—De Quincey cannot do without this social structure. This crowd's excess is exactly cognate with what any literature of power produces: a sense of the world when that world is no longer present.

The dreamscape of opium finally allows De Quincey to align the work of his own text with London crowds, which are so useful to him because they represent the world's frustrating tendency to fluctuate between one state of things and another—or to seem more than one thing when viewed through more than one lens. After all, members of a crowd are undeniably disaggregated individuals at the same time as they are part of a depersonalized social phenomenon, and that dual status can neither be denied nor, in De Quincey's account, readily explained. Align the crowd's instability with the process of self-creation and the result may look like an optimistic account of the self's power to resist tradition. But the *Confessions* never lets its reader forget that memory traces are saddled permanently with the problem of lost tangibility. De Quincey conceives of crowds as extant both out on the streets and inside his brain: it is that doubleness which makes their quasi-tangibility such a permanent irritation and opportunity. The crowd and concomitant markers of partial tangibility (Ann most importantly) assumes enormous weight because the crowd, like the text itself, is not readily catalogued as external or internal to the mind, not readily placed on the ground for the "literature of knowledge" to classify.

The text claims the sanction of the "literature of power" to step above the earth just far enough that its reader will be uncertain of what exactly is occurring during the reading process: Am I the reader? Am

I in fact undergoing the experiences here depicted? But these questions cannot even be posed, let alone answered, in a pure vacuum of mental speculation. So London crowds and allied phenomena are summoned. The recollected experiences of crowds without and within, of Ann, and of the vanishing Malay are indispensable representations of the irritating intangibility of mental activity without a physical referent.[28] Crowds in De Quincey are thus directly connected to the mental processes that fuel the work itself. Like Walter Pater, De Quincey externalizes mental sensation by way of physical reference.[29] Unlike Pater, however, he finds the physical referent for his "impressions" in a phenomenon that in its most palpable incarnation—as the daily reality of the London streets—already carries with it the dream logic of quasi-tangibility. The permanent uncertainty of sensation that haunts the *Confessions* depends on nothing so much as the tyrannical London crowd.

PART 2

1839–1849

London's crowds—and Ann, the singularity extruded from those crowds—pervade the *Confessions,* producing everywhere a sensation of lost solidity. Like Wordsworth's representations of city crowds whose chaos and dissolving power both challenge and undergird poetry's power, London's tyrannical human faces are a marker of Romantic interest in a crowd that fluctuates, terrifies, and insidiously structures the lives of city-dwellers—and of readers more generally. Wordsworth's and De Quincey's texts from this era, then, share a few features that Edgeworth's *Harrington* decidedly does not. Presumably in large part because the generic requirements of the novel forced Edgeworth to consider other aspects of the London crowd, her 1817 book already shows some awareness of the crowd's nascent order as template for novelistic organization. Edgeworth's erotic solution to the novel's problems of too-rigid separation betokens an interest in representing the crowd as potential model for a kind of novel that is required to be both scrupulously privacy-loving and intermittently intrusive. What Wordsworth, Edgeworth, and early De Quincey have in common, however, and what all three reveal about the twenty-year span that their work covers, is an interest in deploying representations of a crowd that can range from pure chaos to moderated lunacy.

This commonality among the three writers becomes all the more striking when one considers the transformation wrought by the 1840s—wrought, that is, even upon the very author whose work best exemplifies the reigning assumptions of the 1820s. In De Quincey's last important work, "The English Mail-Coach" (1849), he switches ground radically in his representation of London's crowds, and of his own indwelling mental crowds. De Quincey proposes a way to stop such crowds from floating forward out of the anchored past and into the unstable present of the dream-writer. By describing a new crowd aggregated around a news-bearing mail coach, he finds a way to justify the temporary bliss the crowd produces, and so to contain its power within that moment.

"The English Mail-Coach" is in telling ways an exemplary work of the Victorian, and not the Romantic, era. The opening chapters of this book have essayed an account of what representations of crowds can tell us about visions of the contested public sphere in an era when organized political working-class crowds had yet to find a national voice. But by 1839, the ground has shifted. Analyzing an 1821 De Quincey text in chapter 3 and an 1849 work in chapter 4 allows an unexpected perspective on ideological and representational changes. Apart from the evolution of De Quincey's own stylistics, the sorts of crowds that filled the fifth decade of the century were different enough from the crowds of De Quincey's youth that there emerges a telling correlation between the decade of composition and the valence each text gives to the crowds represented. My claim is not that there is some strict correspondence between the positive facticity of the crowds that filled London's streets and the ways that those crowds took shape in literary works. Rather, the sorts of pressure that new forms of representative crowds put upon the process of literary composition leave important indirect traces on the works produced.

By the 1840s, enough had changed that generalizations can be drawn on the basis of what might almost seem a generational split. The differences might be written off as simply personal, even as contingent and accidental, if De Quincey did not so neatly straddle the line. A phenomenon that in the early 1820s carried with it the strongest signs of mental imbalance and associated irrationality now in the late 1840s can successfully be linked to a striking way of representing the nation as a whole. It is not, as Tarde claims, that crowds have been replaced by a dispersed, rational public. It is rather that in the 1840s the crowd—along with allied phenomena such as the demonstration, rally, and assembly—has come to seem an available medium for the working classes to articulate shared grievances. That change precipitates in turn a radically changed paradigm for literary representation in the Victorian era. De Quincey's 1849 "English Mail-Coach" lends itself as fruitfully to comparisons with Charlotte Brontë's and Thomas Carlyle's works of the 1840s as it does to De Quincey's own work of the 1820s.

"Grand National Sympathy" in De Quincey's "The English Mail-Coach"

UNIFORM ANONYMITY

The 1849 essay "The English Mail-Coach," De Quincey's last major work, returns to the space of limitless crowd possibility through the unlikely mechanism of patriotism.[1] "The English Mail-Coach, or the Glory of Motion" was the work's full title when it appeared in *Blackwood's Magazine*, and each section comes back to the "glory" produced on the moving coach, a sensation inextricable from its national patriotic role, and from the delighted attention the coach invariably attracts. Half of the glory comes from the thrill of a wind-whipped ride that goes up to a spine-tingling thirteen miles an hour.[2] But the other half of the pleasure is the thrill produced when the mail coaches "published" the news of great British military triumphs in the Napoleonic Wars (that is, in the 1810s, about thirty-five years before De Quincey wrote the essay). Such mail coaches inspired the bliss of a national crowd, and for De Quincey that crowd is the only phenomenon capable of overcoming the sense of continued responsibility to an inaccessible past that had haunted the *Confessions*, the only way to replace interior fragmentation and external intangibility with a transitory but complete union of all Britons.

The essay is divided into five sections. The untitled first section sets the stage for the movement of the "national organ" as "great respiration, ebb or flood of national intercourse" and describes De Quincey's own delight as a college student in riding outside those coaches, whose "organic power" he vastly prefers to the mere "potboilings of a steam train." The section titled "Going down with Victory" describes bringing the news of a British victory against Napoleon to, among others, a coach filled with beautiful women, and a mother whose son had almost certainly been killed in that very victory. "A Vision of Sudden Death" switches ground to tell of De Quincey's memory of riding a mail coach that, while traveling at great speed with a sleeping driver, strikes and possibly kills a young woman on the road. Finally, the "Dream-fugue: Founded on the Preceding Theme of Sudden Death" brings together the glory of motion, national triumphs, and the price exacted in the form of a young woman's possible death, into a participle-heavy ("rising, sinking, falling, raving") poetical effusion of sensational grief, triumph, and sublime awe: a confused congeries of emotion in which the pleasures of the national joy and the price paid for that pleasure are inextricably intermingled.

In "Going Down with Victory," the mail coach comes flying through a town decked out with flags and banners that can convey nothing to onlookers but that a great British military victory has been gained. In such moments of exultation, a great national crowd erases all identifying marks but those of Englishness, and engenders in all participants a pleasurable and a patriotic temporary anonymity. The essay's central pleasure is encapsulated in De Quincey's impression that, during the mail coach's victory rides, "all smile on each side in a way that nobody could misunderstand, and that nothing short of a grand national sympathy could so instantaneously prompt" (13:296). In that moment of perfect accord, smiles cannot be misunderstood because they do not, they cannot, have anything personal about them. Haunting images of faces from past crowds are replaced in "The English Mail-Coach" by a national solidarity that applies only as long as the ride lasts, and carries with it no larger moral burden. The temporary national crowd has an aesthetic and a political use. The curse of intermittence in the *Confessions*—that the crowd's identity can never be a stable one, that last names are incompatible with the London crowds—has here been recuperated as a form of power. The crowd that hails the news of British victories is an important source of national unity.[3] However, De Quincey makes it clear the crowd is not typical of everyday social intercourse. He presents the crowd as deeply anomalous within an England that remains generally resistant to the dissociative logic of rapid "electrical" connection that the crowd brings with it.[4] One can be British for a moment, and a private individual otherwise.

In order to arrive at this entirely new conception of national (and personal) unity, "The English Mail-Coach" introduces a few deceptively familiar elements. It early on seems to be recapitulating a problem familiar from the *Confessions*: how is an individual to react when his insides fail to behave as an individual self? The same tyranny that had haunted the opium dreams—a self shattered into crowds that mirror the crowds of an intangible London—threatens to become central here as well:

> The dreamer finds housed within himself—occupying, as it were, some separate chamber in his brain—holding, perhaps, from that station a secret and detestable commerce with his own heart—some horrid alien nature. What if it were his own nature repeated,—still, if the duality were distinctly perceptible, even that—even this mere numerical double of his own consciousness—might be a curse too mighty to be sustained. But how if the alien nature contradicts his own, fights with it, perplexes and confounds it? How, again, if not one alien nature, but two, but three, but four, but five, are introduced within what once he thought the inviolable sanctuary of himself?[5]

Indeed, the 1856 revision of the *Confessions* retains this very anxiety, explicitly grounded in his pursuit of Ann through dreamscapes, and the reemergence of imagined London crowds in De Quincey's present. In the *Confessions*, the pursuit of Ann across the featureless faces of the past denotes the intangibility of the mental landscape.[6] With a "mere numerical double" De Quincey's worries might have seemed akin to those raised by James Hogg's *Private Memoirs and Confessions of a Justified Sinner* (1824), or even by Dostoyevsky's "The Double" ([1846]): the psyche's split into psychosis. But the infinite regress of mental action threatens to turn the mind into a crowd against itself, as it had in the *Confessions*. In the persistent worry behind "but two, but three, but four, but five," we hear the opium-eater's worry as well: the self can be *pre*occupied by a welter of voices that came from without, but now live within. As the *Confessions* had shown, those voices—the supernumerary threes, fours, and fives—become a nightmare when detached from the solid external world that gave them birth.

However, this is only a residual concern of "The English Mail-Coach," which discovers a situation in which the multifoliate self can be turned "solid" again (as Goethe was turned solid by his passage through Naples). The crowds that gather around the mail coach now can delight the narrator, the writer, the reader, with the reassurance that all who catch sight of it will be amalgamated. They are united in the singularity that their being English produces all along the coach's run. Like Thomas Carlyle's invocations of a sublime unity at the heart of the roaring working class (see chapter 5), De Quincey's vision of a seamless national unity provides a telling insight into the various ways the figure of crowd was put to political as well as to aesthetic use in the 1840s, as it had not been in the 1820s.

"ONE ACKNOWLEDGED SOLE INTEREST"

"The English Mail-Coach" begins by establishing that the experience the coach has to offer is quintessentially unified, in time, in space, and most of all in emotion. The effect of the mail coach's passage is to draw all attention to itself. Its power as an electrifying conveyance of national news is enormous, so long as it retains its monopoly on going thirteen miles an hour: hence the numerous anecdotes that early in the text establish the coach's speed advantage over any private conveyance. When the mail coach was replaced by the train, De Quincey writes with nostalgic fervor, what "perished" were

> multiform openings for public expressions of interest, scenical yet natural, in great national tidings,—for revelations of face and groups that could not offer themselves amongst the fluctuating mobs of a railway station. The gatherings of gazers about a laurelled mail had one centre, and one acknowledged sole interest. But the crowds attending at a railway station have as little unity as running water, and own as many centres as there are separate carriages in the train. (13:284–85)

The dispersed centers of attention that go along with a train are inherently inferior to a coach's centralization.[7] The train—like a newspaper—may seem to act as potential bearer of national news but it can never coalesce all attention to a single point. When one can be sure that all eyes are drawn to a single center simultaneously, the national crowd can gel. The coach's capacity to counter the fears of interior fragmentation is precise: this public homogenization of all minds into one population perfectly counteracts the threat of "horrid alien natures" within a single mind. When all are united in their interest, the dream of difference that makes the London crowds such a recurrent fixture of the *Confessions*—and other De Quincey works—cannot begin. If all the country has only a single thought, then it seems that nobody can be afflicted with a multiplied interior.

Even in ordinary circumstances, the coach draws to it all eyes as an unfocused train cannot:[8] how much more so when the "great national tidings" turn the coach into a mobile performer of the meaning of the nation, into the instant of unity moving through a standing wave of active unification? The coach is then no longer a passive recipient of the gaze: it captures and stores the collective sound, the "continual hurrahs" of the crowd, and returns them to every succeeding onlooker, congealing in itself the long, serialized whole of the crowd. In fact, it becomes an occasion for what Elias Canetti describes as the most powerful crowd phenomenon of all: the crowd that gathers strength from watching itself, that depends on the shared celebration of its own existence.[9]

This sense of national power impresses most of all those who ride the outside of the coaches, among them the author himself.[10] "The outside of the mail had its own incommunicable advantages" (13:275). The incommunicable in De Quincey, like the sublime, is qualitatively different from other systems of value; it has no cash nor prosaic equivalent: the experience of being part of the haze of glory cannot be exchanged for anything. De Quincey gives four explanations for the sublime "agency" that mail coaches have upon riders like himself. They work:

> 1st, through velocity at that time unprecedented—for they first revealed the glory of motion; 2dly, through grand effects for the eye between lamp-light and the darkness upon solitary roads; 3dly, through animal beauty and power so often displayed in the class of horses selected for this mail service; 4thly through the conscious presence of a central intellect, that, in the midst of vast distance—of storms, of darkness, of danger—overruled all obstacles into one steady co-operation to a national result. (13:271–72)

This typical De Quinceyan catalogue of reasons—typical in its imperfect parallels and repetitive reasoning—suggests the rapid, fluent, and overbearing movement of both coach and essay. At the heart of De Quincey's pleasure—in riding and in writing—is the fact that in the conveyance of the national tidings all those who travel along with the coach are also encompassed in the national glory of motion (one version of the essay even offers as the fourth reason "the function, almost a consecrated function, of publishing and diffusing through the land the great political events, and especially the great battles, during a conflict of unparalleled grandeur"). This lends the private rider a connection to the "apocalyptic vials" (13:272) of the nation. To ride on the outside of this coach is to participate in the rush of solidarity that blends news, messengers, and recipients into the single fact of English nationhood: the haze of glory. "No dignity is perfect which does not at some point ally itself with the mysterious" (13:279).

The mail coachmen's apparel is the best symbol of the drive to ally the coach-ride with both martial victory and (domestic) national unity. This uniform—like De Quincey's own delighted cheering—is meant not to impersonate but to extend the martial force of the victorious British army even onto the vehicles that publish military triumphs. The passage that justifies such an extension of solidarity lies at the heart of this text's intentions. The uniform establishes a form of long-distance vicarious connection that annihilates the "horrid alien natures" inside the Englishman or Englishwoman who has not yet experienced the mail coach with its glorious news. To begin with, uniforms promote uniformity.

> Such a costume, and the elaborate arrangement of the laurels in their hats, dilate their hearts, by giving them openly a personal connexion with the great news in which they already have the general interest of patriotism. That great national sentiment surmounts and quells all sense of ordinary distinctions. . . . One heart, one pride, one glory, connects every man by the transcendent bond of his national blood. The spectators, who are numerous beyond precedent, express their sympathy with these fervent feelings by continual hurrahs. (13:293–94)

Heart, pride, and glory: these three qualities—seemingly both internal and incommensurable—are universally distributed among all those who witness the coach's passing, transforming what was moments ago a collection of private citizens displaying the "usual reserve" of British "manner" into a spectacle of homogeneity. The spectators, who might seem to want nothing more than to enjoy this splendid passage alone, instead find themselves forcibly recruited into a peripatetic crowd phenomenon. That the arrayed citizens seem at first unmanageably variegated ("numerous beyond precedent") only makes stronger the power of their conversion to an unprecedented solidarity. The transformation is marked in the curious confusion of the "continual" noise of hurrahs. Each person's "hurrah" is multiplied by the other voices shouting "hurrahs," yet reverts to continuity (a form of singularity) because of the great numbers yelling. The magnitude of the shout produces not division, but a higher unity.

That continual set of hurrahs signals more than merely a maelstrom encircling the mail coach at one moment of delivery: De Quincey figures the long entrainment of national celebration. As the news is spread all over the country, the joy of each celebrant is enhanced by the knowledge that all along its long route the mail coach will create a continuation, rigidly demarcated in space and time, of the same celebration crowd. The power of the mail coach "going down with victory" is to create a traveling procession of good news, a procession that is made possible, and vigorous, at every moment of its existence by the assurance that all along the line similar celebrations will be triggered ("three hundred miles west and six hundred north").

> The half-slumbering consciousness that all night long, and all next day— perhaps for even a longer period—many of these mails, like fire racing along a trail of gunpowder, will be kindling at every instant new successions of burning joy, has an obscure effect of multiplying the victory itself, by multiplying to the imagination into infinity the stages of its progressive diffusion. (13:294)

The fractalization of the mail coach's stages into an "infinity" of diffusing moments is telling. For an ordinary coach a "stage" occurs every eleven miles (when horses are changed), but for this coach a stage occurs each instant that another viewer becomes part of the unified rejoicing in a continuous line along its path. The tidings turn out to be worthy of celebration precisely because each celebrant can be sure that others along the way will feel the same need to celebrate. England is united—but not by way of what Benedict Anderson has described as the concurrent or parallel consumption of news distributed in identical form in a thousand newspapers. Instead, De Quincey imagines the moment of serial diffusion along a single line, with each English citizen corporeally connected to the projected joy of the citizen next down the line, or one hundreds of miles away, who will receive the same tidings and rejoice in the same manner because of the same mail coach.[11]

De Quincey's interest in anatomizing sensation still drives this text as it had driven the mental explorations of the *Confessions*. But there is an important difference: that sensation has now been nationalized, made available to the crowd that both witnesses and produces the coach's act of spectacular solidarity. Clinging to the outside of the coach, De Quincey finds his pleasure in the fact that the coach's speed means it precedes any other medium in transmitting the news of victory. Both the claim of top speed and the continuity from one moment of notification to the next are crucial. The absolute conviction that they are watching the beginning of a national train of notification means, for the London crowds, that their joy at witnessing the coaches is already shared, proleptically, with those unknown other Britons who they know will hear the news later. The exaggerated exuberance in London derives from the assurance that the exuberance down the line will seem to happen as an extension of the very same event, an unfolding of sympathy along the "electric nerves" that post horses (and not the mere "mechanical potboilings" of train engines) are capable of providing:

> ... the sympathy of our Lombard Street friends at parting is exalted a hundredfold by a sort of visionary sympathy with the yet slumbering sympathies which in so vast a succession we are going to awake. (13:295)

Waterloo does not even exist as a British victory until it is thus transmitted. More generally, the joy of the transmission depends on the news's reception elsewhere. The "vast succession" that triggers urban celebration is integrally part of a vision of a crowd truly national.

That vision of the crowd creates a paradoxical relationship between the actual physical fact of crowded London, and the larger vision of a whole nation waiting to be waked with the news.[12] The coach moves away from Lombard Street, "liberated from the embarrassments of the city" (13:295), so that it can spread its news to the whole nation. But after describing the liberation from London's embarrassments, in the next paragraph De Quincey describes what are still unmistakably city crowds:

> broad uncrowded avenues of the northern suburbs ... in the broad light of the summer evening. . . . Heads of every age crowd to the windows; young and old understand the language of our victorious symbols. . . . Women and children, from garrets alike and cellars, through infinite London, look down or look up with loving eyes upon our gay ribbons and our martial laurels. (13:295–99)

The coaches may have left London's "embarrassments," but they have clearly retained its "infinity."

The glory that the coach brings, then, retains all the favorable qualities of the *Confessions* crowd before it returned transfigured as a "pain." This crowd is impersonal (no last names here), it is joyous in inception, and it provides an aesthetic pleasure that exactly breaks down conventional social bounds—a cat can look at a king and anyone can look at a coach. But it has also moved beyond the aimless peripatetic pleasure of the *Confessions* crowds: the coach has a purpose, a direction, and substantial content that unifies the crowd's participants;

the crowd can imagine an extended spatial and temporal existence (as the coach sweeps out of sight those in the crowd know that it will be continued elsewhere); the crowd perfectly justifies its own intermittent status (no one could expect a coach ride to last forever). This crowd has established, then, a seeming solidity of national character. But it has done so without creating the possibility of the return of responsibility, of the haunting sense of ongoing loss that the *Confessions* had demanded.

"HUNDREDFOLD EXALTED VISIONARY SYMPATHY"

Once the pleasure of the "national crowd" has been set up, it may seem a relatively straightforward matter for De Quincey to evade the sense of haunting responsibility that the intermittent (and vanished) crowds of London had produced. It may seem that a permanent national unity via the news of Waterloo victories simply avoids any of the aesthetic pleasures or problems that had shaped his conception of the crowds of London poor and London streetwalkers. After all, when the coach pulls out of Lombard Street and heads off into the countryside, leaving "the embarrassments of the city" (13:295) behind, it seems to move straight into national history, making all those who see it feel connected to "one heart," a British one.

But a consideration of the representational problems raised by the recurrent presence of crowds in the *Confessions* will reveal why De Quincey neither yearns for nor discovers a permanent transformation of all private citizens into a melded British nation. If the transformation into a "national crowd" were to be made permanent, De Quincey's problems would not be solved, but spread generally to the external world at large. It is exactly the persistence of images of crowds that De Quincey fears—the haunting phantoms that mean something to him, yet hover untouchable by his own actions. The entire appeal of this new national crowd is its intermittence. National news must remain, like the opium rambles in the *Confessions*, an interlude. What the mail coach rides establish, that is, is a temporary glory in being English that in the cooler light of dawn will be replaced by the same private identities that people possessed before the mail coach came flowing through. These rides are explicitly a temporary phase of national glory, which lasts only until the thought of being English is replaced in the participants' minds by more specific thoughts of personal duties, specific social stations.

The most important corollary of De Quincey's insistence on intermittence is that it is not the content of the news, but the mere fact of
its distribution that the essay means to celebrate: not the message but
the medium. It is not enough to remember that on a certain day in
1815 all of England came to know that Waterloo had broken Napoleon's might forever—in fact it is scarcely anything at all. It is the
cresting wave of notification that appeals to De Quincey here, because
he is precisely not celebrating the power of England to communicate
within itself, but rather the power of the mail coach to bring a particular piece of news that had a powerful, partially aesthetic effect.

The effect of any given piece of news, then, is to establish a national
connection among all those who listen. But it is also precisely to establish what is not true in the *Confessions*. Here, the full experience
of victory is realized in the instant of its being conveyed. The successful
aesthetic production that is both the mail coach ride and the text of
the essay itself ensures that any effort to personalize the news, to make
any connections other than the purely general one of shared Englishness, will fail. In the *Confessions* the tyranny of a human face had
really begun only when that face had gone. Here, however, the full
import of the news can be registered and dispatched in the moment of
passage.

Both the efficacy and the generality of this power of aesthetic intermittence are forcibly confirmed by the two central anecdotes of notification around which the first section of "The English Mail-Coach" is
built. The first—that of De Quincey passing on news of victory to a
mother and her two beautiful daughters in their open coach—goes only
to establish that the best freedom allowed by this national crowd is a
familiar temporary anonymity: under its unifying thrall all may look
at each other with frank pleasure. But the second—that of the mother
of a soldier who has died in Spain sharing in the joy of his victory
before she hears the news of his death—serves to emphasize the necessary transience of this moment of crowd-based, glory-covered news
transmission.

The first instance operates perfectly as a textually dilated instant. It
is explicitly described as having taken far less time to occur than it can
to describe: the accumulation of such details is one way the text establishes a crowding-in of this all-too-rapid coach ride. By witnessing three
beautiful women reading the signs of victory and beginning to rejoice,
De Quincey exercises what might be called his *droit de citoyen*. He
takes the pleasure of reading their transformation into loyal national

subjects: "one may read, as on the stage of a theatre, everything that goes on within" (13:296). The result is that all the ordinary embarrassments that would prevent this kind of frankly sensual interchange are dropped immediately and those in both coaches all smile "in a way that nobody could misunderstand, and that nothing short of a grand national sympathy could so instantaneously prompt" (13:296). The relation is made familial in the same sense that the French Revolution spoke of fraternity:

> Will these ladies say we are nothing to *them*? Oh, no; they will not say *that*. They cannot deny—they do not deny—that for this night they are our sisters; gentle or simple, scholar or illiterate servant, for twelve hours to come, we on the outside have the honour to be their brothers. (13:296–97)

The fraternal time is stretched to twelve hours because of De Quincey's position on the moving coach; his "sisters" assume the role only while the coach passes.

The temporary leveling powers of notification precisely annihilate any personal character to the national news. That annihilation is clearer still in the second extended example of transmission, in which De Quincey tells the news of victory to a woman whose son has been killed in the very Peninsular Battle that the mail coach has gone abroad to proclaim. To that woman, who will read tomorrow or the next day her own son's name on a newspaper casualty list, De Quincey feels obliged to bring a brief interlude of national joy, disconnected from any sense of personal loss. Rather than tell her that her son has likely been killed, De Quincey folds her back into the unified body of the rejoicing nation:

> Did I tell her the truth? Had I the heart to break up her dreams? No. To-morrow, said I to myself—to-morrow, or the next day, will publish the worst. For one night wherefore should she not sleep in peace? (13:299)

This illuminates the general power of the mail coach to erase distinctions, and its use of victory bunting to make "washerwomen and charwomen . . . feel themselves by birthright to be daughters of England and answer to no humbler title" (13:297). This moment of national crowd formation is not dependent on a system that is dedicated to the rapid distribution of all news. Rather, De Quincey praises here the rapidity of national news-transmission and the retardation of personal news: "This brief respite, let her owe this to *my* gift and *my* forbearance. But, if I told her not of the bloody price that had been paid, not therefore was I silent on the contributions from her son's regiment to that day's service and glory" (13:300).[13] It suddenly becomes clear exactly what the appeal of the "one sole interest of the mail coach" is over the "fluctuating mobs" of the railway station: railway mobs can hear a gamut of news (personal or even partisan), while those around the mail coach can hear only what the nation has at this moment chosen to signal by banners and bunting.

The creation of a moment of national solidarity thus turns out to hinge precisely on shutting down the possibility that the mail coach might be used to convey any news which was not of the nation. The news carried by mail coach is an exact inversion of the railroad-borne news in Charles Dickens's *Dombey and Son* (1844–46). Dombey sees his own son's death marked by crepe and mourning when he travels—a purely personal matter has entered the national medium of circulation. That seems to Dombey an abomination, but for Dickens it is a moment to applaud the possibility of good sentiment moving with salutary melodrama through the nation. De Quincey, however, is on Dombey's side: "The English Mail-Coach" indicts the railway's ability to choose odd bits of personal news to publicize.

The mailcoach only publicizes what already belongs to the nation. The coach's exterior must trump its interior. It is thus inconceivable that the truly admirable, truly national mail coach could bring any other news at this moment—although the newspapers with their casualty lists will be brought down as well in the fullness of time. What is offered to the soon-to-be-grieving mother instead is De Quincey's certainty that her son's regiment's valor is "the foremost topic of conversation in London" (13:300). And that reward of national publicity is augmented by the reaction of the "poor woman," who accepts the national news gladly in place of the personal and "gave to *me* the kiss which secretly was meant for *him*" (13:300). If "secretly" the private identity is allowed to continue, it is buried in a public display that is an ostentatious affirmation of the need to be nothing but English in this moment. Shared feelings win by preceding the delivery of the news that would produce private ones. Consider how far De Quincey has come from Edgeworth's notion of a family member who can be "good to you" only within an enclosed space. De Quincey's notion of a shared national good postpones even the responsibility of a mother to mourn for her son. Being "good to" a son (in this case by mourning him) may ultimately be no less important than taking part in the good of the nation, but it is necessarily subsequent to such shared national rejoicing.

It is precisely because news of the nation as a whole overleaps the "bloody" personal news of a son who lies "mangled together" with his horse that the mail coach is able to act as a unifying messenger of rejoicing. To release in London "a grand national sympathy" (13:296) which is then carried "down" through the country to those who know no facts but the victory (and De Quincey is at pains to point out that no "unauthorized rumor" was able to "steal a prelibation from the first aroma of the regular dispatches" [13:293]) is to heal the nation and say to it "be thou whole" (13:296)—for as long as only that news is heard.

Only in the national crowd, therefore, will the unease of self-fragmentation and the possibility of other forms of personal loss be dispelled. Only in the transient speed of the unfolded moment of national joy—here prolonged into an entire long coach run, and hence into an entire hundred-page literary work—can the self find sanctuary in an annealment of reader, writer, text, crowd, and British nation. To give up distinctions—as all those who see the coach do momentarily, and as those who ride the coach do for long hours—is also to give up selfhood, and to live only in the reflection, the re-creation, of the glorious death of the latest regiment that has become "the foremost topic of conversation in London" (13:300). In Edgeworth's *Harrington*, to become such a topic was to be a laughable prodigy: when Harrington is likened to "George Psalmanazar . . . with his . . . pounds of raw beef" (12), Edgeworth means to mock him for allowing himself to descend into public awareness. Public conversation has gone from the ridiculous to the sublime.

A LOST LADY

Yet even at the moment that a national mission has seemed to provide a way to obviate the guilt associated with a blissful plunge into the crowd, even when the purely national quality of the news has seemed to ensure that a transient state of self-forgetfulness and utterly blissful solidarity can be instituted, even here De Quincey feels impelled to return to his nagging sense that there must be a price to pay for this pleasure, a memory trace as enduring and exacting as the tyrannical memory of Ann among the crowds. The recollection of the woman who must serve as ransom for this unity, then, is the one alien presence that continues to haunt this dream, and thus to hold off the possibility of a unification of all the nation in victory. In the *Confessions*, the sense of nagging responsibility and fated mortality in the floating res-

idue of the crowd was figured in the "perpetual farewells" (113) that
came back into De Quincey's psyche to mark the loss both of Ann and
of his childhood. The "perpetual" quality of the farewells marked, in
passing only, the way that loss could be turned into a permanent, ongoing internal process. That narrator could never stop mourning what
was clearly lost in time—and yet just as clearly lived agonizingly on in
the palimpsest of his mind.

"The English Mail-Coach" does threaten the reader with the recurrence of that experience of "perpetual farewells." The orgiastic celebrations of victory are linked, as De Quincey often links his representational crisis-points, to the sacrifice of a young woman. To forge this
link, De Quincey establishes an exceptionally tortuous chain of connections. It begins in "A Vision of Sudden Death," in which De Quincey describes riding on a mail coach, years after the Napoleonic coach
rides, that either kills or narrowly misses killing a woman in a light
carriage. He knows no more of her fate than he does of Ann's, because
the coach he is riding in fails to stop and a turn in the road prevents
his witnessing the result of the collision. In the concluding "Dream
Fugue: Founded on the Preceding Theme of Sudden Death," De Quincey juxtaposes this image with that of coaches "going down with victory." In the initial telling, the accident was not connected to the
patriotic "glory of motion": it occurred when De Quincey was traveling to Lancaster on a sleepy summer night. But when he again finds
himself invaded by the "horrid alien natures" that fill his head with an
uninvited crowd, her death returns again and again ("into my dream
forever"), and this time juxtaposed to the triumphant news of Waterloo. In De Quincey's dream, the mail coach that either kills or does
not kill this young woman has no ordinary news to deliver, but this
national mission alone: "At midnight the secret word arrived; which
word was—*Waterloo and Recovered Christendom*" (13:322). This removes the young woman's possible death from the realm of industrial
accident, and juxtaposes it directly to the glorious national crowds that
De Quincey has established as the central ethical purpose and aesthetic
pleasure of the mails.

> "Oh baby!" I exclaimed, "shalt thou be the ransom for Waterloo? Must
> we, that carry tidings of great joy to every people, be messengers of ruin to
> thee!" (13:324)

The trade is explicitly articulated here as one between national glory
and personal mortality (for a beautiful young woman who is also a

"baby"). There is something that seems almost consciously false about the equation. Should not the price of Waterloo be assessed in battlefield deaths, rather than on the roads of England? Yet in De Quincey's dream logic the connection rings true. Because he imagines that Waterloo becomes a great British victory only when it is celebrated, it is only when those on Lombard Street know that others all over the country will soon hear the same news that it is certified and passes into fact—the fact of shared belief. By that logic, it is only the creation of a domestic crowd that can truly approbate the doings of the nation. And by the dream logic that makes De Quincey return repeatedly to the lost woman, it is only in witnessing a near-death that he can be sure the national news about Waterloo will be spread.

Thus the possible death of the young woman, reenacted again and again in the dream fugue, becomes De Quincey's most important figure for the glory of the continually unfolding but temporary news-delivery of the national mailcoach. The near-death moment perfectly captures a central rhetorical strategy of the essay that might be called the "perpetual present progressive." That is, the ongoing, continually unfolding revelation that the passage of the mailcoach represents is reflected in the fascinating lists of participles with which De Quincey describes his visions of the woman as she hovers near death. She is described as, for instance, "rising, sinking, fluttering, trembling" and "tossing, falling, rising, clutching" (13:320, 321). In piling up these participles, De Quincey manages to convey linguistically the effect of simultaneity in repetition. The "-ing" overload works both to unhinge temporality and to foreground it, for the action entailed in "sinking," "rising," or "trembling" can be taking place at any time, but the participial form means the action seems always to be occurring within the time of the sentence itself. Like continual hurrahs, this death-experience happens in a single moment, and yet in his imagination is always happening. Because it is in this fugue of almost-death that De Quincey imagines national news can truly be spread, he here provides an account of public news distribution that is crucially at odds with Benedict Anderson's metaphor of "parallel" readerships. This is the experience not of newspapers distributing the same news everywhere at the same time, but of the mail coach linearly distributing identical news—national victory—in an infinity of "stages." The recurrence to this image captures the very sensation of immediacy provided by the experience of going down with victory, or of watching the celebration occur.

There comes, however, a convincingly fatal conclusion, at once confirming and upsetting the moment of news-revelation. The certainty always denied in De Quincey's dreaming of Ann in the *Confessions* is achieved here. After glimpsing this woman in dreams for years, De Quincey finally sees a vision of God picking her up, redeeming her as national barter and as national treasure. The whole ride of the mail coach has taken place, in this final account, "only that at the last, with one sling of His victorious arm, He might snatch thee back from ruin, and might emblazon in thy deliverance the endless resurrections of His love!" (13:322). The plural *resurrections*, like all the earlier participles, marks a single and yet infinitely repeated action.

But it also marks an inversion of that past repetition. If endlessly repeated death is, like the loss of Ann, an infinity of anguish, the "endless resurrections" now seem the property of an overarching national logic that posits the sudden death of this woman as the necessary and sufficient price to be paid for Waterloo. Rather than simply evading his traditional recourse to the figure of the vanishing, dying woman, De Quincey reuses that figure but not as a cipher for uncertainty. Instead, her possible death into certain resurrections restores certainty to the national news-ride, making its crowds an aesthetic summation of patriotic pleasure.

An utterly suitable, if macabre, dream logic follows in the essay's concluding pages. The unity that De Quincey believes can be attained only in the present-participle moment of motion through a crowd returns, in an alienated form, in his final vision of the news of victory. He imagines the news being brought into a giant national necropolis, down an avenue lined with sarcophagi of the glorious dead of the national cause: "a city of sepulchers, built within the saintly cathedral for the warrior dead that rested from their feuds on earth" (13:323). In an explanatory footnote De Quincey explains, unsurprisingly, that St. Paul's in London had supplied the original vision for this part of the dream. St. Paul's—for Wordsworth and De Quincey as for many others—stood for the "urbs within an urbs," the city of God parked within an uncontrolled city of man. As a child, on his first trip to a London far too big for him, De Quincey had entered St. Paul's with a sense of relief ("Nation of London," [1:186]). For De Quincey, to enter St. Paul's is to find national unity and blessed quiet among the crowds of those who are entirely homogenized by their martial glory in the service of the country.

The death of the woman in the carriage is resolved in "The English

Mail-Coach" as the death of Ann could never be in the *Confessions*. But it is resolved in a way that depends on all the power of the nation to justify. The danger put forward in the dream is redeemed on that *camposanto* in St. Paul's, in that vast cathedral armory of national victories, which is also an entrance into the one place within all of London that belongs unalloyedly to a common English identity. Among the crowd of the dead—Canetti allows them an entire chapter in *Crowds and Power*—there are no horrid alien natures nor private familial concerns.

RIVAL PUBLICATIONS AND
THE CROWD'S AESTHETIC POWER

One heart, one pride, one glory, connects every man
by the transcendent bond of his national blood.
                              (13:294)
Did the reader ever happen to reflect on the great idea
of *publication*? An idea we call it; because even in our
own times, with all the mechanic aids of steam-presses
&c., this object is most imperfectly approached and is
destined, perhaps, for ever to remain an unattainable
ideal. . . . Yet, on the other hand, publication in some
degree, and by some mode, is a *sine qua non* condition
for the generation of literature. Without a larger
sympathy than that of his own personal circle, it is
evident that no writer could have a motive for those
exertions.
                    ("Style" [1841], 10:231–32)

In the temporary national crowd, patriotism justifies the ecstatic solidarity that had come at such a high price in the London of the *Confessions*. The distribution of national news provides legitimate boundaries: as long as only national news is known, each witness is both self-unified and united with others in the glory of being English. It is universally known that no one thinks of anything else but the joy that is expressed in each eye, seen in each smile, heard in each ear as a series of discrete and yet "continuous hurrahs." Glimpsed from an era that no longer spreads its news by coach, this spectacle has all the glamour of nostalgia. This nostalgia is both England's for the Napoleonic Wars, when the nation's unity was unquestioned, and De Quincey's for the Romantic era, when his writing circulated among a public whose sentiments he felt himself sure of sharing.[14]

However, De Quincey is bent on comparing the power of this new national crowd to not one but two rival phenomena. Clearly, one comparison is intended back to the static swirling of people with no beginning and no end that doomed the partially tangible London of the *Confessions*. That purgatorial time and space explicitly returns here as the "embarrassments of London," where there is no rapid directed motion. Without such rapid directed motion, crowds cannot expect the arrival of news. But there is another implicit comparison at work here as well: the newspaper-constituted public sphere. In Benedict Anderson's influential and generally convincing account, it is "parallel readerships" created by national newspaper distribution that become the inevitable site both of nation-formation and class-consciousness.[15] Newspapers being read at the same time in various places—newspapers circulated within the state, but potentially at odds with it—may attest not only to a nation, but to the parallel structure of a movement or of a class.

A world in which the news is distributed by the mail coach is exactly antithetical to the vision of a world of parallel events unfolding in the safely separated, socially discrete spaces that Gabriel Tarde in 1901 was to label the "public." The most obvious difference between that public and the physical ingathering of the "crowd" responding to the mail coach is that the latter needs to feel that a vital, nervous link exists between themselves and the point at which the news originates. Only in the establishment of this vital, nervous connection can Waterloo cease to be merely a battle and become an English victory. In order for the mail coach—and De Quincey's essay about it—to be counted as successful, then, it must differentiate itself both from the milling, disorganized, news-less London crowd of the *Confessions* and from the remote "public" distribution of the same news via a hundred newspapers read in a hundred towns. De Quincey finds a way to delineate both its difference from and its superiority to those two rival forms in an elaborate encomium to the temporality of the crowd phenomenon that is both described and inscribed in "The English Mail-Coach." The logic is fundamentally hybrid: in this one peculiar instance of crowd-production around a national news flash, crowd temporality comes to be defined (as a newspaper or market crowd never could be) as linear, continuous, and sequential.

One can begin the enumeration of these qualities by comparing the spatial chaos of earlier De Quincey crowds to the crystal-clear linear logic of this crowd. If murder can take place in secret amongst the crowd in his "On Murder Considered as One of the Fine Arts" (1827), for example, it can do so precisely because the crowd is a scrum and tumult out of which no single vector emerges (13:23). And though there may be a center of attention in the crowds of the *Confessions*— De Quincey himself moving among shoppers—what the reader gets is only a center of subjective attention. That is, the crowd is defined by wherever the eye of the writer happens to light, and it is centered on him only out of the purely methodological necessity of creating coherence within an inherently unbounded event—a coherence clearly shattered in the retrospective dreamscapes of multitudinous tumult. "The English Mail-Coach," by contrast, with its electric extension of that single piece of news out from London to every protuberance and outcropping of England, offers a figure analogous to the reader's glorious experience of the unfolding linearity of De Quincey's text. Just as the crowds in Lombard Street can celebrate with greater vigor because of the anticipated celebrations all down each line, so too the reader's pleasure in the first page of De Quincey's essay is intensified by the secure knowledge that a fourth and fifth and fiftieth page will follow—each experienced in immediacy, yet each in its linear place.

The effort on De Quincey's part to differentiate his own writing from the world of newspaper notification is clear. The coach's ride creates a sense of organic connection among those who experience it, as parallel publication of newspapers does not. Every member of this drawn-out crowd—and De Quincey himself as rider and author most of all—is connected continuously to one event, one single publication that is never divided, never paralleled, never interrupted. The direct physical proximity that made the crowd such a remarkably pleasant experience in De Quincey's earlier writing is preserved, even as its dangerous blurriness is dissolved. The national glory that De Quincey describes, in 1849, as being most perfectly present in 1815 is a glory of unity without recourse to the fragmented public realm of newspaper reading and political colloquy. The affirming national crowd is both the object of this news, and its constitutive subject.

De Quincey's incarnation as a Victorian author, we might say, explicitly demands that he summon up his own past as part of an available realm of nostalgia. To write as a Victorian is precisely to lionize the Romantic era, but to lionize it as the irretrievable past.[16] The mail-coach itself may have no more work to do in the present of 1849 than the vanished school-cap would have had in the present of the *Confessions*. But its departed glory has a worthy successor in De Quincey himself, a self-styled residuum from that physically departed age.

This distinction between what the newspaper offers and what De Quincey posits as the power of the mail coach is thrown into sharpest relief if we compare his valorization of the mail coach to an 1834 essay that praises instead the existence of perfectly interactive national media. De Quincey himself had fifteen years before the publication of "The English Mail-Coach" posited instantaneous communication as the nation's greatest possible good.

> Conceive a state of communication between the center and the extremities of a great people, kept up with a uniformity of reciprocation so exquisite, as to imitate the flowing and ebbing of the sea, or the systole and diastole of the human heart; day and night, waking and sleeping, not succeeding to each other with more certainty than the acts of the metropolis and the controlling notice of the provinces, whether in the way of support or of resistance. Action and reaction from every point of the compass being this perfect and instantaneous, we should then first begin to understand, in a practical sense, what is meant by the unity of a political body.[17]

This may not seem at first glance all that different from the glorious message of the mail coach. Both, after all, are concerned with the highest form of communication possible. But it quickly becomes clear that each feature of this new utopian communication system operates to remove an essential quality of the pleasure inherent in the coach ride. The crucial difference is that the system imagined in "Travelling in England in the Old Days" eliminates any possibility of excessive attachment to the messenger, any possibility of becoming one with the process of communication itself. Such perfection of communication would remove the presence of the messenger from the process of message-making. The result is a corporeal dialogue, but one that lacks the pleasure that those who are not in fact face to face can imagine (via the mail coach)—that of being face to face. In the new dispensation

> every part of the empire will react upon the whole with power, life and the effect of immediate conference amongst parties brought face to face. (1:271)

Such instantaneous perfect communication—better replicated in the train than the mail coach—would be a form of death to just the experience with which De Quincey is infatuated.

The possibility of telegraphic "systole and diastole" also highlights, by contrast, another important quality of the mail coach. The telegraph allows back-and-forth communication, but the mail coach by its nature must be nonreciprocal. Publication via the mail coach—or the production of a glorious national crowd through the mail coach's passage—produces only attention, never a response. In that respect, then, it might even be called an aesthetic spectacle, which forces all who watch to be moved, and leaves them no conduit back into the event other than to register their being moved.[18]

All of these differences, moreover, return to the fundamental fact of national unity implied in the coach ride. The pleasure of rapidity, the uniqueness of the news, and the knowledge that others down the line will behave as one does: all unleash the crowd renewed, metamorphosed into an enduring figure for national unity. But this national unity—the logic turns back to justifying De Quincey's own writing here—is quintessentially shaped by being channeled through an aesthetic experience. Without rapidity of motion, without the joyous intersection of all the celebrations that are magnified "a hundredfold" by the knowledge of the celebrations that follow elsewhere, without that assurance of a continually unfolding crowd defined for that night solely by their Englishness, without what can finally only be described as a temporally limited, spatially disaggregated, aesthetic vision of the crowd as a long line of anonymous English citizens—without all of this, English society would be riven into heterogeneous parts, lacking the "organic unity" that De Quincey believes is essential for the final image of redemption.

Hence the 1834 vision of instantaneous rational communication is replaced in 1849 by an avowedly nostalgic evocation of the very non-instantaneous image of a physical crowd unfolding into anonymity all along the path of the traveling mail coach—as long as it keeps up its glorious motion. The "language of our national symbols" (13:294) is in the figures of Waterloo, of St. Paul's, and of the speeding mail coach whose passage inspires a temporary but nationwide crowd of patriots. The sublime pleasure that in the *Confessions* had been De Quincey's alone—since he alone, at the subjective center of a milling crowd, could appreciate the highest pleasures in its disunified unity—has here become through the medium of a national consciousness an unapologetically intermittent but vital sensation for the nation as a whole.

De Quincey here imagines that the "public" will depend upon the always temporary joy of a crowd experience. And the moment which he has imagined as best elucidating that creation of a crowd-borne public is not the redemptive death of the fallen girl/woman, but the very instant of her death in "endless resurrections" that follow that fall, a perpetual present at celebration. This repeated unfolding of a single moment, so that it can be returned to and recreated, makes it of a piece with the "endless resurrections" of that same moment in De Quincey's own crowded essay. In its own purely temporary enactment of the literal transport induced by the mail coach going down with victory, it recreates textually that momentary, linked, invisible but inescapable pride De Quincey credits to the mail coach and to moving crowds.

By riding along with the crowd-creating coach, De Quincey's text has overcome the dilemmas associated with the pleasures of the crowd in the *Confessions*. If De Quincey had simply avoided representing a dying woman, his figure for omnipresent loss, the sense of effective exorcism would not have been so strong. Mere absence would not have proved the point that presence followed by "endless resurrections" does. De Quincey's essay is pointedly distanced from the diastolic system of perpetual circulation, which is endlessly reduplicated in the world of newspapers and telegraphs. Instead, it claims for itself a living, organic, unique status, half tied to the crowd and half to the driving purpose of the national news system. To be akin to but not of the journalistic world, akin to but not of the organic power of celebratory masses, leaves his writing in a curious but enviable space.[19]

The comparison that De Quincey institutes between his own writing and the onrushing crowd that the mail coach produces is striking. This mail-coach-plus-crowd is, like a written text, linear. The coach, like the text, produces its glory as it goes. The text works so successfully because one feels enraptured in the midst of it—enraptured by its swift organic speed. Losing oneself in the essay—whether to a sense of renewed patriotism, or merely to a textual sublimity like the sublimity of motion—the reader can feel in good company with everyone else who falls under its spell in exactly the same way. The crowd here has the power to produce something that is very like the "literature of power." Yet the essay also has an instantaneously agglutinative power—the power of nation-formation—that De Quincey had never before shown operating within his own writing. This new national crowd produces a sublime publication which while it lasts unites all English viewers in a subjective, but a generally shared sensation.

Charles Rzepka has recently argued that De Quincey's anxiety about entering his work into public circulation impels him to create what Rzepka calls "publication as sublimation." That is, the author's assertion of power causes the reader to forget that the author is "a worker or retailer" rather than an "origin and bestower" (9) of language. In Rzpeka's provocative account, De Quincey chooses to label his work part of the "literature of power" rather than of the "literature of knowledge" (34) because such a claim will cause the reader to overlook the author's simply material ambitions and the book's simply material presence. "Once consumed, the literary text, like ingested opium, seems to take on a life, a persona, of its own to which that of the owner is, paradoxically, subsumed" (31).

Rzepka's model has a fascinating, if partial, application to the sequential, performing text in "The English Mail-Coach."[20] The relevant claim is that the writer of the "literature of power" is concerned not with producing a direct verbal fact, a residuum of bare "knowledge" or "information," but instead aims to convey what Rzepka calls "raw ontic and affective energy" (35), to overawe the reader with a sensation that cannot be simply verbalized or translated. Both the sublimity of publication and the sublimity of such a confusion are activated in "The English Mail-Coach." Its themes are the loss of identity into news-transmission and the delightful confusion that is associated with the "glory of motion," in whose aura the mail coach riders travel, reveling in their inarticulable (but delightfully national) prestige.

This moment of sublimity, in which the crowd is fully justified by the delightful national news, and the national circulation is fully returned to a moment of aesthetic performance, does not directly glorify the author: rather, it glorifies England. And it is exactly this inescapable content that will provide the most compelling rationale for De Quincey's claim to "power." Both the carriage and the freight are patriotic: the text's power thus putatively glorifies not (or not only) its author, but England. The mail coach crowd represents a sort of publication that plunges into the subjective centers of dispersed consciousness, and yet still resides in a shared public world—a publication that validates each internal moment of ecstasy with a generally noted "smile which no one could misunderstand." After such blessed smiles, blessed peace and endless resurrections follow, rather than "everlasting farewells." One should not wonder that the funeral bells are sweet. They toll for England.[21]

CONTESTING THE PUBLIC SPHERE: THE VICTORIAN ERA

To the degree, however, to which philosophical and
literary works and works of art in general were
produced for the market and distributed through it . . .
they no longer remained components of the Church's
and court's publicity of representation: that is precisely
what is meant by the loss of their aura of
extraordinariness and by the profaning of their once
sacramental character.

> Habermas, *The Structural Transformation*
> *of the Public Sphere*

The presence within De Quincey's work of a cultural logic that favor-
ably compares mail coaches to trains, and national crowds to dispersed
publics, opens up a fresh way of analyzing the public sphere in Victorian Britain. Because De Quincey exemplifies an important strain of
thinking about what sort of power literary textual production might
have in a world of parallel readerships—and thus more generally what
place the "aesthetic" might have in the public sphere—"The English
Mail-Coach" suggests that we need to find ways to talk about a whole
variety of competing discursive attempts not merely to fill but to constitute a public sphere—newspapers, literary texts, and demonstrating
crowds among them.

"The English Mail-Coach" asserts the strength and importance of
literary texts by presenting a certain sort of crowd as the validating
somatic presence that is vital for representing authority in the national
arena. Such a model rejects the possibility of a national communicative
network built on the cool exchange of reasonable thought. "The English Mail-Coach" substitutes for a systolic-diastolic system of trains,
telegraphs, and newspapers a corporeally incarnate chain of linked signifying bodies, nervous horses, and cheering crowds, in whose visceral
exhilaration the actual work of both national information and nation-
formation is accomplished. It then proceeds to claim for literature itself
the power to subsume such organic power within a textual production
printed for distribution through a textually constituted public sphere.
In De Quincey's attempt to textualize a living, applauding, news-
creating crowd, Habermas's normative ideal of a realm where speech
acts come unhinged from bodily presence is explicitly denied at a historical moment at which logic would seem to dictate that it be fully
ascendant.[22]

"The English Mail-Coach" does, however, seem to me to corrobo-
rate a relatively underdeveloped (and underappreciated) Habermartian
analogy: that between the notion of waning aristocratic power and the
advent of a new kind of aesthetic power in the early nineteenth century.
The Structural Transformation of the Public Sphere briefly analyzes the
moment in Goethe's *Wilhelm Meister* in which Wilhelm decides to perform theater before admiring audiences because he cannot, at his late
date, hope to be an aristocrat and perform aristocratic power before
an admiring court (34–35). Habermas argues that in Goethe the fading
conception of aristocratic power can be directly replaced by an aesthetic performance which has the power to move, persuade, or impress
its audience precisely because vestiges of the now extinct aristocratic
privilege of display are transferred to it.

Though this analogy is marginal to current understandings of Habermas's central claims (see such sharp indictments as those of Negt
and Kluge and of Fraser), it seems to me that Eley's recent work points
us toward an account of Habermas whereby such subtle observations
about the mixed nature of the public sphere could clarify our notions
about public space in the nineteenth century. By way of the analogy
between aesthetic and aristocratic power, Habermas offers a plausible
explanation of an aesthetic sphere which, in Britain at least, waxes in
strength and in display precisely as the notion of a "rational-critical
bourgeois" public sphere comes into being. In this account, the literary/
aesthetic sphere becomes a parallel form of public interaction, rival to
the rational-critical sphere, and equipped with its own cultural logic.
That account is borne out in De Quincey's nostalgic mail coach, with
its seriality, its living autonomic nervous system, and all the appurte-
nances of aura. The royal mail coach has by 1849 become an essay,
and De Quincey's own ride to glory on it thirty-five years earlier has
become his present-day ride on a glorious construction of prose. As the
actor is a substitute for the aristocrat in *Wilhelm Meister*, the essay
"The English Mail-Coach" is a substitute for the old conjunction of
coach and crowd.

In a world of railway trains and of no-longer-electrifying transmission of news, De Quincey is able to tap into a whole reservoir of regret
for past grandeur by placing this moment of extraordinary national
display in a golden age—the period of the Napoleonic Wars—when
the government still aspired neither to persuade nor to converse with
its citizens, but to dazzle them by parading before them its power and
its glory—a glory which in its turn produced "the glory of motion."

And, having established by this glorious nostalgia the fact that the power of such display no longer inheres in the body politic, De Quincey's text is all the more poised to make of its own performance a spectacle. The past conjured up and controlled its crowds with the help of the mail coaches of His Majesty; but the present's crowds are conjured up, and compelled into a patriotic-aesthetic rapture, by De Quincey's own story. De Quincey claims, that is, that his own essay counts as a potent rival to newspaper-based information by virtue of having assimilated the power of past crowds.

This claim clarifies the enormous range of ways that De Quincey's era defined presence, speech, and action within the public arena. Would an assenting crowd of the "English Mail-Coach" variety count as a discursive presence in the public arena of 1849? By De Quincey's account, it could no longer do so: both because trains have now replaced the old coaches, and because his own essay has internalized such crowds. One might also ask how De Quincey would account for a Chartist procession, assembled peacefully to represent its own desire to be represented in Parliament, or for simultaneous meetings of protesters in town squares all across England. My reading suggests that De Quincey would deny such new crowds discursive presence, but for a different reason—they are unsubsumed rivals to his own work. To the extent that those assemblies are precisely oriented toward inclusion in an arena—exemplified by the newspaper—of rational conversation without somatic presence, De Quincey's account would, I believe, reject them: they represent such a potent rival to the powers of the aesthetic text itself to perform a vital and moving role in the public arena. That literary works such as De Quincey's "English Mail-Coach" stake their claim for importance on waging a struggle with ultimately imitable rivals like political crowds does not prove Habermas's account of a contested public sphere wrong. But, as the readings of Thomas Carlyle's *Chartism* and Charlotte Brontë's *Shirley* that follow suggest, we do need a broader sense of what it means to appear, speak, and act in such a sphere.

CHAPTER 5

Discursive Competition in the Victorian Public Sphere

Thomas Carlyle's Chartism

CROWDS AS SPEECH

With a petition in one hand, and a musket in the other.
> Feargus O'Connor, paraphrased in
> *The Northern Star,* July 6, 1839

Chartism with its pikes, Swing with his tinder-box, speak a most loud though inarticulate language.
> Thomas Carlyle, *Chartism,* 180

In 1837, James Bronterre O'Brien spearheaded a petition campaign.[1] But O'Brien cared less for the fact of the petition itself, or even for the number of signatures, than he did for the procession which he imagined might accompany it, a procession anticipating the Chartist petition processions that so unsettled London between 1839 and 1848.[2] O'Brien's petition would in a certain sense claim to do less than similar contemporary petitions to Parliament. It would request not a specific parliamentary action, but a change in Parliament's notions of what constituted a valid petition. O'Brien proposed that the people of England themselves be allowed to petition for redress in a more substantial form than signed paper:

THAT THE POOR OF ENGLAND SHALL BE HEARD BY COUNCIL AT THE BAR OF THE HOUSE OF COMMONS AGAINST THE LATE TYRANNICAL AND INHUMAN ENACTMENT MISCALLED THE POOR LAW AMENDMENT ACT.

> A petition of this sort, accompanied to the House by 200,000 people and headed by all the popular leaders of good repute throughout the country, would be worth ten thousand of the ordinary kind.[3]

This is a significant innovation in petition-making because it suggests that the assembly of massed men themselves be construed as representative of a desire to be represented. What makes this assembly a significant departure from both the bread riots of an earlier age and the radical assemblies of the teens is that it envisions the living act of representation both as a contribution to the language of political debate and as a presence in the streets. In this duality, it poses a threat to Parliament's claim to represent the working classes vicariously—that is, through the votes of their betters.

O'Brien wants Parliament to acknowledge that political discourse must be expanded so that 200,000 men peaceably assembled in the streets of London can be counted as a speech act as comprehensible as any written petition—and ten thousand times as effective. He is demanding that a movement that makes its supporters physically present in the streets be granted proxy authority to speak for the larger body that its crowds are meant to represent. O'Brien was among the first to articulate the principle on which the "mass platform" of the Chartists was built: crowd deeds serve as a sort of collective speech. As Thomas Attwood said when he presented the first Chartist "National Petition" in July of 1839, "they would prove that the men of Birmingham *were* England." What is visible in the streets, by this account, is only a representative *tranche* of what lies beyond: the threat is not so many thousand massed bodies, but so many millions of potential voters here signified corporeally.

That claim, however, was no more easily accepted by the mainstream Victorian press than by the middle and upper classes. The crowd's dual character—both speech and bodily presence—might seem, depending on one's political perspective, like the paternal rod sitting untouched in the corner when a child is asked politely to obey, or like the brutal club brandished by a brigand when asking for a "loan" on a moonlit road. As a typical *Times* of London description of a Birmingham rally-turned-riot suggests, middle-class observers were inclined to remain aware of the assembled Chartists' capacity always to "attend to [their leaders' speeches] in a very different manner" (July 17, 1839): the threat of action underpinned the overt claim of any demonstration.

Though the rules of the public sphere in which this crowd acted were not yet entirely legible, it was clear in any event that the introduction of a crowd-borne form of signification had substantially altered the grounds of political debate in the mid-Victorian period. Friedrich Engels, in his *Condition of the Working Class in England* (1844), nicely captures this distinctively English form that protest now took:

> That they protest in this way [strikes and marches] and no other, comes of their being practical English people, who express themselves in *action* and do not, like German theorists, go to sleep as soon as their protest is properly registered and placed *ad acta*. (228)

These crowds must be understood as an active form of language, whose effect cannot be compared to the merely paper logic of protest through newspapers. These demonstrators are themselves *ad acta*, and do not concede the validity of mechanisms of judgment that exclude their physical presence from the debate.

Over the decade that followed O'Brien's proposal, the Chartist movement put the notion into practice, pressing their demands for six reforms—which together added up to guaranteed adult male suffrage— by way of repeated petitions backed both by signatures and massive but orderly demonstrations. These demonstrations came closest to success in 1839, but endured in various forms until the backlash of 1848 rang the changes on peaceable public demonstrations (see Finn). Comparing these demonstrations to the crowds that surrounded Parliament during the Gordon Riots of 1780, it is immediately clear that those sixty years had radically changed what Charles Tilly has usefully labeled the "collective repertoire of gestures" (41) available to a political protest crowd. Gone were the attempts at forcible entry, the attacks on entering Members of Parliament, and the clumsy attempts at a pseudomilitary formation. Gone too the parliamentarians with drawn swords threatening to skewer the parliamentary supporters of the petition should the crowd enter.[4]

Instead of the anarchic looting so luridly evoked in Dickens's novel about the Gordon riots, *Barnaby Rudge* (1841), the petition crowds of 1839 and 1848 were characterized by elaborate precautions by the organizers to avoid "all excuse for the Magistrates legally or illegally exercising their authority" to end meetings; by intricate plans to produce "simultaneous meetings" elsewhere in the country as an additional sign of support; and by a highly developed figural language by which banners, cheers, and marching orders conveyed messages about

the intent of the men and women on the streets.[5] The age of the organized crowd had arrived.[6] Demonstrations that far surpassed the radical demonstrations of the teens in their size, their organizational structure, and their orderliness were put together by a movement that had
swollen into an improbably huge juggernaut dedicated not to a collection of social grievances (workplace reform and poor relief) but to
universal adult male suffrage.[7] This movement set out to make its demands known, as one Chartist leader put it, with the weapons of the
"petition, the meeting and the procession."[8] It spoke through the various activities that make a mass of people visible in all its magnitude,
among them torchlight assemblies, family meetings and post-work
meetings, collective church-going, selective shopping, and strikes.[9]

"Great Britain led the way" because its laboring classes had discovered a way to air grievances not through the old forms of parochial
politics, nor yet by way of violent uprising—as on the frustrated Con-
tinent in 1848—but through paraparliamentary meetings like the
Chartist Convention, with its "quasi military" marches and potentially
violent convocations that remained peaceful.[10] It was due to this transformation, and not to the underground radical politicking of the first
two decades of the century, that Great Britain of the 1830s "stood
dramatically closer to something we can reasonably call mass national
politics" (Tilly, 15).[11] The English working classes, under the tutelage
of three decades of radical activism and public contention, had per-
fected a new form of speech, the *demonstration*: "gathering deliberately
in a visible, symbolically important place, displaying signs of shared
commitment to some claim on authorities, then dispersing."[12]

Denis Donoghue asserts that Marx and Engels "set out to give the
masses their own narrative"[13] but by late 1819, when the first great
Charter convention was held, Chartism had already supplied many of
that narrative's verbs. What Mary Ryan has called "both the vocabulary and the syntax" of "social and cultural order" were being formed
in the processions, parades, marches, and assemblies of the Chartists.[14]
In the development of the mechanisms of public meeting, open petition,
and "paraparliamentary action," Chartism laid down a pattern that
virtually all later American and Western European crowd activism was
to follow.

Note, however, that the transformation in the meaning of Chartist
actions is dependent not simply on the inherent power of the signs that
Chartists made, but also upon changes in the media through which
such signs circulated. The triumph of Chartist claim-making in the pe-

tition presentations of 1839 is not simply that their processions were more pacific than those of the Gordon Riots. It also depends on the fact that those demonstrators were met not by swords but by receptive legislators when they reached Parliament. If the newspapers of the 1780s could see in the assembly of demonstrators nothing more than an attempt at an insurrectionary army, those of 1839 saw in Chartist crowds a new form of public speech. The message and its medium had altered together.

The claims made by the Chartist crowds as they entered the public sphere—and those made by Carlyle as he strove to provide a new account of the "clamour and struggle" of those crowds—can best be explained, I propose, by turning to Geoff Eley's provocative suggestion that the nineteenth-century public sphere consisted of various competing discursive formations—rather than, as Habermas would have it, of a "bourgeois rational critical conversation" that operated with varying degrees of success.[15] Eley's work describes a largely print-mediated public sphere that, at least by the mid-nineteenth century, was filled with competing ways of producing political power in public. In Eley's account, the public sphere is "the structured setting where cultural and ideological contest or negotiations among a variety of publics take place, rather than . . . the spontaneous and class-specific achievement of the bourgeoisie in some specific sense" (306). Among the discourses available for claim-making, I propose, were not only the "rational-critical" mode prevalent among newspapers and in parliamentary debate, but also two innovative forms: the representative sign-making of Chartist crowds, and the reactionary claim by Carlyle to deploy an aesthetic text—his *Chartism* (1839)—in order to understand and to explain the crowds of Chartism better than they understood and explained themselves.

Before exploring Carlyle's remarkable appropriation of Chartist crowds to further his own aesthetic claims, it is worth considering in some detail the set of Chartist claims against which he operated. The key to those claims is the fact that the availability of a discursive space oriented toward national representation had fundamentally altered not just working-class claim-making, but the nature of those who made the claims. In September 1819, for instance, the radical Francis Place wrote a revealing letter to Thomas Hodskin that encapsulated fifty years of changes in the nature of public gatherings. In the old days in Lancashire, Place wrote,

an 'outcomling' was sometimes pelted with stones. . . . it would have been
dangerous to assemble 500 of them on any occasion. Bakers and butchers
at least would have been plundered. Now 100,000 people may be collected
together and no riot ensue, and why? Why, but for the fact before stated,
that the people have an object, the pursuit of which gives them importance
in their own eyes. . . . the very individuals who would have been leaders of
the riot are the keepers of the peace. (Tilly, 260)

As Alexander Somerville put it after the Edinburgh illumination riots
that followed the passage of the Reform Bill in 1832, "the greater the
number of men enfranchised, the smaller is the number of
'blackguards'" (132). No longer, Place believed, were protest crowds
to imagine that their purpose was to gain direct redress from a reluctant
landlord for an overbearing local official. The action of bringing grievances before the bar of a Chartist demonstration could be parsed as
itself having a "civilizing influence." That influence derived in part
from the decision of the Chartist movement to make, as Tilly puts it,
"Parliament an object of claims" (260). The crowds had become not
simply the injured clumping together to cry out, but an exemplary
portion of the "masses," choosing freely to congregate to assert a
shared and general claim to justice.

Equally importantly, the government had decided that such demonstrative claims were a valid form of expression before the national public. The dual change—in the event and its interpretation—can be seen,
for example, in the gradual shifts in the legal decisions regarding what
sorts of demonstrations drew prosecutions, and equally well in the laws
governing what sort of communication could go on between Chartist
groups. Thus it is profoundly important that the Seditious Meetings
Acts as they were enforced in the 1830s did not allow private correspondence between Chartist organizations but did permit newspapers
to publish announcements of simultaneous meetings (Yeo, 111 and passim). It was very difficult, therefore, secretly to assemble a conspiratorial cadre: but it was comparatively simple openly to call for a public
show of Chartist enthusiasm. The implication is that demonstrations
were a far more plausible way than secret conspiracies to agitate for
change in such a political climate. As long as the government knew as
much of one's plans as one's supporters did, practically any form of
public *non*violent convocation was permissible. And what was permissible was also what was effective, as Tilly's work on the increasing
importance of nonviolent, nationally oriented protests shows.

Such factors, as well as the intentions and practices of the Chartists themselves, were instrumental in shaping the nascent Chartist movement. The demonstration discourse I describe may have been oppositional, but it was the product of a collaboratively constituted public sphere. And, as one tactic after another was tested, discarded, or strengthened, that public sphere came gradually to be transformed by the nature of the demonstrations themselves.[16]

If the Chartists drew on a signifying repertoire that had evolved in the 1820s and 1830s, they nonetheless refined and transformed that repertoire as it went along, adding what would draw peaceful crowds, discarding what drew little attention or caused government crackdowns.[17] The tensions within the movement itself—and the indecision about what sorts of demonstrations work to make a legible gesture before the nation as a whole—become visible when one anatomizes the various tactics that arose, flourished or failed, and effected change or provoked violent reactions.[18] In *The Northern Star* and other Chartist newspapers, one finds speakers establishing a relationship with their audiences that allowed them to be seen not as leaders but as an extension of the people's will (Vicinus, 486, 488), or assembling them into something like a martial formation. But one also sees the crowd becoming vehement in its protests whenever local problems and national grievances happened to coincide.[19] One speaker proposes going to church in great numbers (Johnson, July 27, 1839); another argues for remaining in the Bull-ring at Birmingham (O'Connor, May 18, 1839); yet another proposes arming for peace (Bronterre O'Brien, May 18, 1839); and a fourth asks how many men will remain standing in the pouring rain rather than moving indoors (G. J. Harren, May 18, 1839). These are debates not simply about the "collective repertoire of gestures" that Tilly describes, but also debates about which of these gestures will effectively both coalesce support and receive a wide national audience and potential approbation. By the same token, the proposals of some Members of the Convention (tellingly styled "MCs" after Members of Parliament, "MPs") to avoid holding even legal meetings because "all excuse of the Magistrates legally or illegally exercising their authority should be avoided" ought to be read as a part of an ongoing discursive dispute in which the opponent is another MC who proposes to assemble at night by torch if necessary, in order to proclaim that "they would have [their rights] in sincerity, peaceably if they might, forcibly if they must."[20]

When debates raged about the tactics a crowd should use, the debate was not simply, Will it work better to petition, or to strike, or to march unarmed, or to march armed? Each such choice signified a decision about the nature of the relationship between the disenfranchised and the nation: Should redress be expected from nearby landlords and employers, or from the nation as a whole? Should redress come from a principle of justice (if so, crowds should use peaceful resistance)? Or should it come from a principle of humanity (if so, bring women and children out into the street)? Should it be granted from fear (forget the women and kids, bring axes, adzes, and weapons of the trade instead)? In each case, what is being debated, and what was enacted in public, was the joint construction of a novel apparatus of meaning.

Consider two popular tactics of late-1830s Chartism: simultaneous meetings and torchlight marches.[21] One can see that while debate about the exact effectiveness of each tactic was widespread, those Chartists involved in creating, participating in, reporting on, and reacting to various forms of demonstration had accepted a great deal about the national significance of demonstrations that would have been inconceivable thirty years earlier. Simultaneous meetings, which seem to have been devised by the radicals of the late teens, proved throughout the first half of the nineteenth century to be a very effective method for proving that one had not only numbers but considerable control over those numbers.[22] In an era without instantaneous, or even very rapid, communications, simultaneous meetings in cities nationwide demonstrated first and foremost a sense of the size of national membership, since no one could possibly attend two meetings at once. But these meetings had a yet wider effect, one suggested by Tilly when he speaks of the turn toward "cosmopolitan" or nationally oriented protests (46). To hold a simultaneous meeting meant that your movement could enforce discipline regardless of local conditions: these meetings would not be swayed by (local) inclement weather, nor would they be scheduled to accord with days traditionally sanctioned for large gatherings in any given locale. The ability to impose a homogenized and abstract national schedule, rather than buckling to local exigencies, was a vital step forward for any demonstrative body bent on making pacific national claims.

By contrast, to organize a torchlight procession was inevitably to ask for trouble in manufacturing towns. Martha Vicinus points out that the torchlight meetings of 1838, for example—the early days of Chartism—were "far more feared" than "the family-based day-long meetings," simply because the decision not to go home from the factory left workers looking like grimy monsters (485). One might also note that these workers retained a trace of their workaday identity at a time—evening or night when work clothes should already have vanished—and in a place—the public streets of downtown—that ought not to have seen such crowds.[23] Dickens's insistence on the terrifying quality of the flame-lit faces in *Barnaby Rudge* is a fictionalization of a widely shared sense of the danger inherent in the presence of working men at an hour when all should have been quiet in such a town.[24] One might compare the decision to hold such a march to the moment in Fanny Burney's *Evelina* (1778) in which Evelina's female cousins elect to walk down dark long alleyways in the Vauxhall pleasure gardens, and their father accuses them of having "a mind to be affronted" (186). There is the same mixture of passivity and activity in the organization of such a torchlight march—it implies an active desire "to be affronted."

It is clear that both of these Chartist tactics were designed and carried out with an eye to proclaiming to England a remediable grievance—but one can go even further. Such a claim of remediable grievance—whether by violent or morally restrained action—only counts as a claim to the extent that the public sphere is already structured in such a way that claims can be "registered" (to borrow Engels's phrase) via demonstration rather than petition. Thus it is not, strictly speaking, prior intent on the part of leaders that is at stake.[25] Rather, as Tilly's sociological work on the evolution of "collective repertoires of gestures" implies, what ultimately matters is what sorts of demonstrations people actually cared to take part in, how they actually transpired, and how they were reported and received.

The implications of the success of such organized collective actions as simultaneous meetings and torchlight marches can perhaps be seen most clearly by comparing them to actions that were pursued by individual Chartists but were—for one reason or another—never really taken up by the national movement. For example, when one overardent Chartist proposed in 1843 that "all male Chartists should grow moustaches, thus ensuring that 'the Charter ever be prominently before the eyes of all,'" the idea failed to take hold (Roberts, 64). Why? There are doubtless many reasons unrelated to the Chartist demonstration crowd, but the salient factor for the failure of that proposal was certainly the absence of any inherent logical connection between the presence of whiskers and the cause of suffrage. Mass demonstrations and simultaneous meetings had it all over whiskers.[26]

The fact that the nation as a whole respected the implicit connection—a logical link that was tacitly accepted by every newspaper—
between massive convocations and the right of the Chartist Convention
to represent working men, is a strong confirmation of my general account of this changed form of representation in the public sphere. For
the first time "the people have an object" (Francis Place, quoted in
Tilly, 260) that is generally accepted by the nation as a whole as figuring a form of representation. It is both in response to and against
this discursive claim that Carlyle's account of Chartism sets to work.

CROWDS AS ACTION

The soul of all justifiable Radicalism . . . continues
dumb.

> Thomas Carlyle, letter to Thomas
> Ballantyne, January 24, 1840

[Beware of the] master of tongue-fence [in] the
National Palaver.

> (*Chartism*, 216)

Both to the Chartists who participated in them and to Thomas Carlyle,
who wrote about them, the Chartist demonstrations of 1839 seemed a
rewriting of the rules of what counted as speech and what as bodily
intervention in the realm of politics.[27] Still, there are descriptions, and
there are descriptions. Even if one grants the efficacy of the mass platform, and supposes that the Chartist actions indeed meant that a crowd
massed in the streets of London or distributed over every Northern
town could now count as a kind of parliamentary petition, the presence
of such signifying crowds in the streets raised a new set of possibilities.
The Chartists had established that demonstration crowds could represent their desire to be represented. But they could not—nor indeed
could anyone—fix the crowd's significance. Having been put into public play, the demonstration crowds were as subject to interpretation,
appropriation, imitation, and even annihilation as any other public
phenomenon. It was clear that the crowds Chartism had brought into
the street were doing or saying something. But what?

This was the question of the moment in 1839, and to it Carlyle
produced a lightning-fast, an influential, and a durable answer.[28] Indeed, even the little phrase that is all that remains to wider fame of
that essay—in it Carlyle first spoke of the "condition of England"—
tells us much. It connects Chartism to that perennial Carlylean concern

with what lay "deep in the heart" of the English nation.[29] Carlyle intended that not only his own text, but also the actions of the demonstrating crowds themselves would be taken as proof of the general veracity of his claim: that the crowd bodied forth the "deep dumb inarticulate want" of the English people, a want deeper than any of the linguistic fluency in the public representations of Chartism itself.

The danger that Carlyle's account poses to the Chartist interpretation of their own demonstrations is enormous. To the Chartists who participated in the constitutive language of demonstrations, acceptance of their discursive logic meant that the crowd would be taken as a form of petition to Parliament. When Carlyle comes to write about the same crowds he inverts all valuation. All this order, this flag-raising, this chanting, this vast public expenditure of energy sounds to Thomas Carlyle like nothing more than "a very slack old drum and shouting round the rumble of it."[30] To Carlyle, the idea that the mob could burst into articulate speech is so laughable that when he talks about Chartists passing resolutions, he describes them as " 'resolutions,' " denying them intention, intelligence, or even the mastery of language by using a protective set of quotation marks. If the "condition of England" depends on Chartism, that dependence has little to do with its words and everything to do with Carlyle's ascribing to Chartist crowds a mystical somatic access to some deeper sort of meaning.

What makes Carlyle's *Chartism* worth reconsidering is not simply its long and largely unremarked legacy in reactionary thought, but the remarkably efficacious logic he finds—on short notice and under the pressure of rapidly changing events—with which to wrest control of those crowds out of the hands of the Chartists who had actually taken part in them. Carlyle's *Chartism* is of extraordinary interest because it stages at once an apparent disdain for and an apparent incorporation of the Chartist crowd's rival presence in the public sphere: it criticizes Chartism's claims, yet depends upon Chartist actions. That dual intent makes *Chartism* an exceptionally instructive showcase of the sort of discursive competition that makes up the variegated public sphere of nineteenth-century Britain.

That Carlyle had preempted his opponents in making Chartism the burning issue of 1839 gave him a certain advantage in defining the terms of the debate.[31] True, the conservative press had fulminated against Chartism, and those in the middle class who had gotten the vote in 1832 declared the Convention's concerns misguided, but the first full-scale response to both the plots and perorations of O'Connor,

O'Brien, and their ilk was *Chartism*. Written in six weeks during the fall of 1839, and published independently that December (Carlyle had first thought of publishing it in Mill's radical *London and Westminster Review*, and then in the Tory *Quarterly Review*), it coupled a surprising sympathy for Chartism's complaints—as Carlyle himself understood them—with a blistering contempt for the remedies proposed by radical parliamentarians and for utilitarian-style statistical evaluation of the plight of England.

Much of the book is forgettable. It was and still is generally agreed that its bogus solutions for England's problems—principally emigration and literacy—convinced no one and made no impact on the day's policy debates.[32] *Chartism* remains memorable, however, for combining a scathing critique of Chartist crowds with a critique of the English status quo, a critique that Carlyle interestingly claims to share with those selfsame crowds. This complicated balancing act begins with one deceptively simple move: every apparent speech-act of the Chartist crowds is reclassified as a form of bodily behavior. Every crowd that the Chartists are inclined to proclaim as a representative form of speech, a discursive gesture, Carlyle instructs his readers to regard as a natural object, an emotional reaction, a speechless body.

Carlyle's redescription of Chartist speech as deed can take place not simply because any demonstration crowd always retains a physical presence, but also because Carlyle, from the very beginning of *Chartism,* introduces a fundamental uncertainty about agency that makes the Chartist claims to be performing legible speech-acts seem absurd. Carlyle vehemently disbelieves in the intended significance of Chartist demonstrations. He doubts not simply their message, but the very medium through which that message is meant to travel. To assign to actions fixed and representative meanings, in Carlyle's account, is at the worst to be doing something impossible, and at best to be reinserting crowds into a diminished world: as *Chartism* etches it, a world of Parliament, statistics, and boredom. Moreover, if the Chartist account of crowd signification is right, then Carlyle's own textual practice seemingly falls apart. That is, a world including actors whose actions could so readily become legible would have no place for the rules by which Carlyle's prose is governed. "Imposture" and "Substance" cannot both be true (183).

From Carlyle's opening salvo, therefore, the key move is to establish a general air of indecision: are there actors or speakers involved; if there are, how many, and who?

> A feeling very generally exists that the condition and disposition of the Working Classes is a rather ominous matter at present; that something ought to be said, something ought to be done, in regard to it. (151)

A whole series of questions is implicitly raised here: where does this feeling exist? What is the difference between saying and doing? What exactly does Carlyle have in mind to say or do? None receives, in the whole course of the essay, a clear answer. In this text the reader is being instructed to accept indecision not even as a problem, but simply as an inescapable ingredient of our knowledge of the world.

Such an account is already at odds with the Chartist account of representation via crowds. Chartism depends, according to the logic implicit in its demonstrations, on making everything that a crowd does a form of representation. If that were not the case, the Chartist claim to reconfigure the public sphere would count for little, their claim that they were representing their right to be represented for less. But Carlyle's opening paragraph uses the trope of depersonalization—already uneasily granted by any reader of the first sentence—to open an enormous gap between rational actors and the world of agencyless acts. Carlyle takes up Chartism's orderly and seemingly legible demonstrations and describes, in the remarkable opening paragraph, a world filled with active objects and silenced human beings, a world where passive verbs and vague abstract nouns stand for the upper classes, while specific heavy and threatening machinery takes the place of the life of the lower-class mob.

> A feeling very generally exists that the condition and disposition of the Working Classes is a rather ominous matter at present; that something ought to be said, something ought to be done in regard to it. And surely, at an epoch of history when the 'National Petition' carts itself in wagons along the streets, and is presented 'bound with iron hoops, four men bearing it' to a Reformed House of Commons; and Chartism numbered by the million and half, taking nothing by its iron-hooped Petition, breaks out in brickbats, cheap pikes, and even into sputterings of conflagration, such very general feeling cannot be considered unnatural! To us individually this matter appears, and has for many years appeared, to be the most ominous of all practical matters whatever; a matter in regard to which if something be not done, something will *do* itself one day, and in a fashion that will please nobody. (151)

We are not, in Carlyle's account, witnessing labor organized behind a rational collection of grievances. Action is taken away from men here, and vested in time ("history"), taken away from time and vested in

machines ("'National Petition' . . . in wagons"), taken away from machines and vested in Parliament ("Reformed House of Commons"),
taken away from Parliament and vested in ambiguous statistical abstractions ("Chartism numbered by the million and half"), taken away
from abstractions and vested in weapons ("brickbats, cheap pikes"),
taken away from weapons and vested in natural phenomena ("confla-
gration").

The pattern established in this opening paragraph is the key to de-
ciphering a great deal of Carlyle's strategy. He wants to strip the crowd
of language while retaining a sense of the importance of the message
it has to convey. Throughout *Chartism* and beyond, various forms of
this interest in making the animate inanimate, and the legible illegible,
recur when Carlyle wants to describe the powers of the crowd—followed by claims to restore the crowd to animation and legibility within
his own writing. The movement into unagencied action allows Carlyle
to deploy his most powerful set of rhetorical operations, because it
enables him to separate the leaders of what he tellingly calls "Chart-
is*ms*" from the true, brute, wordless action of the Chartist crowd itself:
on one side lies the passionate, writhing, "deep dumb inarticulate"
English crowd, an embodiment of Truth. On the other side, the enemy:
"These Chartisms, Radicalisms, Reform Bill, Tithe Bill, and infinite
other discrepancy, and acrid argument and jargon that there is yet to
be, are *our* French Revolution" (181). Carlyle sets out in *Chartism* to
find a way to separate the true anterior content of Chartism, the acts
that occur without agency or conversation, from the various sign-filled
"Chartisms" that hover above it.

That Carlyle is able to effect this separation—and to do so without
seeming even to be in dialogue with the rationalist claims of Chartism
itself, to do so without seeming to hear the enemy to whom he is
constantly attending—is proof of what is always noted and often
praised about Carlyle: his masterful *style*.[33] It is in fact the greatness
of his style that allows him so effortlessly to make a claim for the
incommensurability between his own account of the truth and all those
against whom he struggles. "Style" allows Carlyle to open the door to
an irrationalist account of what language can do as it circulates in the
public sphere: it is a proof of his triumph and not of his failure when
an early reviewer remarks that "We do not understand Mr. C nor are
we quite sure he understands himself." Carlyle's notion of what his
own irrational prose can do in the public sphere depends on his inimitable, unmanageable style's being praised and noticed, not anato-

mized. His nebulous gesturings and sublime rantings can ultimately be parsed as part of Carlyle's overall strategy to displace other claims to the real—the parliamentary report, the statistic, even the Chartists' own description of their action. The very nebulousness of *Chartism* is part of its concrete meaning.

The fact that Carlyle strives to carry his points by getting carried away does not, however, rule out a careful reader's discovering his direction. Consider the seemingly trivial detail above: that Carlyle claims to be able to rescue England from the "Chartisms, Radicalisms," etc., that beset it. Why is the pluralization telling? Though Carlyle calls the book itself *Chartism*, when he sums up the activities of its leaders, the "Chartisms" go into plural along with "radicalisms" and the ceaselessly pluralized acts of Parliament itself. That pluralization reflects one of the book's underlying patterns: the solid monolithic block of revealed truth on the one hand, and the multiple, untrustworthy power of pluralized speech on the other: one crowd, many Chartisms. The interpretative agency of Chartist leaders is as doomed to failure as are Parliament's "ceaseless blue books."[34] Chartism's leaders have in common with Parliament that they pluralize problems, rather than focusing on the one true fact: the "deep dumb inarticulatable want" that lies buried deep within Chartism, close only to Carlyle's own account of it.

Carlyle's style requires such a scrupulous, even an overzealous sort of reading because attention to the almost unmentioned is the only way to parse the underlying logic of a style that strives to mark itself as illogical. For instance, one of the clearest views we can attain of *Chartism*'s account of the difference between Carlyle's own writing and the representational system of Chartism against which he is arguing comes in a careful analysis of a single word. In the triple use that Carlyle makes of the word "figure," he creates a version of the "real" that is inherently linked to the featureless, agencyless space of action, against which all "figures" flatten into mere superficial scrawl. Doing so enables him to make with renewed force the point with which his essay opens: that the intellectual efforts of "Chartisms" to ascribe meaning to Chartist crowds are doomed, while his own intuitive understanding of the interior of those crowds will grant him a "true" understanding apart from such excessive ratiocination.

At the end of chapter 1, Carlyle disparagingly compares working-class self-consciousness to the truth about their condition (and England's):

> Why are the Working Classes discontented; what is their condition, eco-
> nomical, moral, in their houses and their hearts, as it is in reality and as
> they figure it to themselves to be; what do they complain of; what ought
> they, and ought they not to complain of? (156)

Once the elegance with which Carlyle doubles the reference to the question of interiority has been noted (if the essence of the working classes
is to be found inside hearts and houses, then what goes on in the streets
cannot truly describe them), the key phrase of the sentence comes
quickly to hand: "as they figure it to themselves to be." This awkward
phrase reveals Carlyle hard at work creating (or perhaps even discovering within himself—who can tell with Carlyle?) confusion about
what that "figuring" actually is. Two possibilities present themselves.
Does he mean that the working classes actually "think" the way that
Chartist demonstrations present their thoughts? That is, that they are
involved in "figuring" about the world by way of the Chartist demonstrations that occasioned Carlyle's essay? Or does he mean that they
only represent themselves ("figure" as in "figure of a cross") in that
way? Either reading of the phrase sets such figuration in opposition to
the question of the "reality" of their condition. Carlyle is at once acknowledging and undermining the approach inherent in Chartist figurations. Chartism's accomplishment is to give the working class a way
to "figure" oneself to oneself, as well as to others. But in Carlyle's
account both ways are inherently specious. No matter how lucid the
process, it is still inferior to Carlyle's own text, which can inform Carlyle's readers about the reality of their condition.

Lest the operative distinction have failed to take hold in a reader's
mind, "figure" is immediately marked again as the property of a misguided intellectual effort. In the next paragraph—the first of chapter
2, "Statistics"—statistics are twice described as figures. First, "A witty
statesman said, you might prove anything by figures," and then twenty
lines later, "With what serene conclusiveness a member of some Useful-
Knowledge Society stops your mouth with a figure of arithmetic!"
(157). Carlyle's widespread fulminations against utilitarianism and the
world of the "Cash Nexus" make this particular turn in some ways
unsurprising. Statistics are always, in his account, "nothing . . . rather
than a something" (159), and the generalized data stored in statistics
are "like cobwebs, like the sieve of the Danaides, beautifully reticulated, orderly to look upon, but which will hold no conclusion," (157),
meaning that anything that takes a solid fact and turns it into figures
will never contain the reality of the fact so adduced.

In a certain sense, then, Carlyle here is only fighting his old battle with his most predictable opponent, the lobby of detail-oriented, committee-loving, statistics-quoting "jabber" and "tonguefence" of Parliament.[35] But by repeating the word "figure" in describing both statisticians and Chartists, Carlyle is building a linkage, continued throughout *Chartism*, between two very unlikely co-defendants: the parliamentary figures are here being allied with the working-class demonstrators who by marching are "figuring" their own desires in public, as well as "figuring" those desires out in their own minds. Both processes, says Carlyle, are failures. Not because they do not do what they say they are going to do, but because they fail at what Carlyle believes to be truly important: in enumerating and articulating their desires and demands, they have deafened themselves to the reality of "wild inarticulate souls, struggling there, with inarticulate uproar." His opponents—and here he means both Parliamentarians and the putative leaders of Chartism— have not grasped the impersonal and pre-figural intensity of a reality that "carts itself in wagons along the streets."

Chartism to this point may seem to confirm an account of discursive competition, but a competition consisting of a simple negation. This sort of opposition would seem to confirm, for example, the account that Stedman Jones supplies of Carlyle's reaction to Chartism: that he "set the terms of the predominant response" (91) of conservatives to crowd action, simply by finding ways to deny that Chartist crowds had any sort of power at all. However, *Chartism* contains something more. Carlyle needs to assert that Chartist "figurations" of the crowd are flawed. But he also needs to provide a new way of placing that crowd within his own rival account of what the public sphere ought to look like. In both reviling and appropriating the Chartist crowd, therefore, in both blaming it for excessive attempts at "figuring" and in making his own attempt to figure it, Carlyle moves on to embroil his text in a curious and ultimately extremely revealing contradiction. And that contradiction is highly elucidative of the logic of rival discourses that compete for logical control of the public sphere.[36]

Carlyle wants to have it both ways: on the one hand to borrow from the crowds their energy and hence their modes of speech; and yet on the other to claim for himself an irreproducible relation to the truth, one fundamentally incommensurable with all the rival accounts that circulate in an irritatingly promiscuous public sphere. On the one hand, that is, he wants to partake of the wealth of a discursively variegated public sphere: its wide variety of ways of formulating what is "true."

In that mode, Carlyle is willing to co-opt not simply the symptoms but the very speech and logic of Chartism. On the other hand, Carlyle wants to make use of such formulations without admitting that his own discourse is one among many in such a public space—that his own "figuring" is not *ipso facto* superior to all of the competing ac-counts. How can Carlyle both retain the magnitude of the phenomenon that occasioned his essay in the first place and deny that his text is in competition with the signifying practices of Chartism? How can he delete the crowd and have it too?

Carlyle begins this task slowly, by trying out a few ways to depict Chartist crowds that gain him a fair bit of rhetorical power. One plau-sible (and widely imitated) tactic that emerges fairly early in *Chartism* is Carlyle's classing Chartism as a disease. Carlyle makes striking use of disease imagery to justify both his work's intense attention to Chart-ism, and to demonstrate his own power to negate the overt intentions and aspirations of articulate Chartist leaders. In his two prolonged uses of disease imagery, Carlyle works to convince readers that, first, what Chartism has to tell us is extremely important; second, it is a sickness, not a form of speech, so we must try to cure it (into silence); and, third, because it is a sickness, the words you hear Chartists speaking mean exactly the opposite what the outbreak of Chartism truly means.

> Chartist torch-meetings, Birmingham riots, Swing conflagrations, are so many symptoms on the surface; you abolish the symptom to no purpose, if the disease is left untouched. Boils on the surface are curable or incurable,— small matter which, while the virulent humour festers deep within; poison-ing the sources of life; and certain enough to find for itself ever new boils and sore issues; ways of announcing that it continues there, that it would fain not continue there. (152)

Reading Chartism as a set of boils not only empowers the speaker to find his own name for the disease within; it also manages to call Chart-ist actions themselves into question in two ways. First, it accords them far more importance than would a straightforward allegation of inex-plicable madness or of dangerous disobedience. By symptomatizing Chartism, Carlyle credits it with the power to reveal the inner disease. But these symptoms, like those of a disease, are signs of a body strug-gling to throw all symptoms off. Second, then, what Chartists-as-symptoms say is that they would "fain not continue there." Chartism speaks, and loudly—but only to call for its own demise.

The same is true in the passage in which Carlyle most openly praises the expressive powers of Chartism:

> If from this black unluminous unheeded *Inferno*, and Prisonhouse of souls
> in pain, there do flash up from time to time, some dismal wide-spread glare
> of Chartism or the like, notable to all, claiming remedy from all,—are we
> to regard it as more baleful than the quiet state, or rather as not so baleful?
> (176)

Even as Carlyle prepares to silence the crowd in passages such as this,
there is no suggestion that he would rather the crowd had not gathered.
Peace and quiet would have been baleful considering England's condition; Chartism is a salutary "dismal wide-spread glare." It is through
Chartism, then that the "disease of England . . . becomes acute, has
crises, and will be cured or kill." Carlyle has recognized a worthy enemy here. Whatever is rotten in England will only be excised with the
dangerous help of Chartism.

When Carlyle begins to describe what the Chartists do as a form of
speech, he is forced to engage in an overt battle with the accounts of
that speech implicit in Chartism itself. *Chartism*'s opening epigraph
elegantly describes Carlyle's strategy of peering beneath the crowd's
sign-making: "It never smokes but there is fire" (151). The smoke of
Chartism does indeed connote something, then, but it requires no
knowledge of the grammar and syntax of smoke signals to parse it:
smoke tells one to look down to the vivid, energetic action of the fire
below, of which any smoke is purely epiphenomenal. In making an
utterly sharp distinction between the fire's meaning and the smoke's
mere signaling, Carlyle establishes an important binary between the
redundant wind that is ordinary human babble, and the deeply significant silence that is the "speech" of the truly heroic.[37]

In such works as *On Heroes, Hero Worship and the Heroic in History* (1841), Carlyle establishes the lonely hero who pours forth silent
truth against the empty wind of the crowd. In *Chartism*, however, the
true voice below the voice is to be found not in a single heroic mouth,
but solidly embodied in the crowd itself:

> How inexpressibly useful were true insight into it; a genuine understanding
> by the upper classes of society what it is that the under classes intrinsically
> mean; a clear interpretation of the thought which at heart torments these
> wild inarticulate souls, struggling there, with inarticulate uproar, like dumb
> creatures in pain, unable to speak what is in them! (155)

"*Like* dumb creatures": the simile is an apt one, because while the
crowd may be "like" dumb creatures, it is in reality clearly comprised
of talking ones. Their uproar seems to the Chartists themselves, and to
at least some middle-class onlookers, to have not only a substance but

a syntax. But Carlyle denies that the syntax has emerged from the "intrinsic" meaning of the hearts of the lower orders. Fire is below their smoke.

Carlyle's distinction between Chartism's "clamour" and its "struggle" is telling in this context: "not for this, however in words he may clamour for it; not for this, but for something far different does the heart of him struggle" (166). That "something"—also described as "the earnest obscure purpose of democracy" and "the soul of all justifiable radicalism"—is Carlyle's way of suggesting that those who hear the crowd should look not to Chartist manifestos but to what they themselves "intrinsically mean" beneath. The effect of such observation will be to turn Carlyle's own text, then, from a form of speech to a conduit directly to that inarticulable insight: Chartist significations will have been undercut by Carlyle's direct evocation of the true voice of the crowd.

This claim represents something a good deal stranger—and more aggressive—than simply a binary between "figure" and "reality." In the inextricable mixture of clamor and struggle, the putative opposition between speech and true silence starts to look a good deal more complicated than it had. For the central paradox is that the "struggle" has finally to be given a voice, and that voice cannot evade being in language altogether: it too must be a kind of figuration. How then is Carlyle to present the discursive claim of the crowd as he interprets it, but present it in such a way that it seems incompatible with the mere "clamour" of Chartism's ordinary demands? The solution Carlyle comes up with is to himself propose a paradoxical formulation that seems to point to a paradox within the Chartists' demands that crowd actions be taken as a form of speech. Disregard all the demands of "Chartisms": were one truly able to hear, one would hear not the clamor or simultaneous assemblies, the torchlight marches (with their signifying moustaches), but

> Bellowings, *in*articulate cries as of a dumb creature in rage and pain; to the ear of wisdom they are inarticulate prayers: "Guide me, govern me! I am mad and miserable, and cannot guide myself." (184)

To imagine a speaker capable of that sentence, one has to imagine a speech which is not out of the speaker's own mouth or indeed his own conscious brain. This voice comes from below, and expresses not the working class's "seeming" demand to govern itself, but its "real" want of a leader.

Notice the odd nature of this imperative: it is not, as in other Carlyle writings, a hero giving orders to his leader. Rather, it is a voice from the crowd giving an order to its own leader: ordering itself ordered, we might say. The very existence of such an imperative constitutes the core of Carlyle's claim to have tapped into a durable alternative explanation for the strength of the crowds on the street, an explanation that is, we might say, at the other end of language from the Chartist account. If the Chartists suppose that such crowds are there to join in a general conversation about peaceable forms of rational representation, Carlyle proposes instead that their presence means something far different, that it counts as evidence for an entirely different claim to authority, a claim bodied forth inarticulately, bespeaking a public sphere that depends not on rational interchange but on the true speech that comes from the body without passing through the conscious brain.[38]

The model implicit in this sentence is of a world where speech can proceed from a site that is impossibly far beyond any sorts of conscious guides, censors, or sites of reason. To make such a cry is to prove the existence not merely of a working-class desire for a strong leader, but of a way that such a desire can, against all logical possibility, be put forth into speech. By claiming to be the "ear of wisdom," which interprets that cry from below, Carlyle has found a way to have his discursive competition both ways: both to borrow what is most powerful of the crowd-speech, and to pretend that he is relaying to his readers the only possible discourse that can emanate from this crowd. Just as Carlyle's discerning in Chartism the virulent symptoms of a systemic disease deep within the English body suggested a scrupulous attention toward such symptomology, so too his role as "ear of wisdom" demands an unceasing and scrupulous focus upon the very demonstrations whose meaning he presumes to discredit. Though all of his stylistic panache urges his reader to regard Chartism as nothing more than one of many "Chartisms, radicalisms, statistics," nonetheless the real efficacy of the essay is that it draws to Chartism itself a special and abiding kind of attention.

That attention seems neatly to negate the peaceable claims that make up the central claims of Chartism's "mass platform."[39] Carlyle has discovered a remarkable way of taking Chartist crowds at their face value, and yet inserting another level below. In rhetorical terms, this may seem a complete triumph. And yet, has Carlyle invented this violence strictly *de novo*? Ironically enough, it is in his own opponents' idea that Carlyle has discovered a way to displace Chartism's claims. For while the

central claims of Chartism may have been peaceable, in its attachment
to the powers of physical presence there always lingered just a trace of
the Carlylean attachment to violence. That is, even those Chartists who
were most vociferous about the power of a peaceful speech act still
remained thoughtfully aware of what Thomas M. Kemnitz has astutely
labeled an "intimidationist" rhetoric of reined-in physical force.[40] The
key Chartist demands, its long marches, and peaceful processions, as
Kemnitz shows, made conscious use of the visceral intimidation inspired by the crowds' presence on the streets, allowing crowd leaders
always to gesture toward the barely reined-in power of the crowd itself:
consider for example Attwood's call for the men of England to rise
with "a petition in one hand and a musket in the other."[41] Even those
leaders of Chartism who preached "moral force" were loath to relin-
quish the unutilized threat of street violence implicit in their marches,
although they realized that to force an actual physical confrontation
would doom their movement.[42]

This convergence between the two sorts of discursive claims is certainly an immense irony: it is not, however, akin to saying that their
two claims are the same. This convergence of the two claims suggests
that a space of discursive competition can produce the seeming paradox
of two rival interpretive claims converging on certain key points. Both
Carlyle and the Chartists were struggling, in the same era, with the
same rules about publication, assembly, and popular reception to discover ways to make their own conceptions of the public sphere emerge
triumphant. The fact that Chartists seeking universal male suffrage
should also at times make use of the idea that there was a gray area
between speech and action—an area where both physical violence and
peaceful demonstrations might hope to effect change—is unsurprising.
It is, however, suggestive of certain advantages that a reactionary embrace of violence might have over a discourse committed to peaceful
redress of claims. The discursive logic of Chartism and the logic of
Carlyle's *Chartism* depended not only on originary principles, but also
on ongoing assessments of what would be effective in the public sphere.
Carlyle's decision to read 1839's crowds as "inarticulate uproar," that
marked true "struggle" below, seems to have been a more effective
discursive strategy than were Chartist claims for a transparently signifying crowd.

CONCLUSION: THE INARTICULABLE
AND AESTHETIC POWER

Fascism sees its salvation in giving the masses not their
rights, but instead a chance to express themselves.

> Walter Benjamin, "The Work of Art in the
> Age of Mechanical Reproduction," 241

It was high time that the people should be represented
in books, as well as in Parliament.

> William Hazlitt,
> "The English Novelists," 819

For several months in 1839 it seemed that the Chartists would succeed
in representing their desire to be represented. That brief period has
often been read as a promissory note that would come due in a later
era of full ballot representation, pointing toward the triumph of the
Reform Act of 1867, or perhaps toward the extension of full adult
suffrage in the 1920s. To a liberal or Whig historiography that reads
the Chartist demonstrations as almost like ballot representation, Chartism is a sort of stepping-stone on the road to victory. In the sort of
skeptical conservative account that similarly reads crowds as a claim
to ballot representation rather than as an undirected visceral presence,
the ethical valence may be reversed, but the fundamental interpretation
is the same. Chartism can be read, in the political register, as an overardent desire for more sweeping parliamentary representation thirty
years before Disraeli saw fit to grant it: premature anti-oligarchism.

However, it is worth bearing in mind that the immediate aftermath
of Chartism's long, hot summer of 1839 was a decisive set of setbacks.
Though the claims of Thomas Carlyle's *Chartism* did not entirely triumph in 1839, those of Chartism itself did go down to defeat. The
public sphere, rather than changing to accommodate the collective repertoire of gestures that had evolved from the Radicalism of the teens
to the simultaneous meetings of the thirties, shifted decisively in 1848
to exclude "mass-platform"-style representation throughout the mid-
Victorian era.

There is a plausible argument to be made that this setback was only
a temporary one. Large political crowds did over the course of the next
century reemerge in a variety of forms, and one might well argue for
tracing a line between the representational practices of Chartism and
the forms of civil disobedience that, in Gandhi's India and Martin Lu-

ther King's American South, did succeed in procuring enduring forms
of civil rights. In fact, a strong case could be made not simply for a
direct genealogical affiliation between Chartism and later forms of civil
disobedience, but even for a kind of structural generalizability: in a
society in which access to unmistakably political channels of communication is relatively restricted, there exists strong pressure for a concomitant exploration of alternative discursive formations.[43] The distance of that claim from the apparent availability of various public
sphere expressions in North American and Western European democ-
racies today ought not to blind us to the fact that the grounds for
discursive competition are still strikingly present in various forms elsewhere.[44]

In noting latter-day successes we ought not, however, to overlook
the immediate aftermath of the failure of Chartism's mass platform.
James Vernon has recently argued that Chartism's fall after the early
1840s represents the hegemony of impersonal bureaucratic party oli-
gopoly over local culture: he thus reads in the mid-century the waning
of something like an "organic" protest movement in favor of the cold-
ness of the modern Liberal state. It is more accurate, however, to see
the defeat of the Chartist conception of crowd-mediated representation
as a reaction against any powerful alternative to the extant discursive
rules of the national public sphere, as represented by Tories and Whigs:
taking the crowd-as-speech into account would have necessitated a different conception of public representation altogether.[45]

The Chartist mass platform is not a residual component of an older
world of "rough music," but a potent alternative both to older and to
emergent forms of politics. The fact that it lived on after 1848, by, in
John Breuilly's terms, "maintaining a political initiative on issues of
metropolitan importance" (12) in London, reflects local successes for
Chartism as a parochial interest group. Importantly, however, it leaves
no site for collective instantiations of the national working class's representability.[46] The possibility of Chartist-style representative claims
had receded; the later emergence of analogous forms may suggest the
enduring power of peaceable crowds as a form of representative speech,
but it does not erase the long decades of eclipse.

The lingering traces of Carlyle's ideas are something altogether different. Carlyle's notion of a crowd that is not an affirmation of but a
threat to the representational ideal of parliamentarianism has left its
traces on a long line of reactionary thinkers after him, from acknowledged borrowings in Taine and Tarde to the unacknowledged legacy

in Le Bon, Sorel, Schmitt, and Mussolini. Carlyle's key legacy is his ability to excoriate the crowd as base rabble while simultaneously depending upon it as an avenue to the "deep, true energy" of the people themselves. This allows Sorel to seek in "violence" purgative redemption from the shallow satisfactions of rational colloquy. It enables Mussolini at once to denounce the dangerous rabble of the working classes (in the hands of outside agitators) and to justify the loyal Fascist crowds who are immunized against outside agitation by their wholehearted emotional connection to the Duce himself. And it allows Carl Schmitt to offer the inarticulate yet truthful voice of "the People" as a (Nazi-inflected) counter to the "jabber" and "tonguefence" of the Weimar Parliament. These thinkers—and a great many others in the same lineage—are ultimately instructed by Carlyle's terribly lucid way of grounding politically conservative irrationalism in a very rational elision of the crowd's corporeal presence and its strength.[47]

The failure of Chartism's goal of making crowds into representative signs, and the comparative success of Carlyle's attempt to do the reverse ought to prompt, I believe, a serious reappraisal of how we imagine the nineteenth-century public sphere in operation. For surely something odd has happened here, something unaccountable given a Habermassian public sphere constituted by "rational critical conversation" or by nothing at all. The Chartist claim to representation by way of publicly accepted gestures pointedly refused many of the complications that Carlyle's far more vexed and paradoxical account produces. If one considers the world of crowd gestures as the Chartists themselves set out to instantiate it, it is quite plausible to imagine a public sphere characterized by "rational-critical dialogue." The Chartists were committed to a model that saw representation as the *pu sto* of any sort of signifying gesture in public. Their account of crowds as a form of public speech, then, seems exactly in keeping with Habermas's axioms about the emergence of public rationality. All that is required is for one to posit—and it is not a difficult hypothesis—that the realm of rational communication can include the physical sign-making of crowds. Such an expansion of the "bourgeois" or of the "proletarian" public sphere is theoretically perfectly compatible with the Habermassian account of the "rational-critical."

The success of Carlyle's *Chartism* in disputing Chartism's claims, however, sweepingly undercuts any inclination one might have to suppose that the public sphere of the period was constituted entirely—or even primarily—by rational-critical modes of communication. Carlyle is brilliant at discovering ways to produce a text that finds its way in that public sphere by seeming to scorn the very process of rational sign-making itself. Chartism can hope to succeed in public if the rest of England is ready to grant a quite straightforward connection between massed bodies and signification: "that the men of Birmingham *were* England." Such a connection is refused. Carlyle depends for his success on a fiendishly complicated claim to contain within his own writing that which cannot be contained in any speech, but which must always be a form of action. Carlyle has found a way to appear to evade "figures."

He has thus presented—as a publicly circulating discourse that proved both portable and durable—an account of crowds that systematically denies to the crowd any representative quality, and that uses the crowd's corporeal "reality" as the justification for a deeply irrationalist account of what "true Englishness" entails. It is not simply that Chartism has failed to speak. It is that any attempt to make straightforward signification by a crowd a form of public discourse will always fail. Only by passing into Carlyle's own aesthetic discourse can any of a crowd's "inarticulate" essence enter into the discursive public sphere. That he was successful ought to make the latter-day critic alert to an exceedingly complicated field of cultural production, a world where aesthetic, economic, and political discourses are not readily separable from one another, where they interpenetrate, compete, and borrow one another's claims as part of the ongoing flux that constitutes the Victorian public sphere.[48]

In fact, Carlyle's move into the depths of the crowd's hidden heart—so as to invalidate the surface claims of articulate Chartism—has its parallel in Victorian aesthetics. The fiction of the day also aspires to represent, below the mere surface of the social realm, interiors seemingly too deep to plumb but not too deep to write up. Of course Carlyle's claims about the essence of (actual) Chartist demonstrators are not quite like Charlotte Brontë's claims about the invisible heartstrings that bind her (invented) Jane Eyre and Rochester together. But the resemblances between the two sorts of writing ought not to be overlooked. Carlyle's claim to reach below the level of articulate "clamour" manifested by a working-class crowd to find their true "struggle" resonates strikingly with the ongoing explorations, in the work of such novelists as Charlotte Brontë, Charles Dickens, and George Eliot, of the interior spaces out of which "deep calls to deep." A trivial example from Dickens (who was often criticized in the period for his comparative lack of attachment to depth): in *Great Expectations,* Pip is described as telling Magwitch, under stern questioning, "what I hardly knew I knew" (21). Like Carlyle's vision of the "struggle" below surface "clamour," the novelistic idea of an interior truth can work to invalidate the mere surfaces of other forms of public discourse: most notably, the novel can aspire to provide depth that the newspaper never can.

The novelistic device of depicting the inner nature of an invented person laid bare under external compulsion or external investigation surely has different antecedents and intentions behind it than does Carlyle's effort to reveal deep corporeal unrest below signifying crowds. But the alignment of strategies here suggests an analogy that elucidates the nature of contests for public sphere legitimacy in the era: as Chartist crowds are to Carlyle's "profound" politics, so newspapers are to the novel. As Carlyle takes Chartist demonstrations as his inescapable antitype, so too do the era's novels invoke newspapers as signs of the evils of merely flat public discourse. In each pair, the former (Chartist crowds, newspapers) is figured as representing the world as nothing more than a set of signs, laid flat for all to read. Thus Chartism asks nothing more than to be completely legible in the public sphere. By the same token, novels often figure newspapers as deliberately striving for a depthless representation of daily public life in a notionally rational public sphere. Anthony Trollope, for example, in *The Warden* (1855), parodies *The Times* as the *"Jupiter,"* a newspaper that superficially knows all, but is blind to affairs of the heart or of the hearth.

Carlyle's *Chartism* and the Victorian novel both operate by at once spurning and copying such a rival: novelists rely on the very same narratives as newspapers, but always leave themselves room for the claim to peer below the story's surface into inescapably murky depths. Like Carlyle, a great many of the most successful Victorian novelists succeed by emulating the triumphs of other public discourses while disdaining their lack of depth. In like discursive struggles, like strategies are born. Carlyle's tract and Victorian novels both shed light, then, on the ongoing struggles, borrowings, shadowings, and alliances that define the age's public sphere—a public sphere that is made malleable not simply by interest-driven politics, but by the rise and fall of various discursive claims, and by shifting notions of what counts as representation, as speech, even a perpetually shifting debate as to what constitutes the public itself.

CHAPTER 6

Producing Privacy in Public

Charlotte Brontë's Shirley

THE CASE FOR CONFINEMENT

In Charlotte Brontë's *Jane Eyre* (1847), there is a reassuringly clear confrontation between public bluster and passionate privacy, between vocation-oriented St. John Rivers and broodingly involuted Mr. Rochester. By choosing Rochester over Rivers, Jane affirms a desire for abrasive intimacy at all costs. Small wonder, then, that much Brontë criticism has the novel pegged as encapsulating, even shaping, an inward-looking Victorian self. True individual identity comes into being, the argument goes, when a connection is forged between two smolderingly silent souls. The connection between the two produces the depth that is the salient characteristic of the era's cloistered femininity.[1] Readers of *Jane Eyre* are shown the enterprise of constructing a self set at right angles to the unsavory public and commercial realm— perhaps even encouraged to try this at home. Brontë's *Shirley* (1849), however, has something rather different to say about making up privacy.[2]

The last two decades have seen the rise of literary criticism that rightly stresses the role that literary texts played in "conditioning" (to borrow Hannah Arendt's term) the views, feelings, and thoughts of their readers.[3] Valuable as this approach can be, it sometimes moves outward from describing the work of literary texts and proposes to assimilate a novel's "conditioning" force to a subject-conditioning matrix of forces that, for all its multifarious manifestations, is beneath all variety homogeneous. One frequent error of such accounts is to overlook the complicated give-and-take of variegated and incompatible accounts of self and world, of public and private, of politics and ethics, that can pervade not only a culture as a whole, but even a single text.

Recent accounts of the Victorian novel's role in the representation or the production of Victorian interiority—like the unapologetically psychological or psychoanalytic accounts that have also held recent sway—are thus often oddly disinclined to reckon with the daily, mundane exigencies of an economic and political world that shapes both individual psychology and novelistic structure.[4] A more complete genealogy of the forces that place pressure on any given text's creation—and of the ways such forces come to be represented within the text itself—therefore seems a potentially productive way of sharpening our understanding of the selves and social roles represented (and putatively shaped) by the mid-Victorian novel. Though *Shirley* is at first glance little more than a peripheral Victorian novel, an account of the competing ideas by which it is structured turns out to have a great deal to say about the implicit logic of the period's public sphere.

Recognizing *Shirley*'s surprising centrality begins with recognition of what historians have known for several decades now: the importance of Chartism's crowds to 1840s Great Britain. As chapter 5 argued in some detail, the political shifts that Chartism and like public protest movements effected in the 1840s bespeak a public sphere that was variegated beyond the assumptions of most present-day critics, and that lent itself to a (variously constrained but nonetheless genuine) ongoing discursive competition as to what would constitute speech or action in the public realm.[5] That struggle left its traces on the period's texts in more or less striking ways; on *Shirley*, those marks are peculiarly legible. Romantic privacy is figured in *Jane Eyre* as the natural convergence of two strikingly synchronized souls. *Shirley*, by contrast, is quite clearly intended as a manufactured response to a tumultuous public realm—a response to petition presentations in London as much as to suffrage marches in Haworth itself. The connection between Chartist claims to represent the working classes and *Shirley*'s claim to represent the Yorkshire Luddites helps to clarify ways in which the era's literature is produced and circulates within an avowedly contestatory public sphere, within which various discourses vie to mandate what might count as public action and what as circulatable private feeling.

Brontë describes middle-class private lives whose treasured forms of privacy and interiority come into being only on account of the actions of the working-class crowd. That peculiar genealogy for bourgeois interiority sheds invaluable light on the contestatory public realm within which the novels of the day circulated—a public realm, that is, within which *Shirley* strove to synthesize a convincing account of the lineaments and the origin of the middle-class domestic realm on which such novels' success ultimately depended.

Novels will presumably always be battlegrounds for various ideas about the shape of the self and of the social, because novels are, ironically, texts whose circulation is sanctioned yet within which privacy and the illusion of absolute intimacy must reign. But that irony is particularly vivid, and its consequences particularly important, in the 1840s. Like various other important literary texts of the day—such as Carlyle's *Chartism* (late 1839) and De Quincey's "The English Mail-Coach" (1849)—*Shirley* bases its account of forms of public action, its sense of what bodies assembled in public may signify or enact, on the strong claims for national adult male suffrage put forth by Chartist crowds between 1839 and 1848.[6] *Shirley* has its ear to a ground that is trembling with a new sort of practice for staking claims in public, a practice that depends on the actions that a crowd may make, whether those be parsed as a form of speech or as a kind of mute "bodying forth" of England's inner essence. As a novel, however, it faces some interesting challenges that neither De Quincey's Romantic memoir nor Carlyle's (quasi-political) essay had encountered.

Shirley (the plot is summarized briefly below) is a striking test case for the project of reading between the lines of domestication and interiorization. Brontë picks out the story of the 1811 Luddite unrest to make it seem that the danger of working-class crowds actually engendered the need for middle-class female domestication. Brontë seems to say: blame stuffy parlors on the mob. Yet there is praise along with that blame. *Shirley* gives an account of the material factors in the public realm that not only dictate a full-scale retreat toward physical privacy, but make that retreat seem a positively laudable move inward—and hence away from merely physical boundaries—to a higher sort of mental freedom. *Jane Eyre*'s great success as a Victorian novel lies in its careful eradication of all traces of a feared underclass in the presence of whose exterior substance emotional introspection becomes a necessity. *Shirley*, however, refuses the easeful solution provided by a domestic retreat from a class-stratified public world. Rather, it finds within the public realm, in the form of the riotous crowd, the necessary paradigm and matrix for the very sort of shared emotional connection that the novel itself strives to establish—ever so gingerly—between select pairs in the upper classes.

Shirley starts with free unattached subjects moving in a landscape of unclear economic utility and political orientation. It ends in a fixed world of respectable marriages, restricted landscapes, and limitless mental space. The space within which the novel oscillates, however, is also exemplary of the conditions under which a novelistic consciousness itself may be produced. The novel navigates between what a safe marriage promises, and what a dangerous factory forecourt threatens. Its brave new world of observant heroines is figured as having been created not only by restrictive industrial spaces, but also by the middle-class character's responsibility to note and to interrogate the power of the extramural crowd that hovers, both tamed and untamed, within its pages.

FROM MARGIN TO MILL: THE EMERGENCE OF THE CROWD

Shirley is set in rural Yorkshire in 1811–12, when Luddite machine-breakers violently resisted the influx of labor-eliminating machinery into the mills.[7] There are four protagonists: half-English, half-Belgian industrialist Robert Gérard Moore, his cousin and bride-to-be Caroline Helstone, Robert's twin Louis, and Louis's former pupil and destined wife Shirley Keeldar, who owns the mill that Robert operates. The plot is twisting and notoriously complex. The quasi-masculine Shirley—modeled on Emily Brontë, with her dog, her cavalier language, and her stoicism about pain—bursts on the scene to begin the novel's business; but there is an involved side-plot about the return of Caroline's long-lost mother; a Shakespearean mix-up about which Moore brother loves which of the girls; and various inconclusive diversions about the ferociously bellicose and patriotic Mr. Yorke and his emigrating family, as well as Caroline's imperious uncle the Reverend Helstone. Still, the central story (which all the subplots echo in various ways) is that of Caroline giving up her girlish freedom and her (quasi-erotic) rambles with Shirley on the open moor and learning to love Robert, the mill operator. This she does by way of a growing admiration for his ability to deal sternly with the dangerous organization of his mill hands. That organization culminates in the novel's most famous moment, a night-time attack on the mill violently rebuffed by Robert—Caroline and Shirley observe it from a nearby hill. Caroline lapses into depression when Robert seems to have eyes only for his mill and his martial duty, but blossoms back into a joyfully passive love when she realizes she is his chosen helpmeet for the industrial expansion that closes the novel.

Though the novel urges readers to lament the passing of the old days of the open moor where Shirley and Caroline once moved joyously with no sense of danger, it also urges them to accept in its place the inevitable growth of new and improved "Hollow's Mill," which will not only prevent further worker unrest but provide new tutelage for workers and their families by way of both a "Sunday" and a "day school" that Caroline and Shirley will administer (598).[8] The novel's ending has bookish brother Louis managing the paperwork so that heroic Robert can continue to embody all that is admirable about industrial masculinity. The chiasmal marriages—that of bold Robert to shy Caroline and that of domestic Louis to adventurous Shirley—thus offer a vivid sense of variation in personality, while ensuring that both women's roles will be essentially passive and observant, both men emotionally stolid, but vicariously attached to a larger world of mills and markets.

As the novel opens, however, none of its protagonists is in sight, and a nearly indescribable crowd sets the scene. No more than a rumor to begin with, this crowd seems diffuse, dispersed, and peripheral, something to be amazed at, but not to worry about. As in William Cobbett's *Rural Rides* (1830), with its musings on the almost-tangible vanished thousands who must once have populated the depleted English countryside, *Shirley*'s crowds begin just beyond the range of definite perception. They are glimpsed or overheard in a distant field when someone is "busy hedging" (49), and if they signify something other than the normal agricultural flurries far from the centers of power, it is not immediately evident what.[9]

Mike Hartley, not simply of the lower classes, but drunk and antinomian[10] as well ("crazed or . . . crafty—or, perhaps, a little of both"[48]), catches sight of the book's first crowd, Luddites drilling on the moors. Relayed through Caroline's uncle, the Reverend Mr. Helstone, Mike's words etch a distant sort of "beyond" for the crowd to inhabit.

> He looked up: all amongst the trees he saw moving objects, red, like poppies, or white, like May-blossom; the wood was full of them; they poured out and filled the park . . . but they made no more noise than a swarm of midges on a summer evening. They formed in order, he affirmed, and marched, regiment after regiment, across the park; he followed them to

Nunnely Common; the music still played soft and distant. On the common he watched them go through a number of evolutions, a man clothed in scarlet stood in the centre and directed them; . . . they seemed passing Field-head, when a column of smoke, such as might be vomited by a park of artillery, spread noiseless over the fields, the road, the common, and rolled, he said, blue and dim to his very feet. As it cleared away he looked again for the soldiers, but they were vanished; he saw them no more. (49–50)

That the blue and dim smoke is as noiseless as the soldiers themselves are ethereal suggests the problem of making such scenes substantial at all. Just before the events narrated in the book, someone "had seen a fairish (fairy) in Fieldhead Hollow" for the very last time, and the book's first chapters seem to situate the working-class crowd as an apparitional replacement for such fairies (599, 294).[11] We stand at a double narrative remove from the stable "real" appearance of the Lud-dites. Readers are left craning to make out the odd flowers that must be armed men, the midges that must be disgruntled workers, the "sol-diers" who must turn back into the neighbors whom the protagonists would be likely to visit on their next charity day.

From its dreamlike beginnings, *Shirley* moves swiftly to become the story of the gradual incursion of numbers of people and of organization into a social realm of dispersed farms and budding mills, a realm that at first had seemed to discourage not only "combination" but even the mere fact of agglomeration in any form. There waxes throughout the book a crowd that never quite manages to disperse. At times it retreats, yet always seems to return in another form, each form disquietingly suggesting a higher degree of order. The working-class crowd is not finally akin to these last few "fairishes"; it has come to take their place. As the novel's penultimate paragraph puts it, "It is altered now" (599). Retrospectively, this crowd seen on the moors is the beginning of a threat that the opening chapters of the book scarcely give the reader an opportunity to comprehend. The safety of the open field seemingly promised by a fairy crowd has, it turns out, been vanishing even with the apparition's arrival. As the novel's own vision of fully domestic social relations comes into focus, so too do the crowds gradually ma-terialize into bands of millworkers.

The enigmatic sight of May-blossom soldiers, silent as midges, is initially the signature only of a world beyond the social, an unfath-omable space where both crowds and ruined convents still seem pic-turesque, even sublime. But when a palpable material presence looms, demonstrably human and yet somehow alien, the meaning is profoundly different. The nature of this difference is registered first by the (excessively) sensitive Caroline. Exactly halfway through the novel, even something as innocent as the assembly of twelve hundred pious children in a grassy field is enough to discommode her. True, her instinct to hide behind a group of her students at her picnic ("she drew near them now, rather to find protection in their company than to patronize them with her presence" [308]) is eventually overcome by *noblesse oblige*: she recalls her duty at the communal tea urn.[12] Yet her performance "*on* duty" can never obscure "her evident timidity when off" (308).[13]

At this point, Shirley Keeldar seems by contrast to promise a better sort of boldness with which to face, for example, the threatened agglomeration of factory hands. But she too, faced with the assault on the mill, will come to accept the necessity of moving indoors. From the first, Caroline and Shirley share an aversion to extended social contact. At first, this jibes well with the fact that Shirley is accustomed to take to the high solitude of the moors "for the mere pleasure of seeing the stars, and the chance of meeting a fairy" (325). Before the mill assault, she and Caroline move through a world of secluded walks in "a deep hollow cup, lined with turf" where the "oldest of trees, gnarled mighty oaks, crowd about." But their anti-sociality can also move them in other ways when etiquette mandates communication.

Like other admirable Brontë characters, they are disinclined to sanction easy communication between people not already tied by blood or love. Such sociability is most charitably described as "a rushing backwards and forwards" or "mutual invasion" (60). When Caroline scorns three small-minded curates, the narrative seems to mock, and yet actually applauds, her discrimination: "What distinctions people draw!" (131). In its context, the evident meaning is: how necessary to draw such distinctions, or risk being drowned in curates. The ethical stance of *Shirley* is nowhere better in view than in Caroline's remark when she bemoans having to meet the husband-hunting Misses Sykes: "but they are different from me" (135). *Shirley* tells its readers from early on that forcible interchange with those quite different from one ought to be shunned.[14]

By midway through the book, indifference to those "different from me" is no longer an option. Shirley and Caroline can no longer be silent witnesses to silence. The novel's overt nostalgia for the cool solidity of a Yorkshire untroubled by "an abundant shower of curates" (39) is replaced with an active engagement in the Luddite unrest of

1811. The apparent stasis of the novel's opening is displaced by working-class unrest, an unrest so troubling to the characters' decorum (and the novel's ethos) that the charitable Shirley now feels moved to vow, "If once the poor gather and rise in the form of a mob, I shall turn against them like an aristocrat . . . [rather than] let Robert be borne down by numbers" (268). The presence of the same poor whom Caroline and Shirley had visited in earlier walks now discourages any such mobility. This confinement both infuriates Shirley and explains her martial inclinations.[15]

In a Yorkshire filled with obscurely troubling Methodist hymns overheard on the roads at night, Shirley and Caroline come to discover the necessity of taking a side, and remaining with it. Nights become the home to strange noises, no longer distantly intriguing, but presently threatening. As Shirley walks by, "Oh, the goodness of God / In employing a clod / His tribute of glory to raise" filters out of a church, followed by a potentially revolutionary and certainly inhuman "interregnum of shouts, yells, ejaculations, frantic cries, agonized groans" at the "climax of noise and zeal" (164). Fervent chapel-goers are drunk with the spirit that justifies the unconscionable assemblies that start to pepper the novel.

The fairy intangibility of blossom-crowds begins to give way to the solidly incorporated Luddite crowds whose public manifestations will justify a variety of belligerent actions to uphold domestic privacy. It is the turn toward encounters with hostile crowds that justifies *Shirley*'s praise of tightly sealed spaces, within which the imaginative life of central characters can find safe harbor. If the crowd glimpsed on the moors in the novel's opening pages had hinted that the realm of the "fairish" was still inexplicable, the next encounter with an outdoor body is palpably, agonistically human. This comes when Caroline and Shirley are leading their Sunday-school children on a picnic. A rival picnic party of children suddenly appears at the other end of a narrow lane: the reader is given only a paragraph of warning. The effect is polarizing upon meek and bold alike. Shirley asks the apt questions— "Is it our double? . . . our manifold wraith?"— but even timorous Caroline frames the question as a martial one: "'If you wanted a battle, you are likely to get one,—at least of looks,' whispered Caroline, laughing" (300). The battle that follows is a comic prelude to the gunfire that is to follow later that night at Robert's mill. The enemy is defined, without any further amplification, as "Dissenting and Methodist schools, the Baptists, Independents, and Wesleyans, joined in unholy alliance, and turning purposely into this lane with the intention of obstructing our march and driving us back" (300).

At such a moment, it helps to remember that Wellington had been Brontë's hero since childhood—she even once trailed him through London crowds. What men will do with cannon and cavalry at the mill later that night, "every child and woman" of the Sunday-school procession is prepared to do bodily at this moment. Sanctioned bellicosity extends even to such seeming noncombatants. The almost indecipherable sentence that summarizes all the action captures well the slightly improbable irresistibility of marching preachers, strong female landowners, and child foot-soldiers. Singing, they stride down upon the unified dissenters:

> And (Reverend Helstone) strode on with such a determined and deliberate gait, and was, besides, so well seconded by his scholars and teachers—who did exactly as he told them, neither running nor faltering, but marching with cool solid impetus; the curates, too, being compelled to do the same as they were between two fires,—Helstone and Miss Keeldar,—both of whom watched any deviation with lynx-eyed vigilance, and were ready, the one with his cane, the other with her parasol, to rebuke the slightest breach of orders, the least independent or irregular demonstration,—that the body of Dissenters were first amazed, then alarmed, then borne down and pressed back, and at last forced to turn tail and leave the outlet from Royd-lane free. (301)

The sentence serves to drag in all participants: tucked into an out-of-place subsidiary clause, the curates have no choice but to watch Helstone and Keeldar, who in turn are neatly metaphorized by cane and parasol, both weapons in this "roadway riot."

This crowd constitutes the opening salvo in a war that can only be won by those who will fight. Conciliation is ruled out. An economy based on active antagonism is here inaugurated; only after a confrontation can reconciliation begin. Recall that *Shirley* begins with various isolatos—Caroline and Shirley prominent among them—who move silently over the lonely moor, their privacy defined by the length of their walks or their skill at deflecting the attention of others. But after this encounter, the novel has unmistakably begun its turn from the solace of private walking to the necessity of containment. By the story's end, there are two stable married couples living up against the confined space of a mill and its newly built additions—workers' cottages, roads, all the trappings of a mill town that is a logical forerunner to the Coketown of Dickens's *Hard Times* (1854), or the Milton of Gaskell's

North and South (1854–55). Shirley, who once kept even her dog bites a secret (a detail that Charlotte had adopted from Emily's life), has now moved into the public eye.

The picnic assault is in a certain sense the best-case scenario for a novel interested in establishing that the dissenting crowd's energy is raucous and its planning haphazard. Were this march against chaotic dissenters simply a picture of the confrontation to come, then the novel could safely choose either side: position itself as the emotional ally of the helplessly confused dissenters, or throw its sympathies with those tucked into the citadels of the middle class. However, Brontë complicates her account: the crowds to follow are not mere disorder, any more than they are idyllic moonshine visions. Between this picnic melee and the mill attack that takes place that night, both bellicose intent and military order strengthen among the lowly. Shirley's "piercing" eyes still had an active part to play in a picnic melee. Faced with a mill assault, however, they must be reassigned merely to witness a battle between a working-class crowd and a middle-class bulwark. Caroline and Shirley may already be inclined to distrust public spaces, but their role as conduits of feeling observation is born only on this nighttime hillside, when the crowd below reveals its own aspirations toward a new sort of industrial participation.

CREATING OBSERVANT WOMEN

The crowd at the mill will eventually serve to drive Caroline and Shirley out of their prior disposition toward unrestrained movement over the empty moors, and into a combative concord with Robert Moore and his mill minions. This transition, however, does not occur as a matter of course. Rather, it is drawn out over several chapters in which mob agglomeration comes not only to justify but even to model a new sort of enclosure. Both Caroline and the novel's readers are somewhat disinclined to trust prickly Robert Moore from the first: both are won over by the events surrounding the assault on the mill.

Brontë methodically sets the stage for this conversion. To implement an immediate conversion, a change of heart simply leaving women weakly waiting for their husbands to return home, would be to repeat the error that had so weakened her fragmentary novella, "The Moores" (1847). The woman who assumes she has no role but to stay inside cannot possibly lead to an interesting tale: in that story, Mr. Moore's simpering wife can ask nothing better of her husband than "I am the best thing you possess, old or new, after all, am I not?" (63). Accepting Mrs. Moore's role as drawing-room fixture, her husband gives her a predictable rating—as well as a "rating" in the sense of "teasing"—maintaining that he loves three things more than her: his mill, his "credit and connections," and his bookkeeper, Tim Steele (64–65). All is as it should be for a thoroughly unattractive man of the new school: his material success should logically precede his love for a wife who took him for his position and form in a world whose rules demand that he value these trappings of that position. No wonder the story was abandoned. Mrs. Moore, in her straightforward acceptance of an instrumental role behind her husband's well-built walls (part of the furniture of his life), could never embody Brontë's alert depiction of a consciousness reaching out just slightly beyond the bounds of the well-regulated social realm.

Shirley raises the stakes by deferring the marriage of Caroline and Robert, and the unconditional assent it implies. Shirley and Caroline do not at first assume that their role is to remain in a locked room divorced from the business, and busy-ness, of the world outside. After the Sunday-school face-off, working-class unrest grows apace, and that night the march of men upon the mill begins. Caroline and Shirley ready themselves for action when they hear outside of Caroline's uncle's house "a nearer, though a muffled sound" looming out of a night that should be as "safe, silent, and solitary" as the moorland paths they walk (329, 331). Action, though, is not ready for them. The tramping sound that Caroline and Shirley hear hours after leaving the picnic-ground, "not the tread of two, nor of a dozen, nor of a score of men" (329), is not at first even palpably human ("Those who listened, by degree, comprehended its extent" [329]). Only when a "human voice" says "Halt!" does it definitively leave the realm of natural or fantastical phenomena. But that human referent at once grounds the source of the disturbance and removes it as an immediate threat to the women. The site of employment (the mill), not of female seclusion (the preacher's house), is the crowd's object.

Though Shirley may not be their actual target, she is quick to identify the crowd on the road as the palpably antagonistic working class she had warned would make her into an aristocrat. She does not give up that plan easily. Indeed, she almost becomes one in earnest, reverting to the forms of valor of a previous generation—or of a Walter Scott novel. Martial like a man of the old school, she has her "finger . . . on the trigger of this pistol" planning "to give that man, if he had entered, such a greeting as he little calculated on" (331). But *Shirley* has other plans for its female protagonists, and its crowds have other enemies in mind. The "measured, beating, approaching sound" dies away, replaced now by "mustering, manifold, slow-filing tread" as the rioters move on toward Hollow's mill where the arsenal of Robert Moore awaits them (329, 330).

Shirley's desire for an old fashioned man-to-man showdown is thwarted—such futile belligerence would embody neither the characteristic feminine nor masculine virtues of *Shirley*. Firing one gun against an enormous crowd would have made a suitable hero for the novels of an earlier generation, but has nothing to do with the new role of encircled mill-owner.[16] Such a shot would have little chance of success: "behind him followed three hundred: I have neither three hundred hands nor three hundred weapons" (331). Shirley voices here the disappointed futility of the old nobility. This is a moment where the supplanting of vestigial aristocratic mores by prudent middle-class ones noticeably displaces questions of gender: a gentleman with a pistol would have had the same problem. Shirley's quixotic and potentially suicidal valor delineates a role that neither men nor women will want to occupy in the citadel economy that impends. Behind his wooden walls, Moore triumphs by virtue of the hired labor and seconded redcoats who are his personal equivalent of three hundred hands.[17]

In the world of "The Moores," the bypassing of the Helstone house would have ended the drama: Mrs. Moore would probably have gone to bed. But Brontë here introduces an important and interesting twist on the seeming irrelevance of the women left to languish in safety. To be overlooked is to gain an unrestricted license to observe. The sympathies of Caroline and Shirley ally them with Moore in his mill, but their sex gives them the license to move to an eagle-eye vantage as a barricaded gentleman could not. Shirley and Caroline dash over the moors (tearing their delicate "silks" and "muslins" [332]) to deliver a warning. But they come too late for action: the men inside are well warned, and the men outside well placed by the time Shirley and Caroline's slow run is done. Thus, while their male counterparts are locked inside the mill, counting on various technical aids to defend them against three hundred hands, Shirley and Caroline—as they so often do at key moments, as they had earlier that afternoon over a crowded church picnic (309)—stand shivering and watching on the bare hill above the scene of action.

Physically superfluous, they perform another sort of salutary action:

they observe, feelingly. Being female here comes to mean finding oneself in the enviable position of being privileged both to observe and to judge without being impelled to act. Their presence is not without its purpose, but that purpose explicitly prevents direct action: "I am glad I came," says the intrepid Shirley. "We shall see what transpires with our own eyes: we are here on the spot, and none know it" (334).

To be there and none know it: the text has begun to define a new role that the presence of a crowd creates.[18] Clearly there is an important self-referential component to such passive involvement: implicit emotional attachment—for example, that of reader to character or of lover to beloved—demands a feeling observation of another's actions from a removed vantage. And the injunction against action recalls the Aristotelian observation that a spectator at drama must accept his or her powerlessness to interfere. But to embed such a claim into the account of an event that seems anything but "fictional" is to provide a far more pervasive account of the situations in which merely observant action will be called for. Silent observation on the overlooking hillside can continue only on the condition that Caroline and Shirley not interfere— that they look, and advocate, and remain aloof. Such observation becomes possible because all parties regard female direct action as nugatory at best, self-defeating at worst. Though Shirley "would have given a farm of her best land for a chance of rendering good service" (337), the offer is as filled with a sense of its own innate futility as was her pistol-toting.

Martial male discipline is all. As men clash, women marvel. Women ought to serve as feeling witnesses, rather than dash into action. Shirley warns Caroline that:

> Instead of amazing the curate, the clothier, and the corn-dealer with a romantic rush on the stage, we stand alone with the friendly night, its mute stars, and these whispering trees, whose report our friends will not come to gather. (334–35)

The explicitly antitheatrical nature of the comparison is apt: like firing the pistol, such a spectacular gesture would be exactly counterproductive, generating chaos and danger instead of resolution, necessitating aid from the men at the mill rather than supplying it.

This is a key point for the novel to reassert its commitment to a process of active watching, a watching that permits feeling involvement even as it discourages a full identification with the energy of the crowd below. Recall that Wordsworth's narrator in *The Prelude*'s "Residence in London" feels free to admire the energy of St. Bartholomew's Fair crowds, but is impelled to invoke the muse's help to ascend above the crowds when they grow too fiery:

> For once the Muse's help will we implore,
> And she shall lodge us—wafted on her wings
> Above the press and danger of the crowd—
>   (7, 656–58)

By the same token, here Brontë prepares the reader to enter the novel's most memorable moment, viscerally shocking, effectively inviting: the Luddite assault on the mill. But an apt *pu sto* is required. Though the report of a fairy crowd on the moors can be filtered through any number of eyes and mouths, this assault scene demands the presence of the two star witnesses, to make the moment into an assimilable part of the plot.

At this moment in which the crowd is central to the action, the reader is reminded that on the hillside above are the characters whose consciousness will channel the novel's account. Though Caroline's love for Robert urges her forward, Shirley's self-restraint, along with an oddly memorable but peculiar natural analogy ("they stood together as still as the straight stems of two trees" [335]), holds them both in place. Gazing down at a picnic field of "nearly a thousand adult spectators" earlier in the day, Caroline and Shirley had used Shirley's "eagle acuteness" to discern the "tall stature and straight port" of the man who would become the defender of the mill, Robert Moore (309). The process is repeated here, albeit with a difference. At the picnic Robert had been out amongst a thousand others, yet distinct from the crowd: "He looks amidst the set that surround him like Eliab amongst humbler shepherds" (309). Here, his very invisibility is his singularity. The one man standing alone outside the mill is only a "shabby little figure of a private soldier"; Robert is surrounded by his delegated representatives, the loyal foot-soldiers who form a part of his elaborate citadel. His place behind his walls makes him both present and absent—literally invisible and yet visible in every gear and beam of a building that stands as the concrete embodiment of Robert's will.[19]

The book's most memorable paragraph follows. The crowd that had only been heard on the road is now seen looming out of the black night, and the noise they make is neither singing, nor tramping, but a yell—a yell reported as rising almost from the body of Yorkshire itself, the signal of the workingmen's final assault on the body of the mill.

The description of the yell besieges not only a mill, but also all stable rules for perceiving space and time:

> A crash—smash—shiver—stopped their whispers. A simultaneously hurled volley of stones had saluted the broad front of the mill, with all its windows; and now every pane of every lattice lay in shattered and pounded fragments. (335)

Like Emily Dickinson's dashes, the dashes in "crash—smash—shiver—stopped" (especially the final one) disorder syntax. They connote connection, but leave causality, even temporality, throughout the passage, deliberately vague: when we hear of "simultaneously hurled . . . stones" the exact nature of the simultaneity (what happens at once? what follows?) is unclear. Though Caroline and Shirley are isolated, they are inescapably involved in this scene, without participating in the active duties of the men inside the mill.

Shirley and Caroline have become the locus for a novelistic gaze that is also the reader's own. Passivity and emotional involvement are concurrent here: to feel for Robert also means not to act for him. The paragraph continues:

> A yell followed this demonstration—a rioters' yell—a North-of-England—a Yorkshire—a West-Riding—a West-Riding-clothing-district-of-Yorkshire rioters' yell. You never heard that sound, perhaps, reader? So much the better for your ears—perhaps for your heart; since, if it rends the air in hate to yourself, or to the men or principles you approve, the interests to which you wish well, Wrath wakens to the cry of Hate: the Lion shakes his mane, and rises to the howl of the Hyena: Caste stands up, ireful, against Caste; and the indignant, wronged spirit of the Middle Rank bears down in zeal and scorn on the famished and furious mass of the Operative Class. It is difficult to be tolerant—difficult to be just—in such moments. (335)

Without this yell there would be no justification for Moore's truculent air of cold command. But that purely irrational yell—witnessed by Shirley and Caroline—underwrites what will follow, and the hauteur that preceded it. It is as elevated observers that readers hear this yell, but the various interpretational matrices presented seem intended to blur into one another: is it Robert, Caroline, Brontë, or the reader who interprets this yell? Mixed metaphors (wrath wakening to hate) and elision of differences between various schemes of value (caste, rank, and class are blurred) abound. "You" react to the threat to your interests, but also to those you hold dear; you respond to hate with wrath, but also to property claims with gunpowder.

The moment of polarization temporarily produces a vision of bodily conflict. The spectral visions of lions and hyenas do not reappear after this moment, but they leave behind them, like an etched negative of their lurid power, Shirley and Caroline's prosaic decision that "all their interest had been enlisted" on Robert's side (337). After the nightmare image of the crowd has faded, that conviction stays. What has been shaped in the molten crowd will stay firmly pressed on the characters when they harden again into coolness.

Unable to go forward or back, the two women are moved but immobile:

> Both girls felt their faces glow and their pulses throb: both knew that they would do no good by rushing down into the mêlée: they desired neither to deal nor to receive blows; but they could not have run away—Caroline no more than Shirley; they could not have fainted; they could not have taken their eyes from the dim, terrible scene—from the mass of cloud, of smoke— the musket-lightning—for the world. (336–37)

As long as that sentence lasts—and lasts—the text is immobilized with them, incapable either of acting or of ceasing to witness. What they witness is both the necessity for someone to defend a space in which a man they love is located, and the impossibility of anyone's doing so without addressing the crowd with "tongues" of fire or with Robert Moore's imperious voice from within. His incarceration in the mill is both a precaution against and a product of the mob's onslaught. Without the onslaught there would be no justification for the elaborate aggression that master must bear toward men.

The reaction of Shirley and Caroline must be read as a two-fold movement, both forward toward Moore, and away from the open moors—a reminder of the pun, presumably deliberate, between "moor" and "Moore." To Shirley and Caroline, the assault seems from the first a stunning justification of enclosure and, by the same token, an abrogation of the former safety of the open empty moors. The enumerated mob outside, called into existence originally by Robert's intense drive to produce a work-space in the factory, now looms beyond that factory—it is what makes it dangerous for women to go abroad on any occasion. Yet at this moment what we hear from Caroline and Shirley is that their "interest" has gone forward to Robert, not that it has been withdrawn from the working classes. The role of the two women who observe the onslaught is to confirm the existence of connection—love, solidarity, and comprehension across barriers—but only between those already united by class and by emotional similarity.

Caroline and Shirley, then, nowhere more so than in this scene, achieve a form of readerly oversight that carries with it a sort of obligatory participation in the fate of those to whom they are emotionally connected. That participation, like a reader's participation in a novel, may never directly affect the actions of those they watch. Yet indirectly such vicarious participation, such complicit assent to the actions of those who move in the public realm, has tremendous significance. The novel's power as a discourse well poised to define a stable public sphere is here underscored, because the novel offers what the crowd cannot: representations at once public and private.

But the novel also offers, in its complicated establishment of implicit contrasts between the powers of text and those of the crowd, something more. To forego a theatrical form of intervention is not simply to retreat into a safe domestic space. Caroline and Shirley have not become "precious things" like Mrs. Moore. It almost seems that the contrary is true: in the reactions of the two principal female characters to the assault that Moore has precipitated and endured is born a new paradigm, that of a strong female role as imaginative observer. To be an observant woman means to witness but not replicate, to admire but not join, the well-structured heroism of the citadelled male.

In the confines of that observational role, Shirley and Caroline are the loci of an imaginative leap that depends upon the impinging crowd: imagination, and the female talent for observation and reaction, can keep alive a vicarious participation in the lives of one's allies that is very close to the sort of vicarious participation in others' lives that a novel supplies. *Shirley* suggests that this is especially true in a world of impinging crowds and the steady collapse of spatial separation between classes. Thanks to the power of such observation, the free-ranging pleasure of the unattached protagonists—especially the unattached woman—may survive once onlooking has been replaced by marriage, and by life in a vastly expanded mill area. The most dramatic, if not the most lucid, exposition of this claim in *Shirley* is contained in the powerful burst of imaginative sympathy produced among the three protagonists by the assault on the mill. As the parameters of the assault itself should suggest, it is the presence of a crowd that threatens both disorder and an alarming kind of revolutionary new order that instigates in *Shirley* the sort of feeling observation associated with Victorian notions of well-guarded interiority.

It is obvious that such an account of interiority refers to the novel-reading process itself, not so obvious what the intended relationship may be. Throughout the novel, there is a conscious effort to distinguish the sort of observation that Shirley and Caroline acquire from the sort of unruly solidarity that is the undesirable property of crowd-members who intend to destroy and then to restructure the factory world. Caroline's observational powers allow her to flee the Misses Sykes; by contrast, the religious drunk Moses Barraclough, one of the crowd's leaders, welcomes preternaturally close contact with his followers, explaining ominously that "I'm a very feeling man." The "feeling" that Barraclough preaches both is and is not akin to the logic of separation and long-distance sympathy that Brontë wants to promote. Where there are crowds, there are feelings: where one goes to escape crowds, there are similar feelings.

If this novel simply confirmed the overall importance of a sharp public/private dichotomy that gives women a laudable private role, one might simply conclude that the long-distance observational sympathy that Brontë advocates was a simple inversion of the crowd's agglutinative logic: a lumpish crowd mind on one side, prickly solitude on the other. But such a reading misses the real strength of *Shirley*, the way it is striving to contain within the confines of the novel a potentially disruptive rival. That rival is the claims for representation that working-class crowds forcefully asserted throughout the 1840s, the claims, that is, that a nonvoting population might find alternative suffrage by making representative claims in public spaces, by way of a widely accepted "collective repertoire of gestures" understood by crowd-members and witnesses alike.[20] These Chartist claims are understood perfectly, but deliberately displaced or discredited by authors intent on putting these crowds to use within their own work for quite other purposes. De Quincey used the power of English crowds to undergird a transformative moment of aesthetic patriotism in "The English Mail-Coach"; Carlyle's *Chartism* had ten years earlier made the "inarticulate power" of the raging crowd a somatic supporter of his own brand of heroic politics. Brontë here employs the Luddite—and the Chartist—crowd in the creation of middle-class domesticity.

There can, however, be no conversion of a rival's claims without an initial acknowledgment, implicit or explicit, that such claims might themselves hold sway in the public sphere: else why bother to turn them to one's own use? We see here not a hegemony engulfing a doomed rival, but the attempted assimilation of an innovative alternative to middle-class mores and mindset. Brontë is far from skeptical of what the massed bodies of workers can proclaim or accomplish. What she demands here is not the power to shut them up, but the power to put words into their mouths. One could certainly try to construct an account of a pervasive binary between public and private that encompassed even this representation of the power of crowds to unsettle public and private. But such an account would have to blind itself to the problems that Brontë has in *Shirley* reestablishing a simple model of private and public.

In fact, the effect of working-class crowds, perhaps not the intended effect, has been to transform the terms whereby such boundaries are established in the novel. The strength of this rival discourse requires Brontë to postulate new forms of bourgeois freedom (not the moor, but marriage to Moore). The central and unavoidable role of the Luddite crowd introduces, in an almost underhanded way, an idea of salutary publicity that makes *Shirley* far from an unequivocal supporter of any simple boundaries between private and public.

A very interesting set of ironies follows from *Shirley*'s commitment both to defending the realm of the private and to admitting the potential power of the representative crowd. The impending presence of an expanded factory world filled with industrial crowds hastens, in *Shirley* as in *Harrington*, the postulation of substitutive imaginary or vicarious connections: between Caroline and Robert, or between author and reader. Yet mills or classrooms cannot dispel the notion that the Luddites' well-drilled coordination and futile unity pose a real challenge not simply to Robert Moore's self-interest, but to the half-emotional, half-prudent disposition of the novel itself. Having raised the problem of this promiscuous presence in the public realm, Brontë does channel some of its energy, as *Harrington* had, into sexual alliance and romantic reaffiliation. But that attempt is far from adequate to undo the impression that the crowd's presence has created. The inadequacy of redress through merely romantic alliance begins to bespeak the strength of this alternative way to imagine public space. The suffrage demonstrations of the 1840s left their trace even on a historical novel both set and composed in rural Yorkshire. The ghost of Chartism, muffled and nearly seeming to preach its own demise, yet audibly speaks in Charlotte Brontë.

CITADELLED MEN

The romantic association that forms between Caroline and Robert across the rampaging crowd does offer a partial solution to the problem of rampant public action. *Shirley* proffers romance as a suitable alternative to a crowd—whether Chartist or Luddite—that is already in the process of subdividing or colonizing the physical spaces around the central characters. Yet there is another half to *Shirley*'s solution and it is contained in an alternative sort of vicarious association, one seemingly open only to those who have, like Robert, thrown in their lot with the invisible extended network of manufacturing worldwide.[21] *Jane Eyre* presents a brilliant example of a world where intimacy is romantic, where privacy hinges on the associative sympathy between a complementary pair. But *Shirley* offers another sort of vicarious sympathy: that between a single mill-owner and his extended, invisible web of business associates. The man in his citadel is no more "alone than he is alarmed," and his sociability begins and ends within his well-armed walls. But that sociability is not cameral: behind his walls lie the correspondence network and the commercial contracts that ensure his dependence on suppliers, and customers, as well as theirs on him. Like readers of a novel, those associates abroad will follow his cause with interest, without being able to participate in it.

The remainder of the assault on the mill can best be analyzed by moving into the well-guarded space where Moore's ego and ambition are couched. Robert Moore has been awaiting an attack since, in the book's opening pages, "the throes of a sort of moral earthquake were felt heaving under the hills of the northern counties" (62). And it is that attack that makes him what he is, all prior dispositions aside. One can begin parsing Robert's character in the early didactic passages, where Brontë stresses his yearning for "silent, sombre, unsafe solitude" (63) or his alarming sympathy with the imperious Coriolanus. But such psychological foreshadowings all lead up to—and fail entirely to predict—this moment, in which the onrushing assault of the angry working class justifies his recalcitrance. Robert earns his identity not by going forward to establish an identity in public, but by lagging behind to defend a newly fortified private space. Robert Moore's function in *Shirley* is to reiterate the necessity of division across the barriers that mark class, vocational, and even dispositional differences: we gentry and industrialists prize solitude, while they, the workers, love their agglomeration, their "fellow feeling."[22]

From early on there have been voices (among them Shirley's) warning against the belief that all incursions by the importuning masses outside must be repulsed violently from the inside. Traditionalists within the novel argue (or imply) that Robert's deliberate actions, not the organized crowds, trigger the reciprocating onslaught. Poor treatment creates misery, and—famously—"misery generates hate." But when the Luddites actually strike, the notion of top-down causation is formally rejected. Shirley's idea of "amiable distance" disappears in the moment of the air-shattering yell. In Moore's defiant voice responding to that yell, indissoluble lines between caste and caste are drawn, and indissoluble links between man and woman within the ruling caste are soldered. Against the incomprehensible scream at the heart of the assault scene, and the nearly illegible demands of the mob's "peculiar" "orthography" when they send a defiant note, Robert Moore has only contempt and defiance to offer.[23] Wearing on his face the adjective Brontë bestows only upon her most-beloved characters, he smiles a "singular smile . . . when he reaches a juncture in his life where this determined spirit is to feel a demand on its strength: when the strain is to be made, and the faculty must bear or break" (64).

In this, his crowning moment, Moore knows how to treat a crowd according to what is represented as its own statistical logic. Though he would not kill any individual member isolated, taking them *en masse* he will kill, without discrimination, one or more. And why can he move to number rather than name that mass? Because they themselves have introduced the practice: "a roll was called over, in which the men answered to figures rather than names" (337). The novel does not assign explicit blame for the deadly result of the assault, which Moore has decided to break before being himself broken. But his justification is clear by the time of the exchange of gunfire volleyed between Moore's men and Moore's enemies, so that within minutes "a human body lay quiet on its face near the gates; and five or six wounded men writhed and moaned in the bloody dust" (338).[24] The numerical blur, "five or six," like the earlier dating of the novel's action to "eighteen-hundred-eleven-twelve"(39), may seem to inject uncertainty into the reckoning, but its primary effect is to draw attention to numbers rather than names. Was it five or six, the reader wonders, rather than "What were their names?"

When it comes time at the end of the novel to welcome workers back into a mill that "shall fill its present yard" (597), the "houseless, the starving, the unemployed" (598) will only return to be enumerated as obedient employees where they had first counted themselves out as rioters. Set against the homogenized nonentities of the Luddite crowd, Moore's individuality is artificially heightened. Though most of the violence comes from merely delegated substitutes who are as little like

Moore as the "shabby" sentry, in this moment, their actions, their bullets, are his. The descriptions of everything, from the structure of the mill to the voices of its defenders, revert quickly, synecdochically almost, to the animating intelligence of that mill, Moore himself. Moore is neither seen nor heard from until after the attack, because he is securely concealed, "as little alone as he is alarmed" (336), with soldiery and stout Yorkshire companions. Against an uncontrolled crowd, he has now summoned—and the contrast is vital—the sort of crowd that Le Bon liked to call a "pack," not exactly coerced but not quite free either.[25]

Against the wounding yell (mere sound, but seeming to threaten ferocious destruction), Moore's mill offers gunfire (deadly, yet ostensibly no more than a counterpoised form of speech). "The hitherto inert and passive mill woke: fire flashed from its empty window-frames" (336). Moore fires, as it were, out of himself. Shirley grasps the point immediately: "Moore speaks at last! . . . and he seems to have the gift of tongues; that was not a single voice" (336). Moore's multiple voice is the only lucidity in an otherwise confusing exchange. In his voice, the yell of the rioters is matched, and undone.

> They heard the rebel leader cry, "To the back, lads!" They heard a voice retort, "Come round, we will meet you!"
> "To the counting-house!" was the order again.
> "Welcome!—We shall have you there!" was the response. (336)

In "Moore's own voice" both Shirley and Caroline recognize a true master whose "soul was now warm with the conflict" (336). The voice and the yell together both define and necessitate this fight.

To understand Robert's behavior as Shirley and Caroline understand it requires something more from the reader than amiable sympathy. It requires the whole work of the book's first half. Within the book's opening pages, Moore's distance from his workers has already been ascribed to his "hybrid" nationality—raised in Antwerp by a Belgian mother and an English father: "he had a tendency to isolate his individual person from any community" (60). From there, the continuing chain of indignities offered to Moore—his inability to move into the world of international finance, the resistance to his industrial improvements among the independent Yorkshiremen—are all understandable developments within an antagonistic industrial milieu. But all these developments are also pitched to set Moore increasingly at odds with his environment.

Moore loves nothing more than to exaggerate his solitude. His defense explicitly depends both upon the reinforcements the government has provided him, and upon the distant reassurance of a market, into which his identity as cloth manufacturer is integrated. Indeed, all recourse to the powers of romantic love aside, this second form of vicarious attachment (manufacturer to manufacturing realm) is thrown into sharp focus by the mill assault. Shirley and Caroline justify their readerly observation of the mill fight by invoking their feeling of sympathy with Moore. Moore finds his strength, by contrast, in looking beyond his surroundings, to the generals in York at whose command, "[s]ilent and orderly, six soldiers rode softly by"; and to the markets of India and America, with whom "[t]rade is likely to prosper for some years to come" (317, 597).

Moore's turn away from his much-vaunted isolation to a strategic alliance with forces outside Yorkshire, forces whose shared interest and shared valor here combine to create an insurmountable barrier against the disgruntled workers, provides a fitting corollary to the sort of vicarious connection that Caroline's act of feeling observation has already supplied from the hilltop. The vital link that Moore silently accepts is his attachment to a market elsewhere, a market whose swings and fluctuations determine not only his actions, but his temper, and his virtues. Courage in adversity can turn to arrogance in triumph; peevishness in defeat can become magnanimity in a good year.

Moore's claim to manhood is staked on his being one among many, part of a cotton and weaving empire that stretches far enough beyond himself that he can denounce even his own king, because his true capitol (and capital) is dispersed among the international markets, not down here in Yorkshire. "Now I, if I know myself, should stand by my trade, my mill and my machinery" (57), he tells an uncomprehending curate of the old school, and the fact that he puts his "trade" first is significant. Here is a man firmly anchored within a workplace, yet attached to a world that is linked at long range to the products of that workplace, a world made up of those with whom he competes. *Shirley*'s emphasis on this unseen world beyond the mill points up an important irony of the male claim of self-standing stability in public performance, of self-created citadel status. Robert can possess the courage and sense of righteousness required to defend and then to expand his mill only because of his attachment to a distant world of commerce, of power dispersed worldwide.[26]

Even Moore's passivity comes to look like activity when viewed in terms of his extra-Yorkshire affiliations. Moore's alien temper is needed for the inevitable challenge ahead: to "double the value of [the] mill-property . . . and pour the waters of Pactolus through the valley of Briarfield" (597–98), though it must also mean changing "our blue hill-country air into the Stilbro' smoke atmosphere" (598). The reader can, like Caroline and Shirley, bemoan Moore's headstrong unwillingness to conciliate his workers, but the novel allows no challenge to his insistence that a peremptory firmness is the only sound basis for an owner's relations with his employees. Neither the protagonists nor readers are given a perspective from which to gainsay his insistence that "radical reform" via capital and machinery is the only viable economic platform, and the general "enclosure" of commons and habitations the only way forward (61).

But it is a way forward that is possible only when the workers have made the first move. When Mr. Helstone says of Robert Gérard Moore, "I call him very careless," he credits Moore with being—to invert the formulation in Henry James's *What Maisie Knew* (1897)—a character on whom everything is wasted. It is Moore who effectively lures the rioters to his home, so that he can triumph against a working class pressed into an agglomerated unity, and thus justify his own oppositional "silent, sombre, unsafe solitude" (63). He is not merely willing but eager to force on his recalcitrant workers a confrontation: his character is well suited not only for entrepreneurial success but for its corollary, direct struggle. He wants nothing more than to present a brave face, an unemotional and "careless" face, to the world—so after courting death threats he makes it a point of honor to "sit in the counting-house with the shutters unclosed."[27]

Robert has taken the law into himself: his coolness preempts any attempt to reach him. He chooses a social face to meet the other faces he will meet, and shapes his conversation as confrontation rather than intercourse. This is a direct challenge to the "good-humored rating" that Shirley is capable of with a crowd of farm women. Robert's coolness supposes that there can be no middle ground between devotion (extended to his sister, his cousin, his brother, and his landlady) and the reserve he preserves toward those who are "different from me." He is uniquely suited to be the novel's paragon of unfellow feeling. "It is likely that he was unapt to attach himself to parties, to sects, even to climes and customs" (60).

When, during a reading of Shakespeare's *Coriolanus*, Caroline charges Robert with enjoying Coriolanus's arrogant and self-contained cruelty to the people of Rome ("I see another glimpse of brotherhood in error" [117]), she calls his crime the inability to distinguish among "poor working people," putting them all "under the general and insulting name of 'the mob'" (118). This is the very lack of distinction that his coolness both demands and rewards. Only under the hostile glare of the mob can this aspect of his character, this unwillingness to accommodate those "different from" himself, become a palpable advantage. In the eyes of Moore, the workers whose livelihood his new machinery threatens must be brought to behave like a "mob" so that they—now become an "it"—can be laid low.

In fact, an earlier encounter has already set the tone for Robert's exceptional willingness to treat his workers as a group. When a delegation of workers comes to negotiate with him at the first arrival of new machinery, Robert commits an apparent error in refusing to recognize that one member of the delegation is willing to break with the others, to forge a compromise. To offer a job to this rebel—William Farren, "a very honest man, without envy or hatred of those more happily circumstanced than himself; thinking it no hardship and no injustice to be forced to live by labour" (157)—would be a small favor. Farren makes it as easy as possible for Moore by explicitly disavowing any connection to an organized protest against the power of the owners. While the rest of the "delegation" stand simply as "eleven behint" (153), Farren explicitly distances himself from the demagogic Moses Barraclough to make a personal plea for mercy: "'I've not much faith i' Moses Barraclough,' said he; 'and I would speak a word to ye myseln'" (156).

With no claim to right, but only to Robert's *noblesse oblige*, he represents a familiar old way between harsh landlord and stiff-necked workers. Yet Moore rejects such conciliation decisively. "Talk to me no more. . . . *I'll never give in*" (157, emphasis in original). Through his attachments and his detachments, through his sympathy to the foreign market and his hostility to the recalcitrant workers, Robert's effort is to foster the unified action of the Luddites as much as to repel it. Even in the book's early pages, when Robert still seems primed for some cavalier action, he will not cross country to arrest those who broke up his machinery. Instead, he waits till they come as a peace mission to his mill, and seizes them within its forecourt. "Repress your forwardness!" might be Moore's credo (383). Should it come to a fight at the mill, he knows that he will have won.

DISPELLING AND CONTAINING THE CROWD

By enduring the mob's attack, Moore allows Shirley and Caroline to witness him in the presence of the crowd's yell. The yell's inevitable effect is not so much to terrify as to polarize. The crowd gradually encroaches, first reported overheard marching and playing music out of the fog, then looming, barely audible out of the dissenting churches, then present but easily vanquished on the roads, and finally armed and unstoppable on the road toward the mill. Each step the crowd has made toward its full concretization (when "blossoms" are rumored, when "halt" is heard on the road at night, or when the collectivity yells) is also a step that forces the men of the rising middle class into a purely defensive posture. Master waits on men. The "mob" that counts off by arcane numbers both justifies and tutors Moore. By counting, by plotting, by drilling on the moors, it establishes a presence that is premonitory of yet more complex organization. It is ironic but by no means paradoxical, then, that by the book's end a mob tamed by imperious management stands revealed as a sort of useful interme- diate step on the way toward a more continuously present and obedient work force. A hostile crowd, as it turns out, is easily transformable into a standing reservoir of labor, which can be imagined counting off, not in headlong retreat, but on the way into the mill each morning.

Shirley upholds the power of private spaces and privatized men and women to overcome dangerous exposure to the public realm, but only through a complicated tangle of ways of conceiving that realm. *Shirley* employs a novelistic discourse that unabashedly aims to use the strengths of discursive rivals. The novel's own powers as an aesthetic document; the powers of the working-class crowd when it manages to make legible claims for redress (or even representation); the appeal of chosen solitude and "singularity" as a middle-class avenue to a higher kind of freedom: all of these competing elements come together to gen- erate the story of a mill owner who first holds off and then rehires a hostile Luddite mob. The contest that the novel stages between various accounts of what makes the public sphere—and the final solution that reconciles without eliminating either of the warring parties—suggests that the novel is designed to move through a public sphere filled with a variety of ways of imagining public action and public speech.

The novel stages a drama of incorporation that subsumes the former logic of the quasi-organized crowd to the overpowering logic of the fully organized factory. That subsumption presumably aims to allocate to the novel the power to overcome crowds, but to retain them as well, to gather their perilous strength into a text that is itself publicly circulatable—yet a text that remains, by generic definition, representative of a telling sort of privacy. The implication of such assimilation, however, is not that *Shirley* is secretly subversive of an otherwise monolithic ruling-class ideology. The point rather is that, in a public realm that contains both the claims of Chartism and the claims of Brontë, Brontë must strive openly, not secretly, to assimilate rival ways of figuring representation. To conclude that the novel finds in a rival discourse the strength to put forward its own claims about the shape of public life does not by any means imply that the overly articulated claims put forward by any one Chartist or Luddite crowd have a greater chance of being adopted. Rather, as in Caryle or De Quincey, the triumph of a public discourse that represents brute inarticulate crowds begins with the realization that publicly oriented, politically signifying crowds are available to be adapted to suit the literary work's requirements.

Indeed, any critic who went looking in *Shirley* for any sign that a "genuine" working-class voice was stored within the novel, a secret history waiting for the right word to unlock it, would have a long, hard search of it. Even under the most minute observation, *Shirley* reveals very little discussion of the "representation" of that working class in more detail than the notion of a patient (or hostile) labor reservoir would encourage.[28] Out of Moses Barraclough's boast of being a "feeling man" and the eerie unity of the mysteriously drilling men of the moors, a composite character is formed, with no head but many bodies. Any claim a crowd could lodge either to political representation or to redress of industrial grievances must seem out of the question when the character represented is barely human at all. No wonder Brontë feels the need to specify that it is a "human body" that lies in the mill yard when the shooting stops (338). The depiction of the crowd is in a sense all contained in that one West Riding yell, in which the possibility for rational action—for anyone—goes out the window. The working class at times looks like little more than what is left over when the mob subsides.

Indeed, the hypostatization of workingmen as "the Luddite crowd" forecloses the possibility of allowing working-class men to enter the novel's reach as fully individuated characters. Shirley pities the assailants in terms that leave them mere components of their "manifold" action against the few men in the mill: "I will not say there is courage:

hundreds against tens are no proof of that quality" (335). That she credits them with "suffering and desperation enough" is scarcely a concession to evoke either understanding or even forgiveness: their attack seems merely animal, a simple reflex action against a perceived hurt (335).[29]

The logic is straightforward: no privacy, no personhood. Lacking the self-contained reflection on one's own autonomy that Brontë prizes above all, Robert's steward Joe Scott, when he bests Robert in debate, knows no better boast than the egalitarian: "there's thousands i' Yorkshire that's as good as me, and a two-three that's better" (88). But such a democratizing vaunt falls flat here: its implication is that the best of the working class aspire to no more than homogeneity. That (distinctly ominous) conclusion reduces any individual workingman to no more than fodder for "feeling man" Barraclough or for the commercial aspirations of Moore. In defeat, the mob is dreadfully reduced to what Moore's multiple voices and guns have made it: "something terrible, a still-renewing tumult" (336).

In striving to incorporate a rival discourse, which offers organized working classes as overt enemies to the stability of a middle-class domestic space, *Shirley* moves from a world in which the classes do not meet—and in which the presence of drilling men on the moors has a half-religious, half-magical quality, a world where hymns overheard on the road at night are the only sign of the working classes—to a world in which "the houseless" are constantly making tracks for Hollow's mill, where Robert Gérard Moore has domesticated Yorkshire. Indeed, by the novel's end the new crowd has come to seem rather called into being by the aggressive industrial action at Hollow's Mill, and by the accelerated entrance of the West Riding into a market of world trade that the crowd's refurbishment signifies.[30]

A space for the working-class crowd does therefore emerge at the novel's end: "the houseless, the starving, the unemployed shall come to Hollow's mill from far and near" (598). But the name "hollow" is all too apt. Within that space, the men who come will find their natures defined by the newly enforced coalition between man and wife, manufacturer and gentry, church and industry: "Joe Scott shall give them work, and Louis Moore, Esq. shall let them a tenement, and Mrs. Gill shall mete them a portion till the first pay-day" (598). Here indeed is the distinctive nondomestic privacy foreshadowed in Moore's earlier commitment to the distinctly commercial intimacy of men tucked behind the walls of the mill. "Nondomestic," that is, because it proposes workplaces and educational structures where the classes will mingle; but "privacy" because the protagonists will retain enough control over physical spaces to regulate when contact may occur, and what it will signify. Lest the prospect still not seem appealing to those women trapped inside the mill-yards and houses, there is a sweetener for Caroline that reverses the violence of the first Sunday-school picnic: "Such a Sunday-school as you will have, Cary! such collections as you will get!" (599). The success of those Sunday collections will depend upon the containment of the destructive orderliness that the Luddites had earlier offered. It is the dispersed crowd that must be invoked in order both to justify and to explain the well-ordered, collected triumph that concludes the novel.

CROWDS AS CATALYSTS TO PRIVATE CHANGE

As a child, Jane Eyre is fond of strangers. It is physicians and passersby who offer her sympathy when the Reeds spurn her. Not because strangers are friendly, however: "If even this stranger had smiled and been good-humored to me when I addressed him . . . I should have gone my way . . . but the frown, the roughness of the traveler set me at my ease" (117). Roughness is the only way to overcome the natural solitude that Mr. Rochester sees limned on Jane's pensive brow; her "inward treasure" will give way only to his "penetrating gaze." The "singular persons" in *Jane Eyre* find their lonely ways disrupted by forceful and antagonistic love: Rochester and Jane are, each to the other, abrasive surfaces in a world filled with comparatively smoother smiles and more unctuous manners. Any sort of real companionship will work to suit people uniquely to each other, and thus ultimately eliminate even the solace in strangers that Jane had initially found so helpful. By the time she loves Rochester alone, strangers have come to mean little more to her than do dumb animals. She has no expectation of relief when alone and hungry near Whitcross: "None that saw me would have a kind thought or kind wish for me" (325) because none was related to her by the close bonds that characterize her relationship with Rochester— beloved or hated. When she does find a suitable place to ask for and receive charity, the importuning of strangers is ultimately justified (or overjustified) by the Dickensian "discovery" that they are her cousins, albeit unknown ones.

The true dimensions of one's soul can only become known in adulthood, when one takes up, antagonistically, with a half-beloved, half-opposed figure. That figure, for Jane, takes two guises, a good private and an evil public one: Rochester the hermit and St. John Rivers the saint. Rochester masters her—from the inside out and with little moral rationale—and she accepts it, but when St. John tries the same trick—from the outside in, with might, right, and God on his side—he fails: "he acquired a certain influence over me that took away my liberty of mind" (400). In contending with Rochester, Jane discovers her own freedom in confinement to a single love: "I have spoken my mind and can go anywhere now." If her brow tells Rochester that "I need not sell my soul to buy bliss. I have an inward treasure" (203), it finally also assures him that such freedom will persist, will indeed be strengthened in marriage to him.

She finds the strength to refuse Rivers and his public calling because she has learned to urge her identity into its finest shape by orienting it to one man alone. Not to God, whom St. John Rivers invokes in an ill-fated bid for her soul and her services, but to Rochester: "every good, true vigorous feeling I have gathers impulsively round him" (177). Jane and Rochester's alliance, then, not the call to public service implied in Rivers's failed courtship, is what ensures the book's afterlife as a touchstone of fierce romantic individualism. Jane and Rochester's final retreat to a shared "audible thinking" (455) in a backcountry house explicitly underscores Brontë's interest in a hermetically sealed, definitively private menage of two well-suited singularities.

It makes perfect sense for St. John to be conventionally handsome, far too handsome for Jane. He represents the vanities of an outer world (even a religious one) that does not have at its center the delighted meeting of two "singular" and privately social hearts. Rivers remains in the public world—albeit an enervating foreign corner of it—because his duty draws him to a task more suited to the outside man than to the inner consciousness which Jane needs most. Rivers is not quite an active male version of *Bleak House*'s Mrs. Jellyby—whose "telescopic philanthropy" makes her famously indifferent to what passes nearby—but he comes close. His flaw is to remain overly fixated on duties beyond the narrow range defined by personal emotional attachment. Rivers wants Jane to perform the outward, public duties that freeze her soul and dry up her liberty. She learns to beware of his impersonal anger, which is so like "the breaking up of the frozen sea" (377), because it has as its object to flood the whole world with Christianity, rather than to win one landlocked heart.

Brontë, however, is not finished with the rejected Rivers. What if

Rochester were to change so that the notion of a professional life, of an interface with the public, were not wholly repulsive? If he were not Tory but Whig, not gentry but rising middle class, and not landowner but manufacturer? That is, what if the heroine stumbled on neither Rivers nor Rochester but on Robert Moore, mill-operator and reluctant member of a worldwide trade? *Shirley*, that is, ought to be read as an attempt to ground the solitary pleasures of *Jane Eyre* in a social realm that necessitates habitual and even violent interaction with the busy toiling classes. It may even be read as an open-eyed reckoning of the cost and consequences of choosing privacy over the public world—just the reckoning that *Jane Eyre* had been able to avoid by the conclusive blindness of Rochester.

Readers clearly respond to the claim of Jane's solitude: she addresses the reader so often because she has no other confidante. By contrast, readers of *Shirley* often tend to reject what they conceive of as the novel's plurality, its unwillingness to settle down with a single plot (see Keen). Ready for another Jane Eyre, whose desires are pointed toward the ultimate satisfaction of her loneliness in union, readers discover instead in Caroline a would-be member of the public realm: a heroine who lacerates herself for her own mooning idleness, who wishes that the world were structured so that she could enter into it via any conduit other than an empty spinsterhood or an unrewarding partnership with a dominant man.[31] Like the professionless Robert Ferrars in Austen's *Sense and Sensibility*, whose great flaw and regret is that he has nowhere to go when he leaves his friends, Caroline and Shirley notably lack a public calling. They find instead an observational role in the assault on the mill, and a complementary vocation behind their husbands in its later administration.

It may be Caroline's longing for a tactile engagement with her surroundings, running at right angles to the marriage plot, that ultimately disenchants readers expecting another version of an isolated soul calling out to same. Caroline spends her empty hours thinking of the work she is not doing, and of the work that Robert has done, far from her. "Fifty times a day" Caroline wants her own introspection to stop, and her attention to "a single tyrant master torture" to be replaced by the "varieties of pain" that life in the world can afford (235). That tyrant master torture is none other than her love for Robert Moore, which ought to satisfy Caroline, and the reader, as a complete replacement for whatever the mundanities of labor and professional affiliation can offer. The two choices Caroline conceives—between "a vacant weary, lonely, hopeless life" and "successful labor"—omit what Rochester would deliver, a tradeless life devoted fully to one person in front of whom she would never have to "repress [her] forwardness" (235, 383). Where is Rochester when you don't even know you need him?

The solitude that Caroline strives to overcome is rich terrain for novelistic speculation, but it is also a troubled sort of blankness that leaves Caroline desperate for just the order that Robert's new mill, and new vocation, will bring. The freedom of motion promised to Caroline unattached comes at a price, including a long bout of gruelingly rendered depression. For each visitation that a single woman gets from "the voice we hear in solitude" she gets as well a depressing vision of her "vacant, weary, lonely, hopeless life" (234–35). While the moorlands unencumbered by factories present the possibility of "lying stirless on the turf, at the foot of some tree or shady umbrage" (237), they also force "from your lips, as you sit alone, sudden, insane-sounding interjections" (236).

For if the crowd is poised between a past disorder, and a present turn into rigid, obedient conformity, Caroline and Shirley are correspondingly on the move between openness—figured as the past, the open moors, and celibacy—and structure, figured as a treeless and well-traveled "hollow," the present mill, and husbands (the Moore brothers). Past openness had promised continued isolation, the present order various inducements for a movement toward intimacy with at least one man (a husband), one woman (a rediscovered mother), and one space (the mill). Undisciplined liberty has passed away and been replaced by a posited liberty within structure: "Her captor alone could cheer her: his society only could make amends for the lost privilege of liberty" (592).

Shirley offers, then, a fairly uncomfortable compromise when it comes to merge its vigorous industrial plot with its scattered romantic intentions. Marrying Robert Moore is marrying into a job. To marry him is not so much to deny the crowd of workers that looms at the book's core as it is to take one's part in administering that crowd. Shirley and Caroline will live out their lives both in their homes and at a distance, down at the mill and among the working-class cottages (which Louis will administer) that will always be a kind of omnipresent absence in their lives, offering proximity without real attachment. By the same token, Caroline learns to witness, if not to share, Robert's impressive mastery of a world beyond. It was an ability to turn formidable sternness on each other that drew Jane and Rochester together—but Caroline finds her mate in her eventual approval of Robert's power over the working-class crowd. Those whom the mob has brought together, no mill, no rejuvenated working class, no social world beyond the marriage can draw asunder. This is the discovery that Gaskell repeats in *North and South*, in which the memorable embrace between Margaret and Mr. Thornton is originally a form of defense against the crowd—an embrace that then engenders the love which it had seemed to reveal.

In *Shirley*, it is not self-consuming love that triumphs, but a marriage whose logic is formed both out of and in contradistinction to the world of work. What Jane Eyre saw exemplified in the devoted actions of St. John Rivers and rebelled against, Caroline rediscovers. Not finding such qualities detestable, she discovers in her marriage a successful blend of blissful attachment to a public man, and sanctioned antagonism toward those whose plans for their own destinies do not suit with the public-controlling ambitions of her husband. One might say that *Shirley* aims to restore to the novel-reader a possibility that *Jane Eyre* seemed to eliminate: a public life doing the work of man (or God) while preserving a fully realized individualism. It was only in 1840, nine years before *Shirley* appeared, that a translation of de Tocqueville's *Democracy in America* (1835) introduced the word "individualism" into the English language, but his definition resonates well with the division implicit in *Shirley*:

> Individualism is a mature and calm feeling, which disposes each member of the community to sever himself from the mass of his fellow creatures, and to draw apart with his family and friends. (506)[32]

Interstitial familial space is all, by this account. The space left between one individual and another, within the family sphere, is just enough to allow the literary imagination to begin to expand. One can find the stubborn individuality Brontë prizes so much, as de Tocqueville did, in the men with family and a home. In *Shirley*, then, the advent of an industrialized Yorkshire does anything but destroy the possibility for interesting individuation of the upper-class characters. The transition from the openness of the moors to a world of humming mills, tightly sealed and interlocked marriages, and rediscovered kinship claims does not destroy the possibility of characters' preserving the "difference" that Caroline so values as a way of characterizing all the world in relation to herself.[33]

But the development of that well-guarded and productive "difference" depends on nothing so much as the initiative of the Luddite crowd. In *Harrington*, strongly built houses serve as insulation against the irrationality present both outdoors among the Gordon rioters and within the unhinged psyche of any potentially irrational individual, so that a well-guarded social realm at first appears to be sufficient protection against the "strong imagination" of the London mob. *Shirley* too seems to promote a form of overt hostility toward the crowd. Is there not, after all, a straightforward distrust of any crowd able to assert (via its interlocutor Moses Barraclough) that it is a "feeling" organization, and (via William Farren) that "so mich louder mun we shout out then" to "t' Parliament-men" (157)? The threat lies in shouts that might drown out Brontë's own voice. It is just such shouting—especially coming from those who might strive for changes that were something other than local, and wage-driven—that Chartism had seemed to threaten. Small wonder that Brontë would strive to make her novel memorable by evoking, in the sort of detail that no other description of a riot could capture, the terror involved in hearing a West Riding yell.

Harrington, however, eventually recuperates a diluted form of the crowd's madness, which takes the form of erotic desires that can erode old-fashioned social barriers. So too, *Shirley* finds ways to turn the inside out, to make the crowd's yell not only an assault upon the barriers of the past, but a corrective to them. Brontë stages the defeat and dispersal of the crowd only as an immediate predecessor to its being fitted into various institutions—a mill, a Sunday-school, and the process of constructing houses for the employment and housing of members of the crowd—administered by those four minds the novel has striven most perfectly to represent. Just as Louis wins Shirley by wooing her in the classroom where he once taught her, so too by the novel's end Robert will have tamed not Caroline but the crowds, filing obediently back into the mill and into the houses and Sunday school he has built or is building for them. What the crowd has threatened to tear down, the novel attempts to expand.

The distinction between overcoming and assimilating the crowd is a vital one. Just as the Luddite crowd had drilled on the moors (remember the haze that opened the novel) and learned to enumerate itself, so too Moore will catalogue, order, and aggregate the mass of workingmen. If workingmen threaten to represent themselves through public disturbance, *Shirley* asserts its own right to represent them, and to do so through the tight, contained spaces that comprise the novel itself.[34] Such spaces are figured at the book's end by the expanded mill, Caroline and Robert's new home, and the new homes of the mill work- ers—all the places that Shirley and Caroline will now need to leave only by way of their more active imaginations. At the end of a speech cataloguing his (extremely boring) building plans for the Hollow's Mill expansion, Moore exclaims, "Extravagant day-dreams!" (598). This odd exclamation reveals something about the fertile imaginations of captains of industry—a new building is always someone's fantasy first—but something more about novel-writing itself. As the novel's opening paragraph puts it, dry realities can make for extravagant imag- inations. To extend the point further: the duller your locale, the more extravagant the daydreams that being placed there will engender. As the crowd presses in, the novel reaches out. The strongest possible re- sponse to the potential public rambunctiousness threatened by a crowd, then, is the private rambunctiousness that goes on in Shirley's, or in Caroline's, or in the reader's imaginative alliance with men building walls.

Yet the novel in general—and this novel in particular—can never be as orderly as the middle-class-protected spaces it so laboriously praises. Though the crowd's chaos disfigured *Harrington*, and offered a new way to imagine imagination, it did not offer the sort of nascent, po- tentially rivalrous, order that the Luddite (or Chartist) crowd threatens to contribute to *Shirley*. In fact, *Shirley* advances a complicated account of the ways in which the novel may come both to borrow from and to resemble the crowd. Both are sites of order and disorder at once, places for emotional release, but also for strict enumeration and re- sponsible self-definition. In reading a novel that teaches one to be self- scrutinizing, a member of the upper classes comes to count him- or herself as part of a certain sort of public, just as a member of the working class "counts off" in joining one of the Luddite bands.

To read *Shirley*'s praise of privatization as a seamless triumph, how- ever, would be to miss the text's persistent reckoning with rival claims for public-sphere action, its intense attention to the Luddite crowd whose defeat only ensures that the big new mill will be filled with a crowd that counts in a different way. It is a solution, perhaps, but also an uneasy admission that the tension between crowd and master has not been laid to rest by building a new mill. *Shirley* articulates the idea of a crowd that can attain real speech only through the act of novelistic representation. In so doing, *Shirley* deliberately opposes itself to a crowd that provides the sort of emotional attachment that the novel also labors to deliver. The novel's act of containment, within the context of a variegated public sphere, can be effected not by negating but by borrowing, redefining, and otherwise interacting with the implicit and explicit claims of alternative public discourses such as that offered by the Chartist crowd. Thus the triumph of *Shirley* is not to have overthrown the claims of the crowd, but to have assimilated them in a way that seems to leave no place for an alternative discursive form to be staged outside the pages of the novel. That *Shirley*'s crowd both rages and counts, that it has a body and a semantic structure as well, is by the novel's account a seeming threat to the novel's own discursive logic, but a threat that turns into an occasion to broaden the novel's claims. In fighting the somatic intimacy and enumerative logic of the crowd, the novel supplies a long-distance intimacy and an orderly apparatus of attachment all its own.

CONCLUSION: INCORPORATING THE CROWD

Shirley offers a more direct representation than the nineteenth-century novel usually allows of the production of mental liberty through marital confinement. In that openness it sheds interesting light on Hannah Arendt's accusatory claim, in *The Human Condition*, that the novel in its nineteenth-century European incarnation both represents and upholds a "social" rather than a political account of the emergence of private identities into the public realm.[35] Arendt accuses the entire genre of being aligned with an account of human identity that strives to make the "obscurity of the heart" serve as a model for public action. To Arendt, the novel can serve as a vehicle whereby people extend "pity" to others by way of a real but "illegitimate" emotional reaction, illegitimate in the sense that a private feeling ought not to structure the nature of relationships in the public realm. By contrast, some political organizations (Arendt invokes the Chartists explicitly though not by name [1958, 216]) can be interpreted as striving to reverse the coercive emotionality of the novel, to establish "solidarity" and reason rather than the compassion novels advocate.[36]

Arendt's work—despite her problematic claims about the innate difference between the "social" and "poltical" realms, which Pitkin rightly criticizes—reminds us that the inherently interactive and contestatory status of various forms of discourse puts all aesthetic claims into political play, all political ones into aesthetics. Therefore, there may be *anti*political claims made within a novel (as it denies its relation, that is, to other documents that circulate in public), but there can be no *un*political ones. That axiom makes it easier to see that *Shirley* advances important and explicit claims about the political power of the novel itself.

Victorian novels were often written to valorize the tight circle of intimacy and shared affect that the loving couple produces. But to show this intimacy as the product of a direct encounter with a hostile crowd, or with a working world that provides vocation and purpose to the sheltered privacy of love, would seem to give a novel's game away. For individual love to differentiate itself from the proximate world of work and workers, of crowded streets and their crowds, there must be a studied indifference and a suitable silence about the conditions of negation on which intimate love depends. Whether they make it explicit or not, Victorian novels generally rely upon the production of self-scrutinizing privacy in a world overfull of unwashed masses, of intrusive industrial crowds. Consider the sheltered forecourt in *A Tale of Two Cities*, or the cathedral close in Trollope's Barchester series: silence about what goes on beyond these sites is critical for the chosen story to unfold. Yet what Victorian novel tells in rich detail the story of how such external presences help shape the growth of interior consciousness? It is just such obliviousness that *Shirley* foregoes, it is just such a trade-off that *Shirley* explicitly diagrams.

In *Shirley* there is a palpable loss of the older order, with its rigid hierarchical distinctions that made contact between the classes subject to a series of physical obstacles built mainly around distance. The old world, the dream of the century's dawn, contained not crowds but fairies and phantasmal spaces. By the end of the novel, though the violent mob has been dispersed, the general presence of crowds is inescapable. By the time the last "fairish that ever was seen on this country side" vanishes, Robert Moore's "extravagant daydreams" will be all too prosaically realized in workers' cottages, Sunday schools, and "substantial stone and brick and ashes." Hobbes writes that locks on a house manifest the vivid presence of crime, even if their intended effect be to discourage it. Just so, the cindered road, the expanded mill, and the space of the novel itself are the living residuum of the dispersed Luddite threat. When exterior space between ruling class and crowd evaporates, a potentially explosive singularity comes to abide inside the deep subjects of the novel. Thus, in the imaginary future *Shirley* projects, the reader is free (indeed encouraged) to imagine that the crowd's powers will be fully incorporated into Caroline and Shirley's happy marriages, observant women allied to citadelled men, sanctioned to observe forever.

But in *Shirley* the crowd still hovers for a moment, both its mutability and its nascent order palpable. The assault on the mill is the single salient moment in which *Shirley*'s notional ideology of containment triumphs. Yet it is also the moment when that ideology becomes most visible. The move inward to a seemingly unnatural life of the mill turns out to be the ticket to a life of the mind. *Shirley* effectively adapts what in *Jane Eyre* had seemed to be a lesson only about the possibility of isolating oneself with a single soul-mate. A public life with its violent crowds or organized labor becomes a test of one's power to exclude, to differentiate, to allow individuals in while denying masses access. This world's rapid fluctuation between emotional license and rigid separation, between enumeration and personal nomination, was both foreshadowed and necessitated by the stirrings of a proto-Chartist crowd. Yet this world still retains the best features of geographical and mental isolation. *Shirley* celebrates both the stimulation and the simulation of the physical world; a triumph over the hostile crowd turns out to be a triumph of the crowd as well.

The time and energy *Shirley* spends in establishing the advantages of sanctioned difference provide a valuable clue to the nature of the hostility that Brontë intends between the promiscuous sociality of the "feeling" crowd and the much-treasured male and female inwardness. That relentless work of differentiation might even lead one to the mistaken conclusion that, rather than being importantly exemplary of Victorian notions of privacy and the discursive contests that underlie Victorian notions of the public, *Shirley* is something of a freak. Its penchant for valorizing separation, that is, may seem beyond the pale of even the Victorian novel's vaunted penchant for solitude. One might conclude that *Shirley*'s creation of a world in which differences are carefully demarcated—and only rarely overcome—distinguishes it from the "surprising effects of sympathy" conveyed in the novels of such Victorian peers and near-peers as Dickens, Trollope, or Collins—not to mention Brontë's sisters Emily and Anne.[37]

If the era was characterized by an increased valuation of privacy, after all, most mid-Victorian novelists still establish within their pages a wide variety of conditions under which a taste for privacy can be safely and charitably breached.[38] Charles Dickens's *Bleak House* (1853), for example, preaches an ethics of intense involvement in a wide range of characters' lives. When Dickens condemns onlookers' indifference to the fate of Miss Flite, the telling phrase "no one knows for certain, because no one cares" (51) creates an obligation to know and to care about London lives—by reading Dickens's eight-hundred-page book. One might even point out that earlier novelists such as Austen or Hannah More, whose works began to set the tone for Victorian forms of sanctioned intrusion, found a variety of avenues to overcome the ideological predisposition to veer away from true breaches of others' privacy.[39]

But to credit—or to fault—*Shirley* with such an uncharacteristic excess of hermetic zeal is to miss the novel's accomplishment entirely. "Magic becomes art when it no longer has any secrets," writes Ben Okri, in a maxim that describes well the operative principle of a great deal of Victorian fiction. Dickens predicts plot twists, Eliot and Trollope show the writerly hand at work with anguish or ennui: morals are pointed out, devices freely admitted. But more secrets by far get spilled in *Shirley*, secrets that make uncomfortably explicit the social, economic, and political location of its characters. True, characters are imagined as unmarked sites of potential attachment. But their "nobodyness" (that is, their fictive status coupled with their sympathizable interiority, to borrow the model of fictional identification developed so brilliantly in Gallagher's *Nobody's Story*) does not, as in *Jane Eyre,* carry with it a glimpse of "inward freedom" divorced from the material conditions that produced that felt freedom. Rather, these "nobodies" are given body via an overt account of the precise material conditions that allow any such middle-class body to come into being. It is a partial account, to be sure. But such partiality and overstated particularity is concomitant with the novel's generic predisposition to embed ideological dilemmas in characters—no ideas but in persons.

Shirley's configuration of private romance and public ruthlessness was uncomfortable for contemporaries to endure, therefore, not on account of its deviation from the novelistic type, but on account of its precision in proposing what many believed and none said. *Shirley* accounts for the manufacture of desirable private space by blaming the loss of past liberty (and the loss of the last "fairish") on a world of shifting public crowds. But the crowd's fault is the crowd's contribution as well. *Shirley* offers its readers a chance to see public crowds as dangerous assailants on private love, yet simultaneously reminds its readers that private love is oddly, indirectly dependent on the existence of those same crowds. That may be one reason that the novel remains, after all these years, more analyzed than read, better known than loved. Unlike most of its canonized contemporaries, *Shirley* claims to leave the material—and marital, and martial—conditions that produced the novel's inward turn alarmingly on view. Walter Benjamin claims that each generation dreams its successor. Perhaps. *Shirley*, however, dreams of no generation but its own.

Notes

INTRODUCTION

1. It was only in the late eighteenth century that Western European cities surpassed those of the ancient world in population. In 1750 the two largest cities in the world were London with 675,000 inhabitants and Paris with 571,000; by 1800 Paris had grown only to 581,000, and London numbered 1,100,000 (Wrigley and Scofield). By 1800, London was self-sufficient (William Cobbett's perorations about "the wen" notwithstanding, London was unlike ancient Rome, which may also have passed a million in population but was always a drain on its empire) and structurally capable of further rapid expansion.

2. If by 1840 such dandies were liable to keep to their clubs when possible, in the century before they had discovered both streets and parks as sites for promenade and purchase: "Since the Westminster Paving Act of 1751 and with the subsequent multiplication of local improvement authorities, it had been possible to walk through the West End for pleasure; until the great sanitary operations of the nineteenth century, the ordinary Paris street was something to be avoided" (Olsen, 219). The nature of street life in large cities of the non-Western world lies outside the scope of this investigation. Outside my scope as well is a field of study that Sharon Marcus's *Apartment Stories* brilliantly articulates: quasidomestic urban spaces.

3. For a description of Chartism's aims and structure, see note 2 of chapter 5.

4. For early radicalism, see Prothero and McCalman; for Chartism, see D. Thompson and Tilly.

5. Nicholas Rogers and Charles Tilly have both recently located in the 1820s and 1830s the crucial break between "direct-action crowds" and new modes of public action. As Rogers puts it in *Crowds, Culture and Politics in Georgian*

Britain, the radicals' so-called "mass platform" (which aimed to make the working class visible in the national public arena by peaceful assembly) "stood in marked contrast to the kinds of crowd politics that had characterized politics since the Exclusion crisis. . . . It had a different associational structure from that of the eighteenth-century crowd" (279). Importantly for my argument, Rogers and Tilly stress that between the nascent organizations of the first two decades of the century and the fully developed mass movement of the 1830s and 1840s a gulf loomed. As I argue in part 2, it is vital both to register the early forms of orderly protest between 1800 and 1820, and to recognize the gap between such protests and the more highly developed forms of peaceful national action introduced by the Chartists, which I detail in chapter 5.

6. For discussions of architectural transformations of cities in response to crowds—e.g., Haussmannization, the building of enormous urban cathedrals and football stadiums in the last third of the nineteenth century— see Harvey and Olsen; for changes in policing see Miller and Hanway. For more general observations about the response to a "mass" public, see Tratner and Barrows, both of whom describe the development of generally shared French and English ideas about crowds from 1870 on.

7. Charles Tilly's enormously helpful work on changes in the form of public "disorder" over the period 1780 to 1830 from "local" to "cosmopolitan, modular and autonomous" is based almost exclusively on newspapers and journals.

8. I have also benefited greatly from the work of thinkers from other disciplines, notably that of the anthropologist Stanley Tambiah and, despite his classificatory rigidity, the early work of Robert Park. Robert Nye's work on Le Bon has been tremendously helpful. Literary-critical work on crowds includes that of Schor, Mills, Reinert, Fisher, Collins, and Esteve. Recent work of note on related topics includes that of Henkin on public texts in antebellum New York.

9. The works of Le Bon, Tarde, and Freud exemplify (and those of Barrows, McPhail, Nye, and Tratner usefully analyze) the relative narrowing of the definitional possibilities by the end of the century.

10. See my "Coriolanus and the Failure of Performatives" for a Shakespearean example.

11. Maslan's work on French theater crowds in the Revolutionary era offers a fascinating account of an angry public presence that, she argues, ought to be read not as representing but as embodying an ideological assertion. Though our terms are clearly rather different, there is an interesting overlap between her claim to parse the difficult and stubbornly unassimilable nature of the theater crowd's claims and my assertion that the implicit claims of a demonstrating crowd are recoverable in a wide range of seemingly illegible actions.

12. The structure I am proposing, that of various discursive logics continually struggling within a public sphere whose boundaries are defined by the nature of that struggle, contains unmistakable echoes of Weber's notion of separate "spheres." But the idea of competing discursive logics seems to me to allow a more accurate description of the actual interplay between the various

ways that an action or a written text can "signify." In certain circumstances, an "aesthetic" object can contain a political argument, just as a political speech can contain something analyzable by the logic of the aesthetic. Spheres are given domains—indeed in Weber they are often described as having been immanent in the structure of society even before their actual moments of origin. But discursive logics run into, and out of, each other.

13. Dror Wahrman, Gareth Stedman Jones, Elaine Hadley, and Joan Scott have also made valuable contributions to a debate that is not simply a "linguistic turn," but also a register of the various languages there are to turn to. By contrast, James Vernon and Patrick Joyce have in different ways reverted to the error of imagining there is a single explanatory paradigm somehow underlying all the period's assumptions and practices.

14. Linda Colley's work on the development of the idea of "Britishness" would be meaningless, that is, if the British had always regarded themselves as a group. Like the theoretical overview provided by Benedict Anderson's *Imagined Communities*, Colley's work aims to document how people came to define their lives by that rubric and no other. By the same token, Davidoff and Hall describe the conditions under which a class identity and an immense respect for the importance of barriers dividing private and public might hold sway. The success of both projects suggests a matrix within which radically incompatible accounts of the grounds for loyalty, behavior, and felt identity can coexist.

15. Alongside Davidoff and Hall (and such important revisionary accounts or criticisms as are made or referred to in Wahrman and Vickery), there is fascinating work, both old and new, on the changes in nineteenth-century labor patterns that forced workspaces and middle-class parlors into proximity, and indirectly engendered strong movements to separate such spaces. See for example Engels, Steven Marcus, and Roy Porter; as well as Dyos's classic *Victorian Suburb* and his *Victorian City* collection, and J. M. L. Thompson's collection, *The Rise of Suburbia*.

1. THE NECESSARY VEIL:
WORDSWORTH'S "RESIDENCE IN LONDON"

1. A summary of the events in "Residence in London" is provided slightly later in this chapter. I use the 1805 and not the 1850 edition to stress that this is a Romantic-era text. But that decision is reinforced by the fact that key passages in Book 7 are decidedly weakened by the 1850 revision. In the 1805 edition, for example, the "London child" is a vividly executed figure for what poetry itself can do to stave off the ravages of the city:

> He hath since
> Appeared to me ofttimes as if embalmed
> By Nature—through some special privilege
> Stopped at the growth he had—destined to live,
> To be, to have been, come, and go, a child
> And nothing more, no partner in the years
> That bear us forward to distress and guilt. (7, 399–405)

While overtly denoting the impossibility of stasis in this busy city, the 1805 lines all the while effect just such a dreamlike arrest of motion, sharpening the contrast between the flux of the city and the reliability of poetry. The 1850 revision is a mere generalized prayer that never creates tranquil lyric beauty.

2. Raymond Williams analyzes this as a progressive loss of connection with the crowd, the self, and thus social life:

> Wordsworth saw strangeness, a loss of connection, not at first in social but perceptual ways: a failure of identity in the crowd of others which worked back to a loss of identity in the self, and then, in these ways, a loss of society itself, its overcoming and replacement by a procession of images: the "dance of colors, lights and forms," "face after face" and there are not other laws. (150)

Astute as Williams is in isolating this passage, however, he oddly understates the sort of dissociation that is going on here. It is, quite explicitly, "past and present" as well as "All laws of acting, thinking, speaking man" that are lost to the narrator. The "perceptual" includes the social and a good deal more in its ambit.

3. From Walter Benjamin's opaque "each generation dreams its successor" to Raymond Williams's "emergent structures of feeling" (which David Simpson has criticized tellingly), models that depend upon remarkable predictive powers for literature—or make unverifiably strong claims for literature's power to shape its contemporary and future readership—generally turn away from solid synchronic analysis. I proceed on the assumption that texts generally reveal more when parsed against their own variegated present than when decoded for attenuated imaginings of their future.

4. See McCalman, Tilly, and Thompson's famous article, "Moral Economy," for various qualifications of that claim: among the lower orders there was certainly an established tradition of mass display or grievances. However, Tilly's work underscores how little developed a public vocabulary of orderly disorder there was before the 1820s, and McCalman shows how distant most members of the upper and middle classes would have been from organized crowd activities.

5. The North American context is interestingly complicated by the American Revolution (see especially Maier and Ryan), and the French Revolution shifted representational practices (see Ozouf, Rude, Hunt) but brought fewer changes in literary representation of crowds than might have been expected.

6. *Italian Journey*, 172–73. The date is March 17, 1787. One should note, though, that five days later Goethe is already complaining of how uninvolved he is in the life of Naples. "It is quite pleasant to be here, but I wish it was possible to establish myself just a little. No praise can be too great for the city's location and its mild climate, but a foreigner does not have much more than this to fall back on" (177).

7. This attribute of a foreign crowd is an oft-repeated trope of European travel narratives of the nineteenth century. One particularly brilliant example is Richard Burton's description of a Mecca pilgrimage, in which the enormous numbers of Muslims converging on Mecca, many as alien to each other as they were to Burton, kept him safe in a way that continual contact with residents of any single Muslim village never would. In addition, the clashes between

rival Sunnis and Shias, besides amusing Burton, kept him safe from charges of blasphemy: alien members of one's own religion are far more likely to appear, en masse, irreligious, than a lone traveler faithfully aping local customs.

8. Georg Simmel's "Metropolis and Mental Life" (1901) is particularly acute on this topic: the "protective antipathy" that he rather grandiosely bestows on all city dwellers is accompanied, he astutely writes, by the inclination to particularize oneself that depends on the knowledge of others' insulation. City dwellers are both allowed and encouraged to make themselves look (and hence feel) different from their neighbors.

9. November 10, 1787. The word "*solid*" rings unmistakably as a foreign one, in a language that has far fewer such obvious loan words than English (I am grateful to Frances Dickey for the observation). Goethe foregoes etymologically German alternatives such as "dicht," "fest," or even "massiv," presumably in order to underscore the foreignness of the feeling.

10. Nor is Goethe describing a nostalgic trip back into the hinterland of Europe. Rather, Naples serves as the best possible precursor to an account of the population explosion of Northern European cities. It had been a great city through the Middle Ages, possibly passing half a million in population, which limped into the nineteenth century diminished but still populous. Naples was still impressively large even in the 1780s, larger than any European cities except Paris and London, larger by far than any German city. In 1750 Naples had about 305,000 inhabitants (versus 675,000 in London and 571,00 in Paris); a 1796 census of Naples revealed 427,000 inhabitants (London 1,100,000, Paris 581,000). The largest German-speaking city, Vienna, had a population of only 175,000 in 1750, and 247,000 in 1800 (Mitchell, 72–75).

11. However, being foreign is not an inherent advantage. The vivid records of city life left in later generations not only by Wordsworth but by contemporaries such as Lamb, Hazlitt, and De Quincey serve as a salutary caution against Donald Olsen's assertion that "the actual resident, his perceptions dulled by familiarity, will have less to tell us than the foreign critic or visiting tourist" (6). Olsen's book, which argues that "societies better reveal themselves at play than at work" (5), assumes that a study of "play" must be separated from any sort of analysis of the worlds of work or of the sensations that an ordinary resident of London, Paris, or Vienna might experience in the city's public realm. His plausible idea of studying the city as aesthetic object is impeded by his idea that the aesthetic nature of a city resides in its "pleasing distractions" (6). This hypothesis eventually leads him to the claim that "a selective blindness is a necessary attribute of the happy tourist" (169), which, while probably quite true about conditions for touristic pleasure, undermines the tourist's credibility as ideal observer.

12. One notable exception may be Edgar Allan Poe, whose London story "The Man of the Crowd" attempts to look at London crowds from inside-out. Even Poe, however, has a problem staging a linguistic encounter: his London is near silent, the only words in quotation marks are in German and are about illegibility ("*es lässt sich nicht lesen*"; that is, "it can't be read"). By the early twentieth century, there were of course comparable urban congeries elsewhere, inspiring a broad range of European writing. Rilke's *Notebook of Malte*

Laurids Brigge is a German novel of Paris, but Andrei Biely could set his *Petersburg* in his home city, as could Robert Musil his *Man Without Qualities* in Vienna, Svevo his *Confessions of Zeno* in Trieste, and Joyce his *Ulysses* in Dublin.

13. Kleist, letter of July 18, 1801, 111.

14. Richard Holmes, writing on the fate of the circle of English writers and revolutionaries who lived at White's Hotel, discusses the significance of the English freedom to leave during the early days of the Revolution. As he points out, virtually all departed or—as in the case of Mary Wollstonecraft—slipped away from the Revolution in other ways (chapter 3).

15. Alan Liu's brilliant *Wordsworth: The Sense of History* argues that from 1789 onward there was a new sort of time introduced into the rhythm of crowd action, which he calls "succession": massacres celebrated leading on to more massacres committed (160–61). This development he counterposes to earlier crowd events which, in England at least, had, in Mark Harrison's words, "occurred in an everyday temporality paced by a practical schedule of holidays, feast days, summer months, and specially turbulent times of day." One need not assume, however, that revolutionary feasts included, in Wordsworth's own eyes, a radical temporality that earlier sorts of crowd upheavals did not. Wordsworth himself conveys here no sense of time violated: the holiday seems part and parcel of a general national and natural rejoicing.

16. Abraham Cowley's "The Wish" (1647), for example, deploys the same metaphor as a complaint:

> And they (methinks) deserve my pity
> Who for it can endure the stings,
> The crowd, and buzz and murmurings,
> Of this great hive, the city.

17. In the 1850 edition it is some seventy lines after this incident that the glories of the convent at Chartreuse are introduced, as a way of expressing disapproval with the Revolution's excesses. Wordsworth wishes to express intense disapproval of revolutionary destruction of sites of "*solitude*" (the word appears twice in three lines, both times italicized [1850, 6, 419 and 421]), which is to say sites antithetical to or exempted from the general rejoicing of crowds.

18. Wordsworth's relationship to the French revolution is a topic explored in recent articles by Geraldine Friedman, Mary Jacobus, Gayatri Spivak, David Punter, John Hodgson, David Bromwich, and Eugene L. Stelzig, as well as by Liu. James Chandler's *Wordsworth's Second Nature* is an exceptionally interesting treatment of these issues.

19. Yoon Sun Lee's recent "Stoicism in Smith and Burke" points out that Burke's famous patriotism takes the form of a felt affiliation with others who share a patrimony "handed down to us": namely, the British constitution. Affective sympathy flows through the same national channels that Wordsworth here envisions.

20. Walter Benjamin's dismissive account of E. T. A. Hoffman's "The

Cousin's Corner Window" seems to me to go slightly astray when he claims that Hoffman fails by writing about a boring Berlin crowd rather than an interesting Paris or London one: "But it is obvious that the conditions under which it was made in Berlin prevented it from being a complete success. If Hoffman had ever set foot in Paris or London" things would, Benjamin alleges, have been different, better (212). But in order successfully to depict a city crowd, throughout the nineteenth century with almost no exceptions, one must write about crowds of one's own nationality. The partial affiliation implied by a shared nationality and a shared language (not always and necessarily over-lapping, but overlapping in these cases) heightens the sort of claim that can be laid against a crowd, making the disturbance the crowd engenders a social, and an ideological, as well as a merely psychological one.

21. My emphasis here on the overt use of national classification in all three writers is not intended to minimize the importance that class differentiation must have played in the decision to use national identity as an organizing basis for claims of similarity and difference. In fact, the explicit invocation of na-tional categories can sometimes operate as a deliberate distraction from other sorts of "barriers dividing" one from another. On the growth of English na-tional identity in this era, see the important work collected in Hobsbawm and Ranger's *The Invention of Tradition* and Benedict Anderson's *Imagined Com-munities,* as well as Linda Colley's magisterial *Britons.* Recent works that ex-plore this issue include those of Stedman Jones, Wahrman, Vernon, and Joyce.

22. Indeed, the sonnets written just after returning in 1802, the "Poems dedicated to National Independence and Liberty," evidence strongly Words-worth's claim to belong in England. If Wordsworth recalls "a homeless sound of joy was in the sky" on Bastille Day of 1790 ("Composed near Calais on the road leading to Ardres, August 7, 1802"), only twenty-three days later (August 30, 1802) Wordsworth paeans England with "Here, on our native soil, we breathe once more" and "Inland within a hollow vale, I stood." Neither is about London, but both partake of the sense of security involved in crossing the sea from France. Simpson's brief account of Wordsworth's localism is help-ful on this point (139–41).

23. John Farrell's insightful criticism prompted this response.

24. Consider, for example, the panic of Anna Maria Falconbridge, in her 1794 *Narrative of Two Voyages to the River Sierra Leone During the Years 1791–1793,* when she sees the chieftain she meets in Sierra Leone conferring with his men. The mere fact of conversation in an utterly alien form of speech convinces her that her life is in danger.

25. Benjamin's work on Baudelaire's representation of Parisian crowds seems to me brilliantly suggestive. But he overlooks a much earlier Anglophone tradition of writing on crowds that, by way of De Quincey, unmistakably left its mark on Baudelaire and beyond.

26. Neil Hertz argues convincingly that the blind beggar exemplifies a gap between signifier and signified. In any case, Wordsworth's attempt to read the beggar and his sign marks the difference between merely gathering information from the world, and truly hearing communication that has been addressed to

one. While the former requires only a sign legible to the reader, the latter requires that the bearer of the sign also know its significance, which could not be true of a blind man with a written sign.

27. Geoffrey Hartman observes that when Wordsworth catches sight of the Blind Beggar, the "abrupt entry-into-consciousness of an external figure marked by its naked or solitary aspect" disrupts the "reverie, that abstracted, dream-like void which enables Wordsworth to pass unscathed through London" (238–39). Hartman also points out that the real shock here is the lack of contrast between the blind man's face and label. "Face and label are equally fixed or affixed: we expect the beggar's face and eyes to be centers of life whereas they are as much a surface as the paper he wears" (241–42).

Hertz glosses the same moment as an instance of "blockage in sublime scenarios," stressing the gap between seeing and reading the face: "In the play between the Beggar's blank face and the minimally informative text on his chest, the difference between what Wordsworth can see and what he can read is hardly reestablished in any plenitude: it is a fixed difference—the text won't float up and blur into the lineaments of the Beggar's face—but it is still almost no difference at all" (59).

28. A letter from Charles Lamb not long before the composition of Book 7 began presumably provided Wordsworth with a Londoner's perspective on the effect the city could have on its inhabitants:

> I don't much care if I never see a mountain in my life. I have passed all my days in London, until I have formed as many and intense local attachments as any of your *Mountaineers* can have done, with dead nature. The impossibility of being dull in Fleet Street, the crowds, the very dirt and mud, the Sun shining upon houses and pavements, the print shops the wonder of these sights impels me into night walks about the crowded streets, and I often shed tears in the motley Strand from fulness of joy at so much *Life*. All these emotions must be strange to you. So are your rural emotions to me. But consider, what must I have been doing all my life, not to have lent great portions of my heart with usury to such scenes?   (Charles Lamb, letter to Wordsworth, January 30, 1801, in *Complete Works and Letters*, 687)

The "usury" that the city returns to a heart lent out in such a way is like, though by no means identical to, the possession of the poet's mind by the city. Both at any rate entail the return of an excess from the outer world to the inner. However, in Lamb's metaphor that seems a welcome addition, in Wordsworth's an invasion.

29. Jonathan Arac's *Commissioned Spirits* and Philip Shaw's "Mimic Sights" both provide brief discussions of some of the sights Wordsworth had in mind in his pleased descriptions of London artificers' "imitations fondly made in plain." Altick has a useful chapter on "Popular Entertainments" (esp. 494–97), which discusses the "learned pig" and other amusements. See also Baer and, by way of diachronic comparison, Ben Jonson's *Bartholomew Fair* (1614).

30. As A. B. England maintains, "Wordsworth here argues that it is possible for the external world to gain an almost complete primacy," although "Wordsworth also comes to doubt and finally to deny this possibility at the end of book Seven" (604). England correctly links such meditations on the

relationship of mind and world to Burke's *Philosophical Enquiry*. England, though, dismisses "sociological" concerns with the assertion that "Wordsworth's primary concern is still with the development of an argument about a relationship between mind and world in the experience of perception." Such a reading misses the necessity of considering on exactly what grounds Wordsworth differentiates between his perception of a lone pedestrian and the intrusion into perception of an unwelcome but forceful London phenomenon such as St. Bartholomew's Fair. Only by considering the "sociological" implications of this new form of material invasion can one begin to understand the exact nature of the struggle between "mind and world" in this instance of forced or unforced perception. E. W. Stoddard also discusses this scene.

Hartman understates the case when he says that in confronting the fair, Wordsworth's "mind wearies at the given, the complete spectacle" (241–42). The sort of "possession" effected by St. Bartholomew's Fair is evidently meant to be more powerful and more alien than are the preceding images.

31. Jonathan Swift's "Description of a City Shower" (1710), with its half-exuberant, half-dreadful catalogues and triplet rhymes, has a similar energy, not localized to the crowd:

> Sweepings from butcher's stalls, dung, guts, and blood,
> Drowned puppies, stinking sprats, all drenched in mud,
> Dead cats, and turnip tops, come tumbling down the flood. (61–63)

32. That crowds are here allied with the "literature of power," which defies mere rational comprehension, is clear when one considers the famous stone/shell comparison of Book 5. Less like geometry than poetry, the crowds of London are like the shell from Pascal's dream: they speak "in an unknown tongue / Which yet I understood, Articulate sounds" (5, 94–95).

33. James Thomson's *City of Dreadful Night* (1874) stages such encounters as well, albeit less memorably. Its most striking passages are those that involve uniquely London situations—for example, the pursuit of a lone figure who is busy marking the gravesites of Faith, Hope, and Beauty all over London.

34. Sharon Marcus helpfully observes that when the mountain has gotten pluralized to "ancient hills," which "give movement to the thoughts, and multitude" (727, 729), a word that seems almost inevitably conjoined to crowds—multitude—has oddly been conscripted to describe the stable harmony offered by mountains without, and ordered thoughts within (personal communication).

35. Compare De Quincey's memory of his early delight on entering London: "It was a most heavenly day in May of this year (1800) when I first beheld and first entered this mighty wilderness, the city—no! not the city, but the nation—of London."

36. But see Walkowitz on the necessary confusion that persists even in a class-segregated London between middle-class and fallen women. Her article reproduces an 1865 cartoon of a woman rejecting an evangelical tract: "You're mistaken, I am not a social evil, I am only waiting for a bus."

37. See Eugene Sue's *Mysteries of Paris*, G. W. M. Reynolds's *Mysteries of London*, Thomson, and Maxwell's recent work.

2. PUBLIC ATTENTION IN A NEW DIRECTION: MARIA EDGEWORTH'S *HARRINGTON*

1. No modern scholarly edition of Edgeworth's complete works exists. All quotations, hereafter parenthetically referenced by page number, are drawn from *Tales and Novels by Maria Edgeworth in Ten Volumes*, Volume 9: *Harrington, Thoughts on Bores, and Ormond* (London: Henry Bohn, 1874), in preference to the 1817 edition of *Harrington and Ormond* (London: R. Hunter) except in cases of obvious error. In the epigraph and in all subsequent quotations, all emphasis is in the original.

2. As Peter Logan's important *Nerves and Narratives* has recently shown, Edgeworth draws her account of "sympathetic imitation" not only from Bacon and his successor Digby, but more directly from the Scottish philosopher Dugald Stewart, a family friend: Logan points out that Stewart's "Of the Principle or Law of Sympathetic Imitation," a chapter in his *Philosophy of the Human Mind*, must have had a great impact on the novel. Logan also helpfully points out that in Bacon the phrase "in concert" referred to a series of experiments performed together but that Edgeworth seemingly uses "in concert" to refer to the sorts of experiments it requires the "concert" of various minds to perform.

3. Gallagher aptly labels public upheaval an "objective correlative for Harrington's earlier intolerance" (321).

4. The best accounts are those of Rude, de Castro, and Hibbert. Edgeworth would have known Holcroft's.

5. One plausible test of how large a role city crowds play in an era's public culture is the presence of what might be called the "urban prodigy figure," which is already strikingly present in Edgeworth, in Wordsworth's *The Prelude* (e.g., the list of marvels in Book 7), and in a great many texts of the 1810s. Many of the observations made famously by Baudelaire about 1870s Paris, and by Simmel about all European cities in "Metropolis and Mental Life," are in fact phenomena already noted in the early nineteenth century (see the Introduction for a longer discussion of the implications of literature's early observations of such shifts). Benjamin notes the lobster-walking flâneur as a marker of late-century urban homogeneity and desire for distinctiveness, but Edgeworth's and Wordsworth's observations suggest that earlier in the century there was already a print culture that plucked out the exceptional prodigy of the moment in London, and that the public's attention, following that of the press, shifted from one new marvel to another with a rapidity approaching that of the late nineteenth century.

I go on to argue in later chapters that the political crowds of the 1830s radically shifted the parameters of literary representations of the crowd, displacing many—though not all—of the representational tropes of the earlier part of the century. Nonetheless, I think that "prodigies" and amusements of the sort collected by Altick can tell us a great deal about mapping such watersheds. For an account that presumes an earlier transformation of the crowd's significance in public discourse, see Reinert.

6. I am indebted to Adela Pinch for excellent recent work on early nineteenth-century notions of the circulation of emotion in the British public

sphere: her discussion of the Princess Caroline affair and her coda on De Quincey are especially important. Like Pinch, I owe a debt as well to Laqueur's work—both that on Caroline and that on "humanitarian narrative." Hannah Arendt's fascinating discussion of "pity" and "compassion" in *On Revolution* also sheds important light on how emotions might be said to circulate in public.

Elaine Hadley's *Melodramatic Tactics* has been tremendously helpful as well: it offers a rigorously historical evaluation of the circulation of various histrionic tropes in British culture. By contrast, the recent work on the question of "melodrama" by Vernon and Joyce, while intriguing and far-ranging, seems to me to misstate somewhat the nature of transmission through a public sphere: each chooses to hypostatize the "melodramatic" as constitutive of the "real" as other expressive modes are not. I suggest instead that we treat melodramatic emotionality as one mode among others whereby claims were lodged and politics contested within a variegated public sphere: see further discussion in the Introduction and chapter 5.

7. In the 1801 Preface to *Belinda*, Edgeworth referred to that book as a "Moral Tale—the author not wishing to acknowledge a novel." As Gallagher puts it, "despite her rejection of the label, however, reviewers and critics continue, quite rightly, to assess Edgeworth's contribution to the English novel" (28on.).

8. Katie Trumpener (128–56) offers the most recent account of the "national tale" as a genre associated with female writers, and existing uneasily as both precedent for and competitor with the historical novel. I have profited greatly from her impressive work and from that of Ian Duncan. I consider it an important turn in Edgeworth's writing, however, that *Harrington* engages, as Scott does, with the intertwined lives of multiple ethnicities within a larger imperium. *Harrington* proposes a fictional solution that differs interestingly both from Scott and from Edgeworth's own paradigms in more straightforward national tales such as *The Absentee* and *Castle Rackrent*.

Other significant recent work on Edgeworth includes that of Logan, Gonda, Hack, Harden, Kowaleski-Wallace, Papy, and Michals. Butler's is still the definitive biography.

9. The snobbiest of the English lords are compared to "Spanish grandees," who allowed the nouveaux riches into their houses, but refused to address them by first names, thus implicitly snubbing those they explicitly tolerate. The comparison is an interesting one because in the context of Spanish nobility, the "new" lords would very likely be Jews: the "New Christians" whose conversions swelled the ranks of the wealthy would never be fully accepted by the (secretly) invidious Castilian court.

10. This might be likened to the use of blackface by Jewish minstrels in early twentieth-century America, allowing them, argues Michael Rogin, to wipe off all racial markings along with the assumed blackness at the end of the performance (426).

11. That it takes a degree from an English university to teach this lesson is an unremarked irony.

12. The status of her black "neighbors" is not touched on in her letters.

13. Lazarus's influence is recorded within the text of the novel itself by a

paragraph virtually borrowed from her letter, describing the heroine's Jewish life in America. There also sprang up between the two families an exchange of letters and plant cuttings that was not halted even by the deaths of Rachel and Maria.

14. In *Harrington* as in *The Absentee* it is a fast moral rule that one cannot possess two identities at once, but *Harrington* delivers the lesson only in passing, in the form of a relatively minor character. The reader is warned off of the transparent hypocrisy of Harrington's seeming friend, the protean Mowbray, who is so anxious to marry money that he would willingly assume the guise of any religion, even Judaism. Interestingly, the leader of the Gordon Riots, Lord Gordon, did convert to Judaism shortly before his death, a fact Edgeworth probably knew (see Watson, 112).

15. In fact, the riots began when a movement to repeal the Catholic Naturalization Bill of 1778 gathered enough steam to bring northern English and Scottish protesters to the doors of Parliament in 1780 (see de Castro, chapters 1–3).

16. Lefebvre's *The Great Fear of 1789* is an acute historical anatomy of forms of the transmissibility of rumors. One of Lefebvre's great accomplishments is to show that even delays in the transmission of news can be the source of increased spread of panic: the very knowledge that there is information elsewhere that has not yet reached a community can spur the wildest of rumors.

17. In *Harrington*, a riot at a cinnamon factory in Gibraltar definitively establishes that the chains of commands entrusted to authority—which might ordinarily be relied on to break the chain of magnified prejudice—are ultimately no more trustworthy than the capricious moods of the mob. After Lord Mowbray publicly displays his racialized contempt for Jacob,

> From that day there was a party raised against us in the garrison. Lord Mowbray's soldier of course took his part; and those who were most his favorites abused us the most. (77)

As a result, there follows an instance of the lower classes following out loyally the *implicit* command in Mowbray's prejudice:

> it was kindled by a party of Lord Mowbray's soldiers, who, madly intoxicated with spirits they had taken from the stores, came in the middle of that dreadful night to our house, and with horrible shouts, called upon my master to give up to them the *Wandering Jew*. My master refusing to do this, they burst open his house, pillaged, wasted, destroyed, and burnt all before our eyes! [H]e died of a broken heart. (77)

18. Logan astutely points out that the insertion of crowd prejudice against the Jews is more or less gratuitous: no real plot development hinges on it, since the attack on the Monteneros' house is triggered by suspicion that Catholics are inside.

19. Davidoff and Hall offer the definitive account of the establishment of encysted space and the confinement of women to the home in the first four decades of the nineteenth century (see especially chapter 3, "'The Nursery of Virtue': Domestic Ideology and the Middle Class," 149–91). They provide a lucid explanatory framework for the movement toward hermeticization and bourgeois production of new forms of privacy in this period. Novelistic prac-

tices are clearly going to have some elective affinity with this movement: the question is how much, and of what sort, an issue I discuss in the Introduction. For revisionist accounts that challenge the dependence of Davidoff and Hall on spatial metaphors and on class differentiation, see respectively Vickerey and Wahrman.

20. See chapter 6.

21. Thus the novel preaches a tolerance of variety, which is slated in its turn to serve the purpose of a greater Britain that tolerates each configuration of ethnic difference and excludes only a single category of intruder: the lower-class, fully British, fully Protestant maid Fowler, who does nothing in the novel that does not foul her own nest. Her exile to that land which is of all lands specifically outside the Empire—America—marks a suitable conclusion to a book that manages to make not Protestant Britons but Spanish, Jewish, and Irish absentees the exemplary Londoners.

22. Daniel Hack's thought-provoking work on nation-formation in *Castle Rackrent* emphasizes Edgeworth's interest in navigating between an Irish and an English identity in order to "perpetuate the anxiety" English readers feel about the Irish identity depicted in *Castle Rackrent*, thus necessitating "repetition, another mediation by the inter-national Anglo-Irish" (162). To that interesting assertion I would add that her later work, more explicitly concerned with delineating national characteristics via overt contrasts between the nations, is perhaps even more helpful in conceptualizing what place an Anglo-Irish identity might have within an empire conceived as ethnically heterogeneous both at its periphery (Gibraltar) and in its metropolis.

23. One important corollary of this preference for a national identity formed by contrast to a potentially hostile world is that a distinctive national identity does not come by fleeing London, but is in effect manufactured there. If national identity grows out of a sense of difference ("the higher classes were generally similar; but, in the lower class [are] many characteristic differences" [*The Absentee*, 209]), what form of difference presents itself in a population that is not juxtaposed to that of other nationalities? Compare Benedict Anderson (especially 131) and Eric Hobsbawm for alternative models of such nation formations.

24. Ian Duncan's interesting hypothesis (one version of which appears in his "Edinburgh, Capital of the Nineteenth Century") that one way Scott constructed a bipolar Britain was to disaggregate it geographically (political power in London, cultural in Edinburgh) might be compared usefully to Edgeworth's idea of "Irishness" as a floating cultural locus within the vast complexity of what might be called an "Anglo-Subject" empire (e.g., Anglo-Irish, Anglo-Indian, Anglo-Jewish, Anglo-Canadian, etc.).

25. Later in the century such liberty of association between classes cries out for correction: compare, for instance, Silas Wegg in Dickens's *Our Mutual Friend* (1865), who asserts an impossible (and incorrect) knowledge of the lives of the family living in the house outside which he peddles: "he always spoke of it as 'Our' house, and though his knowledge of its affairs was mostly speculative and all wrong, claimed to be in its confidence" (88). By the same token, when one does know something of others' lives, it bespeaks a deeper connec-

tion. In Francis Hodgson Burnett's *A Little Princess* (1911), the affluent in-habitants of the house next door are (almost correctly) named by the Princess-turned-pauper who spies on them. The Little Princess has an almost uncanny inside knowledge of another house's interior: that knowledge is predicated on her ability to think herself into the shoes of another bourgeois family (unlike Wegg). Having been part of one interior, she can correctly map another. *Harrington*, however, clearly belongs to an earlier era in this respect. The knowl-edge of one class's life is unproblematically available to a good character from another class: the widow Levy has an outsider's knowledge of the household's inside information, and there is no reason for a rebuke, or even for surprise.

26. My argument is analogous to C. L. R. James's provocative claim that the black slaves of the West Indies were avatars of the modern, the first instance of a fully mechanized, industrialized, collectivized body of people: "The Ne-groes therefore, from the very start lived a life that was in essence a modern life" (392).

27. The tacitly assumed gap between classes of English here suggests that there is an implicit analogy between the wealthy and the alien—both are trapped in the presence of a vast majority that is fast becoming innately hostile to them.

28. In fact, the same sorts of mental flaws that have dogged Harrington reappear. However, this time they are displaced onto the De Brantefields, who have until now been the book's model for a dignified and traditional anti-Semitism. The Protestant ladies, frozen like statuary, are in effect mirror figures of the mob itself. If the mob is burning with its prejudice, the De Brantefields are frozen by theirs. When Lady De Brantefield "walked up and down the room, with the air of a princess in chains" (157) she has cast herself into a Gothic captivity of her own making. They cannot even communicate their own plight; in order to get through to the widow Levy, Harrington is forced to translate their story into the argot of the public sphere.

29. I am influenced in this account by Gallagher's brilliant account, in *Nobody's Story*, of the contemporary debates on the distinctions between alienable and inalienable property (e.g., 110–25).

30. Of the many recent works on Victorian-era notions of privacy, truth, and where personal integrity demands that the line between the two be drawn, I have found Welsh and Kucich (1994) especially helpful.

31. Contemporary usage allowed the word "apartment" to mean either simply any room within a house or a "particular" room set apart; the ambi-guity works nicely here (*Oxford English Dictionary*, s.v. "apartment").

32. Cf. Susan Stewart on collections (chapter 2).

33. Both are explicitly labeled "Christian" artists, and the fact that Montenero obtained their works as family legacies from previous intermarriages only serves to further the suggestion that there have been plausible forms of interaction between the religions even in Inquisition-haunted Spain. It is re-vealing to compare the only description given of Spanish life in *The Absentee*, in which any thought of social mixture would have been inconceivable (cf. note 10 above).

34. The phrase is from Ragussis, whose analysis of later British texts about

Jewish conversion seems consonant with what Todd Endelman has described as Victorian England's interest in producing a textual anti-Semitism which is out of all accounts "disproportionate" to the actual treatment of Jews in Victorian England (personal communication). Seen in those terms, even seeming philo-Semitism might be part of a Victorian cultural tendency toward fixing on the Jewish character as a site of all of a mobile society's worst vices. But that explanation is not, I believe, apt for what Edgeworth does here, deploying the Jew as a figure for what ethnic integration within a larger British nation might look like, and hence looking not toward conversion but toward tolerated alterity.

35. Among the novels that treat this phenomenon are Balzac's *Cousin Pons* and Huysman's *A Rebours*.

36. Rubin offers one convincing account of the implications of marriage as exchange.

37. I have more to say below about Berenice's ability expertly to "collect herself," retaining a reserve that is not broken even in the most trying social encounters.

38. This vision of Jewish education in limiting circulation must also be seen as a corrective to any account of *Harrington* that would stress the fact that Montenero will have no Jewish children to continue his Anglo-Jewish lineage. Edgeworth explicitly figures the Jewish lineage as intellectual here: if it is passed on to Harrington as collection, it is almost as strongly passed on to the reader of the book as well, who can learn the lesson of being "a good Jew" in a way that ensures the cultural survival (in Edgeworth's account) of the most Jewish legacy of all: collection-making, and confident use of cash. That is, Harrington and Berenice—and the readers after them—are charged with the rather larger cultural task of continuing Montenero's legacy of integrating himself, as it were, into their new English identity of collected selfhood.

39. Barthes suggests in *Sade/Fourier/Loyola* that most French writers of the nineteenth century saw money as purely liquid, a medium that moved toward the fulfillment of various desires. Fourier saw it as a dry, hard, *nonfungible* item, valuable for its own sake. In Montenero's conception of money's possible solidity (that is, the ways it may be used to secure rather than dissolve accepted institutions), Edgeworth may well intend to depict someone concerned to shore up the bulwarks of a society whose very solidity offers to those of his ethnicity their only hope of safety. Just as in the Middle Ages there were "King's Jews," Edgeworth may be proposing an identity as something like "Banks' Jews."

40. On the function and place of money in nineteenth-century Europe and in America in recent years, see for instance Shell, Michaels, and Goux. Georg Simmel's magisterial *Philosophy of Money*, with its claim of money's progressive "idealization" into a purely detachable realm of value is (along with Marx) the relevant proof-text. See also Davis (esp. 65–70), Zelizer, McLaughlin, and Jevons.

41. As Gallagher puts it, "To reform the order of representation, then, Montenero is given all the powers normally attributed to conspiratorial manipulators of signs in general and economic markets in particular" (318).

42. The threatened storming of the Bank of England triggered the bloody suppression of the actual Gordon Riots.

43. Electability is another sort of nonfungible wealth that is nonetheless subject to these exchanges. True, a Jew could not be elected to Parliament, but without Montenero's quasi-fiscal assistance neither could this Christian.

44. Moreover, Montenero's ability to act quickly and decisively is intimately related to his skill as a collector: Jacob, "who goes everywhere and *sees* everywhere he goes" (123, emphasis in original) is able to ensure the destruction of "The Dentition of the Jews" precisely because he has gotten his training helping his master to spend money in the preservation of other paintings.

45. Edgeworth evidently means to link the presence of Jews within England to a valorized world of trade, economic fungibility, and a laudable cash nexus. It would thus be interesting to compare Edgeworth to Scott and to Trollope (conceivably to Dickens as well), each of whom deploys Jewish characters to mark selective disillusionment with certain aspects of a market economy that Edgeworth by contrast seems quite ready to praise. The comparison was suggested to me by Gallagher's striking overall argument, in *Nobody's Story*, for the surprising valorization, by women authors of the eighteenth and early nineteenth century, of the public market's anonymity.

46. An ambassador is in attendance. The repeated appearance of ambassadors in this novel signals Edgeworth's vision of a world in which vastly different nations must always be interacting with one another in various ways, with a modicum of strangeness but a minimum of hostility. For example, it is an ambassador's daughter whom Montenero married, and it is the Portuguese ambassador's wife whose rosary touches off one dangerous flurry of Gordon rioting.

47. Scarry's summary of the imbrication is helpful: "Ian Watt's *The Rise of the Novel* has at its very center the demonstration of the way in which the formal properties of the new genre required that both romantic love and marriage exist, and that the two entail each other. The recognition that marriage is a made thing, that the novel is a made thing, *and that the second made thing only gets made by incorporating into its interior an image of the making of the first made thing*, is perhaps at least latent in our endless critical attention to endless love triangles in endless novels and periodically surfaces in brilliant explicitness as in Tony Tanner's *Adultery in the Novel: Contract and Transgression*" (61, emphasis in original).

48. The passage certainly bears comparison with De Quincey's strolls, in *Confessions*, into London crowds for the purpose of "sharing" joy or grief: see chapter 3.

49. This was evidently grasped by the Victorians, as responses such as Thackeray's *Rebecca and Rowena: A Romance upon Romance* (1850) demonstrate.

50. For an extended analysis of the comparison between aesthetic texts and newspapers, see the conclusion to chapter 4; for an analysis of Habermas's historical assumptions, see the introduction to chapter 5 (and Eley).

51. If cash and cache are thoroughly Jewish developments in Edgeworth's account, the theater at least appears safely Shakespearean and hence English.

And yet Montenero is quick to point out that the "original" for the play had been Jewish, a fact Edgeworth confirms in one of the book's few footnotes. The significance of this is not simply to invert the valence of the story (in the story on which Shakespeare based his work, the Antonio figure was a Jew) but to assert the continued primacy of the Jewish example.

52. What that countenance says reinforces the paradoxical quality of such legibility: he reads "an anxious desire not to give trouble, and a great dread of exposing herself to public observation" (62).

53. I am grateful to Ivan Kreilkamp for this observation, which brings closer together the two linked phenomena that I argue constitute this novel's production of a crowd-like energy: reading and romance.

54. One reason that Edgeworth, like Sir Walter Scott, remains of interest in the story of emergent British notions of nationality is that the purpose of the national tale is to represent the continuation of the very friction that the novel's happy romantic ending would seem to erase. One might for that reason be tempted to say that national difference—Irish and English, Jewish and English, or what have you—and not romantic infatuation, is at the heart of *Harrington*. The conclusion I would draw from this genealogy, however, is a broader formal one that necessitates no choice between rival forms of exemplarity, national and romantic. Where the plot hinges so heavily on the reconciliation of two national groups, the thematization of ongoing interaction must be the norm. Perhaps the single vital ingredient of such a plot is friction, which allows the story to continue by keeping the two groups together without fully reconciling them.

55. Mary Ann O'Farrell's account of blushing is helpful in understanding the era's interest in producing signs of somatic authenticity. A sigh might be "put on," but a *suppressed* sigh seems as innately credible as a blush.

56. Indeed at times the cure can match the disease. The image of Mr. Montenero cutting an anti-Semitic picture to pieces and burning it, saying as one would over an execution "so perish all that can keep alive feelings of hatred and vengeance between Jews and Christians" (106), suggests the counterforce that seems justifiable even against the near-living force that a two-dimensional misrepresentation can have. To fight a theatricalized anti-Semitism with theatricalized anti-anti-Semitism is not only permissible but laudable.

57. Compare for example the cautious (and tedious) distancing of irrational crowds from sensible interiors that characterizes Harriet Martineau's *The Rioters* (1827).

58. Logan argues that by the end of the novel Montenero alone stands for a fully desirable rationality: "He retains his vulnerability to the crowd without being written upon by it, and so escapes the pattern of prejudice and enthusiasm that leads to the larger crowd's immersion in party spirit. Though the crowd believes itself to be judging for itself, it is always imprisoned within prejudice written on its body by prior representations; the crowd is always prisoner of representations rather than its critic" (132–33). Logan accordingly reads the crowd as a residual form, and Montenero's reason as emergent. Logan's account of the novel is immensely learned and almost entirely convincing, but here I disagree. From the novel's first suggestion that Harrington gets well

educated at Oxford not by pure self-control, but by imitating the right types, complicated feelings toward the avatars of sympathetic imitation are central to this novel. If imagination is censured when it manifests itself strongly, as in a crowd, the weak version of sympathy reemerges in the sexual desire for Berenice that moves the novel forward. Crowd energy in one form or another turns out to be not residual but rather every bit as emergent as reason.

59. Matthew Lewis's (ultimately unsuccessful) attempts to publish a bowdlerized Bible, on the grounds that children should not hear certain stories, is an interesting instance of turn-of-the-century concerns about stories' effects upon the untrained reader.

60. In *Harrington*'s paradigm, the grounds for distinguishing between mob and novel may even come to depend upon little more than the novel's claim to be at least relatively consistent. For example, when the mob decides to pardon the falsely accused Montenero, because "in England the mob is always in favor of truth and innocence, wherever those are made clearly evident to their senses" (165), the relief at a just decision is palpably tinged with contempt for those who fluctuate arbitrarily between deadly intent and wild approbation. Compare the French mob that first accuses, then hails, then damns, those on trial in Dickens's *A Tale of Two Cities*.

61. "Bartholomew Fair Insurrection and The Piebald Pony Plot" ridiculed the government for its quickness to treat celebratory crowds as insurrectionary ones: "[The Lord Mayor] had arrived about halfway, when a fellow was detected in looking at his Lordship, and making insurrectionary movements with his face. This, with the impossibility of turning fifty thousand people out of the fair in order to keep the peace, sufficiently proved the inflamed state of the populace that night." To the government, the mere fact of assembly proves criminal intent. But, the pamphlet implies, governments that assume that "a clown outside one of the conjuring shows, who attracted a crowd by incessantly playing on the salt-box, was Cobbet in disguise" produce rather than detect a resentful and conspiratorial lower-class. The radicals retain the upper hand, in this radical account, by their ability to recognize apolitical agglomeration as a daily presence in the rousable but as-yet-unroused city.

The fact that peaceful demonstration crowds were in actuality on the rise (Tilly, Rudé) would not of course prevent Edgeworth from portraying them as archaic, but it does encourage us to read for the ways in which Edgeworth works to come to grips with the abiding presence of London crowds.

3. CROWDED IMAGINATION: THOMAS DE QUINCEY'S *CONFESSIONS OF AN ENGLISH OPIUM-EATER*

1. The epigraph is from Thomas De Quincey, "The Nation of London" (1834; revised 1853), *The Collected Writings of Thomas De Quincey*, edited by David Masson (14 volumes [Edinburgh: A. and C. Black, 1889–90], 1:178). The forthcoming scholarly edition of De Quincey, edited by Grevel Lindop, will presumably supersede the editions cited here, namely Lindop's 1985 Oxford edition of the *Confessions*, hereafter cited parenthetically by page number only, and, for all other texts, Masson's edition of *Collected Writings* (1889–

90), hereafter cited parenthetically by volume and page number (e.g., 1:178). All emphasis in quotations is in the original.

The best contemporary accounts of De Quincey are those by Barrell, Rzepka, Russett, and Leask; Jacobus, Clej, Black, McDonagh, and Cafarelli have also recently published influential work. Other recent work includes that of Burwick, Coates, Needham, and Levin. North offers a valuable assessment of the critical heritage. Earlier important work includes that of Abrams, Miller, and Sedgwick; the definitive biography is by Grevel Lindop.

2. De Quincey's famous distinction, laid out for example in an 1848 essay titled "Alexander Pope," is between the literature "of knowledge" which only tells of the physical world and hence is ultimately forgettable, and the "literature of power," which is unique, unrepeatable, and conveys the subjective experience of the author (11: 56).

3. The stylistics are vintage De Quincey. The metaphor of the lost cap and the rest begins lightly, takes a turn toward the ludicrous, which continues just a bit too long to remain really funny, only to deviate again into a conceit that seems to De Quincey's foes ponderous, metaphysical, or forced, to his advocates an instance of language being tortured into a new kind of sense.

4. Bromwich's account of the singularity of the romantic self thus reads this turn toward solipsistic recovery, and self-justified morality, as less problematic than I take it to be: "The belief in the self is thus the only faith still available that makes the sort of universalist claims we usually identify with religious commitments or with moral duties" (72).

5. Critics have rightly noted that in his "The Palimpsest of the Human Brain" (1845) De Quincey claims that the "earliest elementary stage" lingers last in the memory: "the deep, deep tragedies of infancy, as when the child's hands were unlinked forever from his mother's neck, or his lips forever from his sister's kisses" (13:349). That his sister's death is at the root of much of De Quincey's own sensation of loss I do not dispute, but my argument is that the "habit of loss," however formed, is fascinatingly articulated in the *Confessions* not by way of the family romance, but through representations of crystallized loss ("perpetual farewells!") in a larger world.

6. As with Wordsworth's *The Prelude*, I here choose the earlier version in order to situate the text within the Romantic rather than Victorian period, but there are aesthetic considerations as well. The interlocutory voice of the 1856 version, with its preambles on childhood and elaborate self-referential commentaries on the ways available to tell the story, does not add much of substance to the core issues in the text, and diverts a great deal of attention from what is of abiding interest. I do however treat the 1856 afterword briefly below.

7. See chapter 1.

8. And not just Wordsworth's: the era's widespread accounts of the upper orders' extending compassion to the poor—such as Maria Edgeworth's *The Absentee* and Hannah More's *Coelebs in Search of Wife*—place De Quincey's claim of being "in sympathy" with their exuberance rather than their suffering virtually on its own.

9. That solidarity may also seem less ameliorative than compassionate ac-

tion, but De Quincey wants here to claim a connection, not to be a conduit of relief.

10. Gallagher's *Nobody's Story* includes an interesting account of the various possibilities that economic exchange offers to the writers of the day. The marketplace's production of fungibility and anonymity is discussed at greater length in my account of Edgeworth's *Harrington* (chapter 2).

11. "The English Mail-Coach" manages to amend the process further, granting to the half-known crowds around the coach both memorability and a purely temporary tangibility, a suitable solution to the falling sensation produced in the *Confessions* (see chapter 4).

12. Of course, the Latin and English words do not mean quite the same thing. De Quincey's Latin vocabulary often functions this way—to allude to the higher realm of the classical, and then to "replace" the Latin word with a more common or apt English word, but a word that intentionally runs slightly askance to the meaning of the original Latin. A peripatetic is no more a "Street Walker" than someone who is pensive is "thinking." This is another instance of the doubling of meaning that allows De Quincey at once to stay close to and to move away from Ann—she is and is not close to him, just as she is and is not in the same category as he, just as a Latin word is and is not the same as its English translation. Thomas Hardy's *Jude the Obscure* (1895) explores the same topic by having Jude discover that learning Greek does not simply involve discovering a code that allows one to transform each English word into its exact Greek counterpart.

13. Walkowitz (1982), Cott, and Finnegan provide important modern accounts of nineteenth-century British prostitution; Nield collects the era's own accounts.

14. Kittler tendentiously characterizes the "discourse network" of the Romantic era as dependent on the production both of national uniformity and of an individual's particularized relationship to language. He thus analyzes "alphabetization" as a national ideology nonetheless implemented through acquisition of the "mother's tongue"—that is, childhood literacy attained at a mother's lap.

15. Dickens's *Great Expectations* (1860/1861) conveys the degraded status of convicts by referring to "the great numbers on their backs, as if they were street doors" (227), a description that successfully heightens the felt dehumanization of coming to know and to catalogue other people by way of cold enumeration rather than by older forms of social congress. Dickens stresses the singling out of convicts for a particularly heartless sort of ordination, whereas De Quincey means to suggest that all such forms of ordering information seem extraneous to the warm bond he shared with Ann. Yet De Quincey means as well implicitly to tally up the costs of such unordered intimacy.

16. Clej reads this as one of the exemplary instances of addiction as modernism, but the social matrix—that is, meetings in an anonymous crowd—seems central to the emotions produced.

17. Lindop points out that there is no extra-literary evidence that Ann existed, and that "De Quincey nowhere refers to Ann outside a consciously literary context." He also opines that if she was invented, De Quincey may have

taken the name from St. Ann's Parish, in which Soho was located: Soho also had an Anne street, a Little St. Anne Street, and a St. Anne's Court (87–89).

18. This passage brings to mind Denis Donoghue's notion that Modernist literature begins as a record of "those who feel *beset* by the city" (xi, emphasis in original).

19. The notion of an enumerable, or a comprehensible myriad took on a peculiar importance much later in the nineteenth century, as scientists and entrepreneurs alike strove to convey to the public the importance of understanding, or of being awed by, the sublimely but enumerably huge. *The Autobiography of James Nasmyth* (1885) contains this revealing anecdote:

> Among the many things I showed Sir John [Herschel] while at Hammerfield, was a piece of white calico on which I had got printed a million spots. This was for the purpose of exhibiting one million in visible form. In astronomical subjects a million is a sort of unit, and it occurred to me to show what a million really is. Sir John went carefully over the outstretched piece with his rule, measured its length and breadth, and verified its correctness.

De Quincey's use of the terms "thousand" and "myriad" is characteristic of his era's interest in a similar sort of amplitude, applied to mundane urban life.

20. The *Oxford English Dictionary* gives the "unrhetorical" value of a myriad as ten thousand; but it also claims the word is used in that sense in English only in a very few translations, and those mostly from before 1700. The "unrhetorical" claim for numerical specificity, then, has a rhetorical swagger about it.

21. At each corner, one flips a coin to determine one's direction.

22. Arjun Appadurai has recently suggested that the desire for a somatic *certainty* is at the root of late-twentieth-century forms of ethnic violence: the paradigm, aside from questions of scale, may well be analogous to the De Quinceyan sense of lost certainty in the socially unmarked space of London.

23. "Prefatory Notice to the New and Enlarged Edition of 1856," 3:222.

24. One might compare two pieces of twentieth-century writing. One is the doggerel rhyme:

> Yesterday upon the stair
> I met a man who wasn't there.
> He wasn't there again today;
> I wish to God he'd go away.

The other is an equally comic if slightly more ponderous passage in Samuel Beckett's *Watt* (1958), concerning his uncertainty as to whether a particular kitchen pot really is, after all, a pot. "It was just that hairsbreadth departure that so excruciated Watt. It was a pot, but it was not a pot of which one could say pot pot and be comforted."

25. De Quincey followed his era's general practice of drinking opium in wine—laudanum. It seems an important irony that the only person seen *eating* opium in the *Confessions of an English Opium-Eater* is not English.

26. Rzepka reads the Malay as a figure for a reading public that digests De Quincey's dreams elsewhere, where he cannot control their response (20). Rzepka's reading is acute, but it lacks an account of the choice to circulate

one's ideas impersonally through the medium of print—of which I have more to say in analyzing "The English Mail-Coach" in chapter 4.

27. Barrell's account is the most recent attempt to analyze the content of the various visions: he describes "sheer terrifying numberlessness of the world's population who are evoked only to be dehumanized" (5). Like Leask, Barrell argues that De Quincey's relationship to the British Empire and to its presence in the Far East is central to his writing.

28. On the related question of "vivacity" of imagined objects, see Scarry (1995).

29. I have in mind Pater's famous evocation of the Mona Lisa, which includes such far-fetched "descriptions" as "like the vampire, she has been dead many times, and learned the secrets of the grave; and she has been a diver in strange seas, and keeps their fallen day about her" (80). The important point is not, as some assert, that such "impressions" fail to correspond to the actual appearance of the painting. Rather, it is noteworthy that Pater finds it necessary to produce descriptions of objects in the outer world (vampires, graves, a diver) even when striving to convey the sensoria of the inner.

4. "GRAND NATIONAL SYMPATHY" IN DE QUINCEY'S "THE ENGLISH MAIL-COACH"

1. With one exception noted below (a citation to the text printed in 1849 in *Blackwood's Magazine*), citations to "The English Mail-Coach" are to the 1854 revision printed in *The Collected Writings of Thomas de Quincey*, edited by David Masson (14 volumes [Edinburgh: A. and C. Black, 1889–90]). Again, the forthcoming scholarly edition of De Quincey, edited by Grevel Lindop, will presumably supersede the editions cited here. All emphasis in De Quincey quotations is in the original. Again, the best contemporary accounts of De Quincey are those by Barrell, Rzepka, Russett, and Leask; Jacobus, Clej, Black, McDonagh, and Cafarelli have also recently published influential work. Other recent work includes those by Burwick, Coates, Needham, and Levin. North provides a valuable assessment of the critical heritage. Earlier important work includes that of Abrams, Miller, and Sedgwick; the definitive biography is by Grevel Lindop.

2. In 1849 trains already went about fifty miles an hour, or four times the speed of the fastest mail coach, a fact that draws attention to the irony in De Quincey's praise of a "speed" that is forty years and a factor of four out of date. On velocity theorized more broadly, see the quirky work of Virilio and Baudrillard.

3. Linda Colley's recent discussion of the formation of national sentiment in the Napoleonic era is comprehensive; however, Benedict Anderson's remains the most compelling description of the underlying ideological formations that produced the invention of tradition and the mechanisms of patriotism.

4. Vrettos has written importantly on the Victorian conception of the danger of electrical or nervous transmissibility, which she analyzes as a form of contagion.

5. This passage is omitted from the 1854 version, but reprinted in Masson as a footnote, at 13:292.

6. Compare Rilke's *Notebook of Malte Laurids Brigge*, which shows its debt to Baudelaire (and hence to De Quincey) by its insistence on the ways that the city "forces itself" into an "interior I never knew I had," describing an urban-crafted interiority that contains not the "authentic" self but external phenomena forced inward that rule one willy-nilly. However, in Rilke this move is clearly allied with pre-Freudian psychological theories that were to shape representations of the city as psychic invasion in thousands of late-century guises and in memorable Modernist works by Eliot, Wyndham Lewis, and (in a different vein) Joyce.

7. Schivelbusch provides the best account of the cultural significance of railways in nineteenth-century Britain.

8. Schivelbusch observes that although American train cars were from the early days one single long open space, British train cars were modeled on dozens of little mail coaches strung together: that is, every coach had (and in many places in Europe still has) a series of "compartments" seating only six or eight people, each with its own entrance. Though such a structure seems to preserve the analogy of the mail coach better than an open car, Schivelbusch rediscovers De Quincey's point: by multiplying spaces the coach-segmented train promotes privatization of travel as the mail coach itself did not.

9. I have outlined my objections to the profoundly ahistorical assumptions built into Canetti's overall argument about crowds in the Introduction, but I still credit him (unlike such successors as Moscovici or such predecessors as Le Bon) with a brilliant eye for the mechanics and the psychology of various sorts of public gatherings. Like Erving Goffman's *Behavior in Public Places*, Canetti's *Crowds and Power* has an amazing ability to describe certain sorts of crowd occurrences. One of Canetti's lasting insights concerns the excitement caused in a crowd by the simple act of self-spectatorship—as who might say, "look at us all looking at us all."

10. Interestingly, in later life De Quincey reports shunning mail coaches because he feared being trapped with long-winded bores, whom he was too polite to interrupt. It is a resonant anecdote because the exterior of the mail coach gives De Quincey all the generic pleasure of a swift passage with news, without any of the burden of actually handling any (merely personal) information himself.

11. One fascinating argument convincingly advanced by Georges Lefebvre's *The Great Fear of 1789* is that the waves of uncontrolled rumor that swept out of Paris in the last months of 1789 had the power to create among those who heard them the illusion of simultaneity. For more than a hundred years it was believed that these rumors had not spread serially from town to town, but must have sprung up at the same time in various places. This historical example suggests that news-hungry people will tend to believe that they are synchronized—in receiving news—with other areas of the nation.

12. Just as the market crowds in the *Confessions* had been compared to an opera, this national distribution is rightly analogized to music, for its rhythmic uniformity (as well as its martial obedience): "This post-office service spoke as by some mighty orchestra, where a thousand instruments, all disregarding each

other, and so far in danger of discord, yet all obedient as slaves to the supreme *baton* of some leader terminate in a perfection of harmony" (13:272).

13. Wyndham Lewis, seventy years later, describes an inversion of the same moment that sheds light on the continuing difficulties of squaring the appeals of the personal and the collective in martial situations:

> But the empty York platform, at 2 in the morning, and this English family, without the wild possessive hugging of the French at the stations, sending off the reservist. It hardly seemed worthwhile sending off ONE. What could he do? The mother's sarcastic grin and fixed eyes, and her big boy, with one shoulder hunched up, almost a grace, like a child's trick, as her eyes wandered, were not easily forgotten. (8)

Even in a world suffused with martial fervor, it is very hard to summon the same rhetoric you can with a mass (in this case, "the French") when speaking of "ONE" son boarding a train.

14. Klancher and Chandler have, like Pinch, been very helpful in elucidating readerly assumptions of the 1810s and 1820s; less reliable work exists on the 1840s.

15. E. P. Thompson (1993) and Negt and Kluge, in widely diverging contexts, have made important claims as well for a working-class version of this public sphere, sometimes called a "second" or "proletarian" public sphere. My analysis of De Quincey's explicit repudiation of the powers of the newspaper-driven "first" public sphere applies with equal force to such an alternative working-class public sphere: see chapter 5 for an extended discussion of the class implications of a public sphere that does or does not include crowds within it. McDonagh's useful work in elucidating other De Quincey works that are deliberately opposed to the existence of a working-class discursive space is relevant here. She reads his "Organology" as a "response to Chartism[and a] use of language which maintained social hierarchies, a use of language dependent on the silent submission of the working class" (137).

16. I am grateful to Sharon Marcus's astute commentary on a version of this chapter delivered at the Modern Language Association conference in 1997, for helping me clarify my periodization of De Quincey's writing.

17. "Travelling in England in the Old Days," originally in *Tait's Magazine*, (1834, revised 1853; 1:271).

18. Ludwig Wittgenstein suggests that the key distinction between the aesthetic realm and the nonaesthetic is that an aesthetic experience precisely forces those who witness or consume it to be moved, while events in the nonaesthetic realm offer the witness a choice in the matter (5).

19. Black claims that De Quincey critiques Kantian ethics by proposing in "On Murder Considered as One of the Fine Arts" that violence can function as a way of underwriting the work of art. This suggests another way in which a literary text might be imagined as located somewhere between journalism and action. James Chandler's fine description of the literary "counter public sphere" (1998, 41) also seems relevant to what De Quincey aims for here.

20. Rzepka is right to point out that the Malay, in "vanishing" (7), is turned from an immediate threat (because of the possibility that De Quincey has killed him with an overdose) to an ominous figure of the effects of publication—"from an immediate threat to the author's godlike reputation into a

(presumably) stupefied dreamer of the opium fantasies brought on by" De Quincey's gift of the drug (7). Yet he misses the salient point about this disappearance: that De Quincey's work is littered with figures who disappear when most in danger, of whom Ann and the woman perhaps killed by the mail coach are the two most important. Putting the Malay in that company would have made Rzepka's claim about the painful effects of publication— once the text has passed out of one's sight—all the more compelling. See Needham for a different account of publication and the "rhetoric of display."

21. Adela Pinch has recently provided an extremely instructive analysis of the debate regarding the way that public emotion spread with the news of the death of the Princess Charlotte in 1817. Pinch parses the following contemporary account of the death by Robert Huish, who is anxious to establish that mourning began spontaneously as soon as the news was heard by any individual, rather than passing from one to another:

> One and all acted from a spontaneous sentiment of admiration and affection for the virtues of the Princess, without waiting to know what had been done by their countrymen elsewhere; for true feeling waits not the authority of precedent to teach it how to weep. (Huish, 664, cited in Pinch, 180)

Pinch is right to point here to the salient claim that "the authority of feelings must rest in their own isolation" (181), in contrast to Barbauld's and Byron's verses on the same occasion, both of which used the figure of "electricity" to describe the conveyance of the news. Two things are remarkable about Huish's reaction, and about the outpouring in the national press at the time of "poems, prints and 'true accounts'" of mourning (though radicals claimed the government had planted them all, Pinch is rightly skeptical of that claim). The first is simply that this outpouring registers at an early date (1817) a highly developed public sphere in which news of simultaneous (and hence presumably "true") emotion was both recorded and disseminated. The second is Huish's insistence that emotional reaction did not spread like wildfire, meaning that, at least in Huish's view, each individual Briton felt a personal connection to the royal family. But note as well that social contagion itself, the spread of news from one person to another, threatens to act as an uncontrollable emotional force. Huish implies that such a contagious transmission of news might potentially be directed anywhere.

The significance of De Quincey's recollections, thirty years on, of the transmission of news through the crowds assembled around the mail coach seems to me to be double. On the one hand, De Quincey is acknowledging what was not clear in 1817: that the transmission of ideas "electrically" through the contagious medium of the crowd is an inevitable concomitant of a social space that includes both public transmission and crowd aggregation. On the other, however, De Quincey offers a new medium (the mail coach ride) which mixes social contagion and the more formal public dissemination of national information. De Quincey aims to put the problematic but unavoidable crowd to use—not by separating it from a pure public sphere, but by mixing crowd and text together under a national aegis.

22. Habermas's ideal is more evident in such later works as *The Theory of*

Communicative Action and *The Philosophical Discourse of Modernity*. For the basis of my claim that one ought to locate the ascendancy of "rational critical conversation," as Habermas defines it, in the nineteenth and not eighteenth century, see Eley, but also pages 50–143 in Habermas's *Structural Transformation of the Public Sphere*, which offers a very clear argument for a "liberal" notion of public conversation that Habermas describes as flourishing in the early nineteenth century.

5. DISCURSIVE COMPETITION IN THE VICTORIAN PUBLIC SPHERE: THOMAS CARLYLE'S *CHARTISM*

1. The epigraph and other quotations are from Thomas Carlyle, *Selected Writings* (London: Penguin, 1971). This readily available edition is based on the "Library Edition" of *Collected Works* (London: Chapman Hall, 1870–71) and checked against the "Centenary Edition" of *Collected Works* (London: H. D. Traill, 1896–99). All references appear parenthetically in the text.

2. Chartism was a working-class suffrage movement with some middle-class support. Its earliest incarnation, in 1839, was focused on petitioning Parliament to pass into law the six demands that comprised its Charter. Its demands, as Gareth Stedman Jones's important article "Rethinking Chartism" has made clear, were from the first political rather than social or economic. They were aimed, that is, at what I would like to call "indirect" redress of grievances. They assumed that the representation of the working class in Parliament would solve problems more effectively than would any movement for "direct" amelioration of hardships related to working conditions or to distribution of property. The demands of the Charter were:

1. universal adult male suffrage
2. suffrage protected by the ballot
3. abolition of property qualifications for members of Parliament
4. payment for members of Parliament
5. numerically equal parliamentary electoral districts
6. annual sessions of Parliament

Dorothy Thompson (ix) points out that one or the other of the demands was sometimes omitted, most often the ballot or the numerically equal electoral districts, so one occasionally hears of the "five points."

3. James Bronterre O'Brien, *Bronterre's National Reformer*, February 4, 1837; quoted in Dorothy Thompson, 58 (capital letters in original).

4. Watson; also see de Castro and Hibbert for accounts of the Gordon Riots.

5. The quotation is from *The Northern Star*, July 7, 1839; every issue of *The Northern Star* for 1839 and 1840 contains descriptions of a range of such meetings.

6. Although Chartism is not utterly discontinuous with what came before it, the novelty of the so-called "mass-platform" years is reconfirmed in such

recent work as Epstein's and Pickering's. Tilly effectively demonstrates that the definition of what crowd action meant was finishing a radical transformation in the England of the 1830s. A greatly expanded electorate, a vast government bureaucracy, and an enormous increase of publicity via the mass media had introduced a whole new set of rules into the political realm. Under those new rules, the powerful "strove increasingly to anticipate popular reactions" and "large-scale coordinated interaction" became the likeliest ways for the un- or underrepresented to make "collective claims" (Tilly, 13).

7. Taking a cue from such sources as Pauline Maier's excellent work on American Revolutionary crowds, Marie Ozouf's work on Parisian festivals during the Revolution, David Scobey's account of the New York "promenade" of the 1890s, and Hobsbawm's, Rude's, Dorothy Thompson's, and E. P. Thompson's meticulous reconstruction of the behavior of nineteenth-century English mass assemblies, the modern student of the Chartist crowds is well poised to see the Chartists' pivotal role in the invention of a mass public discourse *not* of grievance, but of representation.

8. Feargus O'Connor, in Dorothy Thompson, 324.

9. See Dorothy Thompson, passim, but particularly 323–28 and all of chapter 3, "We, Your Petitioners," 57–76.

10. Tilly, 18. Tilly notes that one piece of evidence for this is the "migration of the English word 'meeting' into French (*meeting*), Spanish (*mitin*), and Russian (*miting*)" (15).

11. Some argue for the importance of the violent upheavals in Ireland as a formative factor in British national politics—and there seems no question that "Daniel O'Connell's Catholic Association played a major role in integrating special-purpose associations into the British social movement on a national scale" (Tilly, 373), as did, interestingly enough, Methodist and Teetotaling activists, by a slightly different example. The 1820s certainly shaped what have been called "the British social movements": "the creation of associations visibly devoted to the promotion of a particular program; the holding of public meetings to publicize the program and dramatize the extent of public support for it; the production of addresses; a search for publicity in newspapers and other periodicals, including periodicals organized deliberately for the purpose by movement supporters; the submission of petitions; the organization of marches, processions" (Tilly, 372). All these components depend on that central notion of dramatizing public support.

12. Tilly, 24. By the term "tutelage" I mean to credit Gareth Stedman Jones's claim that the ideology of the Chartist movement was shaped by Owenite radicalism and entirely to agree with him that the shape of the new labor consciousness was determined by the language of national protest labor had inherited. But Stedman Jones, for all his attention to language, underestimates the importance of the process of *sign-formation*—the Chartist demonstrators, by convoking publicly, were engaged in the joint "production of cultural meaning." That meaning was not inherited by rote from Radicalism, but reshaped by public meetings that were effectively guided by plebiscite, an element that must be factored into any account of the movement's ideology. James Vernon's more recent work does attempt to account for such alterations,

but his account of popular protest runs the risk of underestimating the wide variety of social milieux from which protests originated: various claims to be "English"—no matter if they be worded identically—mean something different, depending on whether they emanate from manse, mill, or the moors. Steinberg is very helpful on this point.

In short, helpful as I find the evidence amassed by Vernon and the like-minded Patrick Joyce, Robert Gray's thirteen-year-old critique of Stedman Jones should still be borne in mind: "Stedman Jones is quite rightly critical of views which reduce language to a simple expression of experience pre-constituted elsewhere. But his own substantive treatment of language is perhaps itself expressive, in a different way: specific utterances are seen as reflective of the fixed categories of an inherited political tradition, and these categories are held to define the possible forms of political mobilization" (368).

13. Denis Donoghue, *The Old Moderns: Essays on Literature and Theory*, 15. The claim that what Chartism changes are the forms of "narrative" is an inaccurate one: as I argue below, the transformation in the public sphere institutes changes in the entire structure of public dialogue. To single out narrative is inexplicably to narrow the range of discursive shifts.

14. Mary Ryan, "The American Parade: Representations of the Nineteenth Century Order" (1989), 139; see also 152. This remarkable essay (like the book it becomes a part of, her 1997 *Civic Wars*) restricts itself to a limited range of American crowd actions: patriotic and ethnic parades of 1825 to 1880 in New York, New Orleans, and San Francisco. It convincingly concludes that the social order was "represented" in such parades, which formed "a detailed, descriptive portrait of the urban social structure" (137), and charts a movement toward avowedly ethnic parades in the latter part of the century. Her work seems to fit into the reevaluation of the nonprotest crowd that Harrison calls for. But her model of "descriptive representation," borrowed from Hannah Fenichel Pitkin's classic *The Concept of Representation*, has interesting implications for protest crowds as well. My claim that the Chartist crowd represents a desire to be represented intersects in a complicated way with Ryan's account of the parade participants' apparently more straightforward desire to represent one trade, or latterly one ethnic group. The political crowd clearly has more invested in demonstrating its own representability, but its tactics for making such a representation do bear remarkable similarities to the more peaceful constitutive marches that Ryan analyzes.

15. Eley's account of Habermas's *Structural Transformation of the Public Sphere* (1962) in relation to subsequent historical work is an indispensable basis for what follows. For my account, Eley's key conclusion about "placing Habermas in the nineteenth century" is that "it is important to acknowledge the existence of *competing* publics at every stage of the history of the public sphere. The public sphere was always constituted by conflict" (306). This revision applies to Habermas's account of the eighteenth century as well—a more widely studied topic—but for my purposes Habermas's claims about the nineteenth century matter more. I differ from Eley in one important respect: rather than positing a variety of given "publics" (a formulation that Eley borrows from Negt and Kluge's model of a "proletarian public sphere"), I argue that

the public sphere was always comprised of a variety of discourses, and that out of those various discourses the notional "publics" were formed. For a more extended account of the debate about this historicity of Habermas's claims, see Negt and Kluge, Kelly, and Calhoun.

The work in the last five years that takes up Eley's claims may quibble about terms, but even such quibbles confirm the underlying soundness of Eley's distinction between a public sphere in practice and an abstract model of a purely rational public sphere. Thus, for example, John Breuilly argues that Eley is wrong to criticize Habermas's conception of a purely "rational critical" public sphere. Breuilly maintains that even where the formation of voluntary associations in Hamburg, Lyons, and Manchester was designed to accumulate cultural prestige and to exclude the poor, "these are secondary features" (38). He also claims that the key facet of such clubs is not that they were sites for argument but that they "were rule-governed associations with specialized objectives, wedded to the idea of rational contemplation and progress and considering 'culture' to be something both autonomous and transcendent" (39). But such a concession exactly confirms Eley's point: the public sphere allowed a great many structures that embraced principles of reason and unfettered communication, but could also be governed by rules that allowed power to be preserved in one status group or another.

16. Aside from a visible decline in the number of violent gatherings from 1820 to 1834, Tilly's statistics also reveal, for example, that the portion of newspaper-reported demonstrations or "contentious gatherings" aimed directly at Parliament or at national officials increased from forty-seven percent in the period 1801–1820 to sixty-two percent in the period 1828–1830, while the percentage of appeals to royalty and local officials declined from thirty to eleven percent (Tilly, 308 et seq.).

17. For excellent discussions of the role of London's radical underworld in developing the techniques that the Chartists made into tools of popular democracy, see McCalman and Prothero.

18. The most noteworthy recent work on the topic is by Pickering, Epstein, and Vernon; but D. Thompson, as well as Epstein and Thompson, still offer very valuable materials.

19. "Unbroken solidarity was their only weapon, for only thus could they demonstrate their single but decisive asset, collective indispensability. Once they had acquired even a flickering of political consciousness, their demonstrations were not the mere occasional eruptions of an exasperated 'mob,' which easily relapsed into apathy. They were the stirrings of an army" (Hobsbawm, 150).

20. *The Northern Star*, July 6, 1839: the speakers are Lovett et al. and Neesom, respectively.

21. Petition presentations and simultaneous mass meetings are innovations in the political realm as important as any of the changes in the rhetoric of written speeches that Stedman Jones analyzes. Pickering strikes a cautionary note in distinguishing between "newspaper articles and editorials which were produced by a comparatively small group of activists; and, on the other hand, the reports of public meetings where the mass following was to be found." But

the implications of his methodological shift go deeper even than he maintains: what is to be found in the accounts of demonstrations he has uncovered is a way of tracking shifting practices—and shifting assumptions—about the exact representational claims implicit in staging demonstrations before a national public.

22. Again, Prothero's account is invaluable. See also Belchem and Mc-Calman.

23. For an excellent discussion of what different times of day and of the week might have meant in industrial towns, see Harrison.

24. Compare also the almost mythic quality of midnight marches in Brontë's *Shirley*, in which the ghostly music of assembled Luddites drilling implies either an angelic or demonic visitation.

25. A great deal of otherwise very powerful work in the E. P. Thompson and Rudé tradition falls victim to this mistake. The critical error is not—as the more ferocious critics of Thompson and Rudé have proposed—that Rudé gives crowd participants "too much credit" for rational behavior. Rather, the problem is that by focusing on prior political identity, one can overlook the transactions, transformations, and shifts in intention involved in the event itself.

26. John Keegan's *The Face of Battle* includes a useful discussion of the analogous question of why war has for so long been accepted as the ultimate method of resolving international disputes: what is it about violence that gives it more standing as arbiter than any other contest?

27. The epigraph is from *New Letters of Thomas Carlyle*, vol. 1, 186.

28. Helpful recent articles on Carlyle's *Chartism* include those by Lamb and Richardson.

29. The essential early biography of Carlyle is Froude's; the definitive scholarly biography is Kaplan's (1983); and the most recent is Heffer's (1995). Important criticism on Carlyle in general includes the work of Levine, Vanden Bossche, Desaulniers, Ulrich, and Lee.

30. Thomas Carlyle, letter to his brother, July 27, 1839 (*New Letters of Thomas Carlyle*, vol. 1, 168).

31. The shift away from Carlyle's account even in British historiography of Chartism is not absolutely certain until George Rudé's work of the 1950s and 1960s. By the time of the publication of E. P. Thompson's magisterial *The Making of the English Working Class* (1963), though, the rationalist account of Chartist demonstrations may be taken pretty much for granted. Tilly's is the definitive current benchmark of this approach. The most notable exceptions are those historians Tilly labels the "social stress" school: those who treat crowds as potential riots, and assemblies as at worst disruptions, at best meaningless alibis for the ruling classes to do what they intended anyhow. See, for example, Jonathan Clark's *English Society, 1688–1832* (374–75), which argues (as Tilly puts it) that "popular agitation provided ruling politicians with arguments and pretexts but otherwise had no significant impact on the actual course of national political life."

One current critic of the shared assumptions of Rudé, Thompson, and Hobsbawm, is Mark Harrison, who argues forcefully that a focus on mobilized political crowds serves to dangerously misrepresent the actual nature of mass assemblies in the late eighteenth and early nineteenth centuries. He particularly criticizes Tilly's work for making violent or political crowds into a model for mass behavior, and argues that what might be called Durkheimian moments— parades, affirmations of regal power, and so forth—are underestimated as constitutive elements of what gathering in public meant. If Harrison has been accused (fairly, I believe) of having less interest in explaining nonpolitical demonstrations than in explaining *away* political ones, his work nonetheless is valuable in broadening our understanding of the realm of public events that must be analyzed in order to comprehend the variegated presence of British crowds.

32. Even the opening chapters, better written by far than the tedious conclusion, led the anonymous reviewer in the Radical *Tait's Edinburgh Magazine* to complain that "he mutters like an oracle and gestures like a conjurer." (Anonymous, "Chartism," *Tait's Edinburgh Magazine*, n.s., 7 [February 1840]: 115–20. Reprinted in Siegel, 164–70.)

33. Kaplan, Rosenberg, Ryals, and Cumming offer useful accounts of that style; see also Lee, "Carlyle's Fetishism."

34. The Parliamentary blue books are on "Cheap Justice, Justice to Ireland, Irish Appropriation Clause, Ratepaying Clause, Poor-Rate, Church Rate, Household Suffrage, Ballot-Question 'open' or shut" (217); these forms of enquiry are what Carlyle calls "not things, but the shadow of things." They are akin to the flaws of statistical tables, which are "like cobwebs, like the sieve of the Danaides; beautifully reticulated, orderly to look upon, but holding no conclusion" (157). That is, they are figures without substance.

35. Carlyle's condemnations of Parliament would fill a book by themselves. At bottom, his account of Parliament with its "jangling hubbub and tongue-fence" (209) is that it always and fatally misses the reality of action in favor of paper simulacra; the endless plural "blue books" are proof that paper multiplicities will always pale before action's striking singularity, that reasoned talk will give way to Carlylean heroics—be those in Carlyle's own words, or in the physical force of crowds. Given such opinions, there is certainly an implied compliment to the forces of the crowd when Carlyle says that he is sure the Chartist crowds mean to do more than to assert the right "to send one's 'twenty-thousandth part of a master of tongue-fence to the National Palaver'" (216).

36. There is a broad range of nineteenth-century texts that employed parts of Carlyle's logic, but such texts often avoid Carlyle's most interesting problems by looking backward rather than at the challenges of contemporary crowds. Charles Dickens's *Barnaby Rudge* is only the best-known of the many novels from the Chartist era that looked back to a rambunctious past for easy examples of crowd madness. Carlyle, unlike these novelists, chose to confront the relevant contemporary facts. One of the few precedents is Harriet Martineau's *The Rioters* (1827), which dealt with the industrial disturbances of the early twenties.

37. This genealogy can be traced more widely in Carlyle: in many other of his works—particularly *On Heroes, Hero Worship and the Heroic in History*—Carlyle proposes that speaking articulately and at length is a sure sign

your words are nugatory, of no more import than statistics. By comparison the highest form of language comes in sounds that at first may not even be recognizable as speech: "The word of such a man is a Voice direct from Nature's own heart. Men do and must listen to that as to nothing else—all else is wind in comparison" (*On Heroes*, 275).

38. Having established this paradoxical connection between his text and the inarticulable "insight" below Chartist dogma, Carlyle hedges his bets by trying again to have it both ways: to distance himself from the very Chartist disturbances that had justified his pamphlet in the first place. Rather than acknowledging the relationship between "his" crowd and the various "Chartisms" visible on the streets, he pushes the "real" rage of English crowds into an ominous and unspecified future:

> Let no man awaken it, this same Berserkir rage! Deep-hidden it lies, far down in the centre, like genial central-fire, with stratum after stratum of arrangement, traditionary method, composed productiveness, all built above it, vivified and rendered fertile by it: justice, clearness, silence, perseverance, unhasting unresting diligence, hatred of disorder, hatred of injustice, which is the worst disorder, characterise this people; their inward fire we say, as all such fire should be, is hidden at the centre. Deep-hidden; but awakenable, but immeasurable;—let no man awaken it! (172)

Chartism is the awakening in question, but Carlyle is playing false to his own terms here: its awakening has already taken the form of disease, flashes of lightning, and the not-quite-speech of animalistic bellowing. Carlyle can claim that it is "immeasurable" as well as "deep-hidden"; he can posit some deeper level beneath, some physical fact not yet touched. But the one thing he cannot do is to deny that the gist of his claim depends not on what some future Chartism may do, but on what this present one has done. That which he negates (or pushes into the future) is that which he depends on.

39. The process is repeated with statistics: after disparaging them all, Carlyle adds "there is one fact which Statistic Science has communicated, and a most astonishing one" (168). That statistic—which turns out to be the amount of time that a third of Irish peasants go hungry—has a different status from any other statistic: it is, somehow, "a fact."

40. Kemnitz introduces the term "intimidationist" as a way of describing a mediating third force between "physical force" and "moral force," the conventionally understood Chartist strategies. My argument is that the Chartist movement as a whole, whether based on physical or moral force, made use of the intimidationist power that crowds, nonviolent as they might be, held for onlookers of this era.

41. Some recent critical work on Chartism questions the conventional opposition between "moral" and "physical" force: Ian Haywood, for example, writes, "The famous distinction between 'physical' and 'moral force' has been exaggerated" (13). But Kemnitz's work has yet to lead to a fully developed alternative vocabulary for describing what emerged both in Chartist publications ("signifier and the signified of the disenfranchised" [Haywood, 2]) and in its public actions.

42. One remarkable Chartist text that evidences the considerable thought that went into analyzing the implications of both threatening and withholding

violence is Ernest Jones's novel, *De Brassier: A Romantic Romance* (1851–52) (excerpted in Haywood, 148–57 and 198–203). Jones imagines a futile violent revolt that is abetted both by the government's deliberate suppression of any leader who speaks for pacifism and by studied governmental indifference to those who preach violence, until "the people were compromised at last" by taking violent action (152). The government encourages violence, which it can violently quell, but fears those who keep just within the bounds of peaceful action. Jones represents one of the central currents of Chartist thought. According to such thinking, the most logical tactic is to devise ways to gesture at the ominous massed potential of a demonstration, but to shun the possibility of turning that mass openly against a government that waits with artillery and "batteries" (156).

43. Mayakovsky's oft-quoted remark, "In Russia alone poetry still matters; in Russia alone it can get you killed," can be read as a perfect indicator of the infusion of political expression into other media when the ostensibly political realm is blocked. The examples from the Soviet empire abound, and are perhaps best summarized by the Czech joke about a man who goes into a bathroom during a Party Congress to find another man leaning over a sink vomiting. He says to the vomiting man, "I know exactly what you mean." In that word (not "feel," not "are going through," but pointedly "mean") is contained the essence of the dilemma of alternative expression: when political speech cannot be political, what other sort of speech (or action) is *not* political?

44. The first examples that will come to mind are likely to be the successful mass demonstrations that toppled (already tottering) governments in Eastern Europe in 1989, most notably in East Germany and Czechoslovakia. In those velvet revolutions, crowds and quasi-organized demonstrations served as a sort of shadow democracy in nations that had, within living memory, experienced representation via more formal parliamentary means. By comparison—still well within the same register of corporeal protest in place of absent suffrage—the widespread strikes and demonstrations in the early 1990s in South Korea, a society with a less well-established "collective repertoire" of representational strategies, came close to succeeding in establishing a new basis for governmental legitimacy, and avoided widespread bloodshed. The 1989 failure of the Tiananmen Square movement, however, was produced by a slightly different orientation of national government and national public sphere to "representative" collectivities: the demonstration registered there as a potential violent act, rather than as an articulate utterance (see the documentary film "Gates of Heavenly Peace"). Each of these non–First World examples suggests that there remains the possibility that crowds can function not only *within* a public sphere, but as a *constitutive* element of public discursive action: crowds can not only petition, but petition to be read as a petition.

45. Elaine Hadley's recent work offers a convincing account of changing mid-Victorian assumptions about public space, describing in particular the ballot box as a site where the privacy of a liberal citizenry could be publicly confirmed.

46. The long-held consensus view, championed by Asa Briggs (1959) and still accepted in Margot Finn's *After Chartism* (1993), the current touchstone

on the period, is that the "mass platform" of the late 1830s and the 1840s gave way to a period of quietism until the struggles leading up to John Bright's efforts to forge a consensus for the 1867 Reform Bill. And even those who wish to argue that Chartism did persist comparatively unabated into the 1850s and 1860s do not make the argument that the power of collective demonstrations as a discursive statement continued.

For instance, in language that echoes—tellingly—the terms with which Charles Tilly distinguishes the great protests of the 1830s from *earlier* local and parochial movements, John Breuilly writes that "Chartism was able to act as a vehicle of protests in a local setting. In London in particular vigorous club and public house culture that had sustained local branches of the movement through the arrests of 1848 enabled Chartists to continue their activities unchecked into the 1850's" (15–16). But the activities that Breuilly has in mind are not truly a continuation of what the mass platform had presented: a viable form of public speech-act that made the representation of representation a viable possibility for the disenfranchised.

The publication of a series of helpful biographies of local Chartist leaders in Dorothy Thompson's Early Chartism series reveals a telling pattern of 1839 mass activism giving way to local orientation. For example, one ardent organizer of "simultaneous public meetings" in the Potteries in 1838 and 1839, John Richards, turned to small-scale activism and public speaking for hire (Fyson, 75–89). I advance his case, as one among many, to suggest that biography is a fruitful method of filling in the picture of how the public sphere changed, because it shows how a man (a woman would certainly not have had the same chance) could, in the right circumstances, make his voice heard within the national arena opened by a certain kind of mass platform. When that arena passes away, the same man must turn elsewhere: the biography points out not failures or triumphs of character, but shifts in what public actions are possible.

47. Herf, Hirschman, Nye and (somewhat less convincingly) Cassirer all provide partial genealogies of this line of reactionary thought.

48. Bourdieu and Klancher are particularly helpful, the one as a theorist and the other as a historian of the formation of such fields of cultural production. I have found Guillory's account of Bourdieu indispensable.

6. PRODUCING PRIVACY IN PUBLIC: CHARLOTTE BRONTË'S *SHIRLEY*

1. The long-acknowledged power of *Jane Eyre* to promote, enforce, and celebrate utter interiority encourages the tendency in Brontë criticism to "hail Brontë as the high priestess of the soul" (Shuttleworth, 245). On "depth," see the instructive discussion in Armstrong, 20 and passim.

2. Gallagher's brilliant work on the discursive presence of economic notions in the period's fiction aside, the default approach for Victorian criticism is often psychologized accounts of novelistic structure. Shuttleworth's important book, *Charlotte Brontë and Victorian Psychology*, for example, is acute in denouncing fallacies about essential selves in Gilbert and Gubar's *Madwoman in the*

Attic ("resolutely ahistorical" [2]), and rightly critical of a past critical over-investment in the "secret, interior realm of essential selfhood" (2). But her intention to "lay bare the inner, psychological consequences of social ideology" (246) seems to me not quite to register Brontë's intricate struggle to justify new forms of interior soulfulness by mapping their relation to exterior material conditions. *Shirley*, like any novel, is a public text as much as a psychological record.

3. Armstrong and Miller are two valuable and influential examples of critics who have argued strongly for such an awareness.

4. In Brontë criticism, one striking example is Eagleton. Such accounts seem quite unlike the work of their putative forbears. For example, although Raymond Williams's *Keywords* and *Culture and Society* suffer from some underlying confusion about what the truly "material" is, Williams generally succeeds in providing supple and nuanced genealogies of how clashing ideas may interlock and aggregate to create or to buttress both ruling-class views and conceivable sites of dissent.

5. As well as chapter 5, see Eley, Hobsbawm (1975), Gareth Stedman Jones, D. Thompson, and Tilly for various accounts of that shifting public discursive realm. Criticism of *Shirley* has often focused on Caroline's mental state, and occasionally on the novel's narrative strategies, both from a formal and from a linguistic perspective. There are a few accounts of the novel that focus straightforwardly on the depiction of the Luddites, though both Briggs and Eagleton bring more complicated historical models to bear. Interesting recent articles include those by Dolin, Argyle, Keene, Greene, Arnold, and Smith. It is presumably because Brontë excludes overt representations of working-class life that both Raymond Williams and Catherine Gallagher decide to exclude *Shirley* from the category of industrial novels, though Gallagher does not say so directly: "I have chosen to exclude it because industrial conflict in *Shirley* is little more than a historical setting, and does not exert any strong pressure on the form" (269).

6. Though ostensibly writing about Luddite upheavals, Brontë was writing in an era of widespread Chartist activity. As I argue at some length in discussing Carlyle's *Chartism* in chapter 5, the Chartists had made what the Luddites never had: explicit demands for political representation of the "assembling classes." Their peaceful demonstrations represented their ability to represent themselves (peacefully) within Parliament: see Tilly, Rudé, and, on representation as a political concept, Pitkin (1972), chapter 1.

7. See Hobsbawm (1964), Thompson, and Peel. The Luddites have come down to us in the era of the Unabomber as machine-breakers motivated by antitechnological utopianism (see Sale). In reality, their 1811–1820 protests, well described in Peel and Hobsbawm, were largely economic: threatened both by the embargo that had stifled trade and by technological innovations that cut labor demand, workers all over the north of England tried to destroy the machines meant to replace them. In part because they did not act in concert, they failed miserably.

8. References, hereafter parenthetical, are to the 1974 Penguin edition of

Shirley. That edition is based not upon the 1849 first edition but the 1853 one-volume edition (London: Smith, Elder), which incorporated some changes by Brontë herself.

9. Tilly distinguishes among various sorts of local, "autonomous," and un-directed agricultural protest crowds, but he also argues convincingly that crowd protests were becoming increasingly nationally oriented and politically charged during the first four decades of the century (1–47). Chartist demonstrations Brontë is said to have seen in Haworth presumably exposed her to both the organizational potential and the overtly menacing aspects of a protest march aimed at effecting national change (Hook, 36).

10. As A. and J. Hook observe, Brontë liked to play up this connection: evangelical fervor and insobriety are frequently linked in her writing (30).

11. At least one Yorkshire paper read more into such appearances than *Shirley* seems to:

> These partial insurrections form but a curtain to cover the horrible scenery preparing behind it for a denouement of this dreadful drama. It is a mere *drilling* of the people for a *Field-day* upon a larger scale. There is a dark, subtle, and invisible agency at work, seducing the ignorant and the inexperienced, and encouraging the profligate and the abandoned. (*Leeds Intelligencer,* April 17, 1812)

But Brontë chose to read only the files of the *Leeds Mercury* in researching *Shirley*.

12. Gaskell's description of a dinner party during Brontë's 1849 visit to London maps a similar scenario. Meant to sit at the bottom of a long table, "she quickly passed up so as to sit next to the lady of the house, anxious to shelter herself near some one of her own sex. This slight action arose out of the same womanly seeking after protection on every occasion, when there was no moral duty involved in asserting her independence, that made her about this time write as follows: 'I like [her] surveillance' " (Gaskell [1958], 285).

13. Davidoff and Hall acutely point out that in a world of decreasing public roles for women, "auxiliaries of the church and chapel provided a space," the most public example of which was "the Sunday school fete, of which the pastor's daughter was the chief organizer" (147). If Davidoff and Hall notice the fete's potential power as one of the most public locales left for female action, Brontë notes its concomitant power to terrify the privacy-trained woman, whom it threatens with a near-obsolete obligatory publicity.

14. Compare the intrusive narrators of Emily Brontë's *Wuthering Heights* or of Anne Brontë's *Tenant of Wildfell Hall*.

15. There are a few moments, even fairly far along in the novel, in which Shirley and Caroline attempt to reestablish what might be called an "amiable distance" toward those with whom they can never find true sympathy. The "good-humored rating" that Shirley delivers to a crowd of gossiping farm wives, convincing them to disperse without gunfire or death, stands as the exemplary counter-instance to Moore's mortal fortification of the mill. "What good does your talking do?" she asks them, and if their talking is diminished by the question (implying that theirs is mere idle gossip), her own by contrast is elevated. With nothing but talk she has dispersed a female crowd (345). Given such an example of successful moderation, the strict division between

"singular" individuals and a mad scurrying world of undifferentiated crowds may seem, early on in the novel, a product of misguided rejection of the social realm. Any inclination toward such pollyannaish thinking is, however, dispelled by the assault on the mill.

16. An earlier generation, or a country unaccustomed to the newly organized industrial confrontations that Britain had in such quantities, might produce such a hero. Compare, for example, the colonel who confronts the crowd in Mark Twain's *Adventures of Huckleberry Finn* (1885), where one man with vim is worth more than the "mob without any *man* at the head of it," and the one "*half* a man" (190–91) who form the mass against him.

17. The incident is drawn from a real occurrence that took place quite near Haworth, the moment on which Brontë clearly did the most historical research. The newspaper Brontë drew on for the story of the siege of Cartwright's mill, the *Leeds Mercury*, fails to mention many details that papers such as the *Leeds Intelligencer* contain: for example, memorable (and widely reported) allegations of torture by the mill-owner of the wounded with vitriol, and the fact that Cartwright had concealed cannon upstairs, hoping for just such an assault. The *Mercury* does, however, note that the Luddites' guns, if they were even loaded, had only powder in them—a detail Brontë tellingly omits (April 16, 1812).

18. In the twentieth century, the "We Were There" books I read as a child repeated the notion, but with children instead of women granted the role of inactive observer. The whole allure of the books would have been ruined, and the reader's delighted identification compromised, had the child protagonists—"we"—become tankdrivers at the Battle of the Bulge, or sharpshooters at Bunker Hill.

19. Shirley too strikingly distinguishes herself here, as she had when she spotted Robert at the picnic: her visual acuity in sighting Robert's sentry marks her as the exemplary observer (334). Compare, for example, the scene in which Caroline looks into Shirley's eyes to see her catch sight of Robert: "Caroline seemed to think that the secret of her eagle acuteness might be read in her dark grey irids: or rather, perhaps, she only sought guidance by the direction of those discriminating and brilliant spheres" (309). In a Thomas Hardy novel, the scene would strike us an acute instance of physical description, but in Brontë, to whom such details are important only as they activate a latent symbolic register, the triangle of Caroline, Shirley, and Robert (the witness, the seer, and the seen, respectively) is meant to make the reader wonder which matters more to Caroline—the fact of Robert's appearing, or the fact of Shirley's marvelously catching sight of him?

20. See Maslan's work on French revolutionary theater crowds for an important and stimulating account of an angry public presence that might be read not as "representative" but as embodying a claim of direct action.

21. Adams offers the most important of recent studies of masculinity in Victorian culture; others include those by Bristow and Dellamora, the collection edited by Adams and Miller, and (though it is not his central topic) that by Kucich. My notion of the "citadelled man" draws especially on Adams's and Kucich's work on "reserve"; while I hope it will prove useful to other

students of the period, I have worked out its implications only in Brontë's novels.

22. In comparable later industrial novels by Gaskell, Dickens, Disraeli, and Eliot, the mill owner's unwillingness to distinguish between the good and bad workingmen is an occasion for the novelist's high moral rebuke: such distinctions, moral rather than class-based, must be made. The point in *Shirley*, however, is that Moore's coolness precisely necessitates his refusing to be drawn to make distinctions in a situation such as the assault on the mill. That potential leveling justifies Moore's higher ground, and underwrites the necessary privacy on which the novel depends: to meet one worker on level ground would be, in the face of a crowd attack, to meet every worker so. In conclusion, I argue that *Shirley*'s apparent deviation from type in this regard is actually the crystallization of assumptions implicit but unspoken in other novels of the era.

23. This note, filled with lines like "your devilish machinery is shivered to smash" is helpfully "translate[d]" by Brontë "into legible English" in much the same way that she modified the dialect in Emily's *Wuthering Heights* (64).

24. In *Barnaby Rudge* as well, the descriptions of the deaths of rioters in the rioting itself are markedly callous: they seem less mourned than do many dying animals in Dickens. When the riot ends, *Barnaby Rudge* regains a fierce hostility toward any pointless death, which only makes Dickens's willingness to catalogue the lurid deaths of rioters the more striking. This callousness may stem from the conviction that what went on during riots was a suspension of the human condition, and that those participating lost what made them worthy of empathy and fellow-feeling.

Brontë presumably drew the notion of the crowd's self-enumeration from an account of another riot in the *Leeds Mercury*, February 19, 1812.

25. Freud borrowed from Le Bon the distinction between an uncontrollable crowd and the disciplined set of followers, the pack. This pack is a crowd as well in another sense of the word: the *Oxford English Dictionary* cites an 1840 usage of "crowd" as synonymous with "company, set, lot," or loyal following.

26. Edward Said suggests in *Culture and Imperialism* that overseas colonies are a silent component to Victorian culture, an absence in the accounts that novels typically give of the economic life that sustains a family, a community, a plot. In readings of the industrial novel, that "elsewhere" may need to be expanded to include European and American markets.

27. Compare William Butler Yeats's "Beautiful Lofty Things" (1938):

> Augusta Gregory seated at her great ormolu table
> Her eightieth winter approaching: "Yesterday he threatened my life,
> I told him that nightly from six to seven I sat at this table
> The blinds drawn up;" . . .
> All the Olympians; a thing never known again.   (303, ll. 7–10, 12)

Here, coolness reappears as an explicitly aristocratic form of courage. While Yeats waxes nostalgic for noble nonchalance, Brontë is sketching a present-day hero of the middling order, akin to Carlyle's "captain of industry."

28. In fact, *Shirley* seems in many ways an early work in a long literary tradition that depicts workers as nothing more than body parts. One plausible

comparison might well be to the most violent march described in Emile Zola's *Germinal* (1885). As that march begins, the perspective shifts suddenly from the working-class characters whose fates occupy the bulk of the novel to a pair of frightened bourgeois girls. They watch the riot pass by, like a procession, outside a barn where they are hiding. They can only glimpse the rioters through cracks in the barn: only disembodied hands, legs, pitchforks waving on their own. It is a cinematic moment (repeated in early crowd films such as "The Riot" [1913] and "Strike at the Mines" [1911]) that well summarizes a whole range of novels about crowds from one sort of bourgeois perspective. Zola presumably shifts focus at just this moment in order to imitate certain bourgeois representations of working-class unrest. What is seen from this distance, at this moment, and with such fractures in the field of vision cannot seem quite human.

29. Charles Tilly nicely separates three historiographic schemas used to read nineteenth-century crowds: the "progression," the "struggle," and the "disorder" model. The third is operative at this moment: the crowd's members are merely reacting blindly to pain, rather than planning a rational response.

30. Eric Hobsbawm's *The Age of Revolution 1789–1848* and *The Age of Capital 1848–1875* remain useful resources on this development.

31. See Sharon Marcus (1995) for an important account of the role of professions in *Jane Eyre* that links the female acquisition of a vocation with "abstraction, authorship, and advertising." See also Mary Poovey's indispensable chapter in *Uneven Developments* on Jane Eyre's role in the mid-Victorian debates about governesses.

32. *The Oxford English Dictionary* (1989) does list a use of the word in 1827, but the meaning is somewhat obscure.

33. The chiasmal structure of Shirley's and Caroline's marriages, far from opening up space between the two social classes of Whig trader and gentry landowner, only reinforces social ties: mill manager marries landowner's best friend, and landowner marries mill manager's brother.

34. Gallagher (1985) correctly singles out George Eliot's *Felix Holt* as a sterling instance of competitive representation. The novel's afterword asserts a fiction-writer's right to do what mere voting cannot: represent the pitiable working classes.

35. Hannah Pitkin (1998), Mary Dietz, Bonnie Honig, and Seyla Benhabib provide important recent assessments of Arendt's contribution to debates on the relationship between the political and the social.

36. Nussbaum attempts, bizarrely, to make the same argument about the difference between the novel and the political, in her *Poetic Justice*, but with the moral valence reversed: that is, she claims for the novel's "compassion" a power to teach caring universally. Laqueur's important work on the "humanitarian narrative" presumably provides the historical basis for Nussbaum's claim, and Smith's *Theory of Moral Sentiments* may seem to provide a philosophical justification for making the claim a prescriptive rather than merely (as in Laqueur) a descriptive one: Laqueur describes the growth of an idea which Nussbaum embraces and advocates. But no amount of Laqueur or of Smith can justify Nussbaum's preference for emotional over rational grounding for

"right action": on what grounds does one trust any given feeling? Her willingness to valorize the novel's compassionating abilities tellingly obscures the political antecedents and underpinnings to any emotional claim.

37. *The Surprising Effects of Sympathy* is the title of David Marshall's excellent book on a related topic in an earlier era.

38. John Kucich's *The Power of Lies* explores tellingly some of the tensions immanent in the Victorian emphasis both on truthfulness and upon privacy.

39. For example, a character's poverty can always validate entry into that character's life—although justifying a more searching look at genteel characters may require some ingenuity. In Hannah More's *Coelebs in Search of a Wife*, for instance, the protagonist, Charles, knows he has found the perfect mate, Lucilla, when he spies on her in the sickroom of an old pauper. Stealing a glance at Lucilla leaning over the pauper's bed, Charles is filled with an indescribable (and clearly prurient) emotion that is sparked largely by the chance to witness someone of his own class participating in a bedroom scene (302).

Works Cited

Abrams, Meyer H. *The Milk of Paradise; The Effect of Opium Visions on the Works of De Quincey, Crabbe, Francis Thompson, and Coleridge.* Cambridge, Mass.: Harvard University Press, 1934.

Adams, James Eli. *Dandies and Desert Saints: Styles of Victorian Masculinity.* Ithaca, N.Y.: Cornell University Press, 1995.

Adams, James Eli, and Andrew H. Miller. *Sexualities in Victorian Britain.* Bloomington: Indiana University Press, 1996.

Altick, Richard D. *The Shows of London.* Cambridge, Mass.: Belknap Press, 1978.

Anderson, Benedict. *Imagined Communities: Reflections on the Origin and Spread of Nationalism.* London: Verso, 1983.

Anonymous. "Thomas Carlyle." *Tait's Edinburgh Magazine,* n.s. 7 (February 1840): 115–20. Reprinted in Jules Paul Siegel, comp., *Thomas Carlyle: The Critical Heritage.* London: Routledge and Kegan Paul, 1971, 164–70.

Appadurai, Arjun. "Ethnic Violence." Talk given at the Center for Literary and Cultural Studies, Cambridge, Mass., April 22, 1997.

Arac, Jonathan. *Commissioned Spirits: The Shaping of Social Motion in Dickens, Carlyle, Melville, and Hawthorne.* New Brunswick, N.J.: Rutgers University Press, 1979.

Arendt, Hannah. *The Human Condition.* 1958. Chicago: University of Chicago Press, 1974.

———. *Lectures on Kant's Political Philosophy.* Edited and with an interpretive essay by Ronald Beiner. Chicago: University of Chicago Press, 1989.

———. *On Revolution.* New York: Viking, 1963.

———. "What is Existential Philosophy?" 1946. In Jerome Kohn, ed., *Essays in Understanding, 1930–1954.* New York: Harcourt Brace, 1994.

Argyle, Gisela. "Gender and Generic Mixing in Charlotte Brontë's *Shirley.*" *Studies in English Literature* 35:4 (Autumn 1995): 741–56.

Armstrong, Nancy. *Desire and Domestic Fiction: A Political History of the Novel*. New York: Oxford University Press, 1987.

Arnold, Margaret J. "Coriolanus Transformed: Charlotte Brontë's Use of Shakespeare in *Shirley*." In Marianne Novy, ed., *Women's Re-Visions of Shakespeare*. Urbana: University of Illinois Press, 1990.

Austen, Jane. *Northanger Abbey*. 1818. New York: Pantheon Books, 1975.

Baer, Marc. *Theatre and Disorder in Late Georgian London*. New York: Oxford University Press, 1992.

Barrell, John. *The Infection of Thomas De Quincey: a Psychopathology of Imperialism*. New Haven: Yale University Press, 1991.

Barrows, Susanna. *Distorting Mirrors: Visions of the Crowd in Late Nineteenth-Century France*. New Haven: Yale University Press, 1981.

Barthes, Roland. *Sade/Fourier/Loyola*. Translated by Richard Miller. Berkeley: University of California Press, 1989.

"Bartholomew Fair Insurrection and The Piebald Pony Plot." London: William Hone, 1817.

Baudelaire, Charles. "Les Foules." 1860? In *Selected Poems*. Chosen and translated with an introduction by Joanna Richardson. Harmondsworth, England: Penguin, 1975.

———. "An Opium-Eater." In *The Artificial Paradise; On Hashish and Wine as Means of Expanding Individuality*. Translated by Ellen Fox. New York: Herder and Herder, 1971.

Baudrillard, Jean. *Simulations*. Translated by Paul Foss, Paul Patton, and Philip Beitchman. New York: Semiotext(e), 1983.

Beckett, Samuel. *Watt*. Paris: Olympia Press, 1958.

Belchem, John. *'Orator' Hunt: Henry Hunt and English Working-Class Radicalism*. Oxford: Clarendon Press, 1985.

Benhabib, Seyla. *The Reluctant Modernism of Hannah Arendt*. Thousand Oaks, Calif.: Sage, 1996.

———, ed. *Democracy and Difference: Contesting the Boundaries of the Political*. Princeton, N.J.: Princeton University Press, 1996.

Benjamin, Walter. *One-way Street, and Other Writings*. Translated by Edmund Jephcott and Kingsley Shorter. London: Verso, 1985.

———. "On Some Motifs in Baudelaire." In *Illuminations*. Edited and with an introduction by Hannah Arendt. Translated by Harry Zohn. New York: Schocken Books, 1968.

———. "The Work of Art in the Age of Mechanical Reproduction." In *Illuminations*. Edited and with an introduction by Hannah Arendt. Translated by Harry Zohn. New York: Schocken Books, 1968.

Black, Joel. *The Aesthetics of Murder: A Study in Romantic Literature and Contemporary Culture*. Baltimore: Johns Hopkins University Press, 1991.

Bourdieu, Pierre. *Outline of a Theory of Practice*. 1972. Translated by Richard Nice. Cambridge: Cambridge University Press, 1977.

———. *The Rules of Art: Genesis and Structure of the Literary Field*. Translated by Susan Emanuel. Stanford, Calif.: Stanford University Press, 1996.

Brantlinger, Patrick. "The Case against Trade Unions in Early Victorian Fiction." *Victorian Studies* 13 (1969): 37–52.

Breuilly, John. "Civil Society and the Public Sphere in Hamburg, Lyon and Manchester, 1815–1850." In Helmut Koopmann and Martina Lauster, eds., *Vormarzliteratur in europaische Perspektive*, vol. 1, 15–38. Bielefeld, Germany: Aisthesis, 1996.

Briggs, Asa. "Private and Social Themes in *Shirley*." *Brontë Society Transactions* (1959): 203–14.

———, ed. *Chartist Studies*. London: Macmillan, 1959.

Bristow, Joseph. *Effeminate England: Homoerotic Writing after 1885*. New York: Columbia University Press, 1995.

Broch, Hermann. *Massenwahntheorie: Beitrage zu einer Psychologie der Politik*. Frankfurt: Suhrkamp, 1979.

Bromwich, David. "A Note on the Romantic Self." *Raritan* 14:4 (1995): 66–74.

———. "The French Revolution and 'Tintern Abbey.'" *Raritan* 10:3 (1991): 1–23.

Brontë, Anne. *The Tenant of Wildfell Hall*. 1848. Edited by Herbert Rosengarten. Oxford: Clarendon Press, 1991.

Brontë, Charlotte. *Jane Eyre*. 1847. New York: Knopf, 1991.

———. "The Moores." 1847 (first published 1906). In Tom Winnifrith, ed., *The Unfinished Novels*. Dover, N.H.: A. Sutton, 1993.

———. *Shirley*. 1849. Edited with an introduction by Andrew and Judith Hook. Harmondsworth, England: Penguin, 1974.

Brontë, Emily. *Wuthering Heights*. 1847. New York: Penguin, 1985.

Bronterre's National Reformer. London: J. Oldfield, 1837. Vol. 1, 1–11.

Brooks, Cleanth. *The Well Wrought Urn; Studies in the Structure of Poetry*. New York: Harcourt, Brace and World, 1947.

Brunton, Mary. *Discipline*. 1815. Introduced by Fay Weldon. London: Pandora Press, 1986.

———. *Self-Control: A Novel*. 1810. London: Pandora Press, 1986.

Buford, Bill. *Among the Thugs*. London: Mandarin, 1992.

Burnett, Frances Hodgson. *A Little Princess: Being the Whole Story of Sara Crewe Now Told for the First Time*. New York: Charles Scribner's Sons, 1922.

Burney, Fanny. *Evelina*. 1788. London: Dent, 1958.

Burton, Richard. *Personal Narrative of a Pilgrimage to al-Madinah & Meccah*. Edited by Isabel Burton. 1855. London: Darf Publishers, 1986.

Burwick, Frederick. *Poetic Madness and the Romantic Imagination*. University Park: Pennsylvania State Press, 1996.

Butler, Marilyn. *Maria Edgeworth: A Literary Biography*. Oxford: Clarendon Press, 1972.

Cafarelli, Annette Wheeler. *Prose in the Age of Poets: Romanticism and Biographical Narrative from Johnson to De Quincey*. Philadelphia: University of Pennsylvania Press, 1990.

Calhoun, Craig, ed. *Habermas and the Public Sphere*. Cambridge, Mass.: M.I.T. Press, 1992.

Canetti, Elias. *Crowds and Power*. Translated by Carol Stewart. New York: Continuum, 1973.

Carlyle, Thomas. *Chartism*. 1839. In Alan Shelston, ed., *Selected Writings*, 149–233. London: Penguin, 1971.

———. *New Letters of Thomas Carlyle*. Vol. 1. Edited by Alexander Carlyle. London and New York: John Lane, 1904.

———. *On Heroes, Hero Worship and the Heroic in History*. 1841. Edited by Carl Anthony Niemeyer. Lincoln: University of Nebraska Press, 1966.

Cassirer, Ernst. *The Myth of the State*. New Haven: Yale University Press, 1946.

Castle, Terry. "Phantasmagoria: Spectral Technology and the Metaphors of Modern Reverie." *Critical Inquiry* 15 (1988): 26–61.

Castro, John Paul de. *The Gordon Riots*. London: Oxford University Press, 1926.

Chandler, James. *England in 1819: The Politics of Literary Culture and the Case of Romantic Historicism*. Chicago: University of Chicago Press, 1998.

———. *Wordsworth's Second Nature: A Study of the Poetry and the Politics*. Chicago: University of Chicago Press, 1984.

Chesney, Kellow. *The Anti-Society: An Account of the Victorian Underworld*. Boston: Gambit, 1970.

Clark, J. C. D. *English Society, 1688–1832: Ideology, Social Structure, and Political Practice during the Ancien Régime*. Cambridge: Cambridge University Press, 1985.

Clej, Alina. *A Genealogy of the Modern Self: Thomas De Quincey and the Intoxication of Writing*. Stanford, Calif.: Stanford University Press, 1995.

Coates, John. "Aspects of De Quincey's 'High Tory' Prose in Theory and Practice." In Bruce Woodcock and John Coates, eds., *Combative Styles: Romantic Writing and Ideology: Two Contrasting Intepretations*. Hull, England: University of Hull Press, 1995, 118–47.

Cobbet, William. *Rural Rides*. London: J. M. Dent & Sons, 1924–25.

Colley, Linda. *Britons: Forging the Nation, 1707–1837*. New Haven: Yale University Press, 1992.

Collins, Christopher. "The Figure of the Crowd in Late Nineteenth-Century America and Its Appearance in Stephen Crane's Writings and Pulitzer's 'New York World.'" Ph.D. dissertation, New York University, 1992.

Cooke, Michael G. "De Quincey, Coleridge, and the Formal Uses of Intoxication." *Yale French Studies* 50 (1974): 26–40.

Cott, Nancy. "Passionless." *Signs* 4 (1979): 219–36.

Crary, Jonathan. *Techniques of the Observer: on Vision and Modernity in the Nineteenth Century*. Cambridge, Mass.: M.I.T. Press, 1990.

Cumming, Mark. *A Disimprisoned Epic: Form and Vision in Carlyle's French Revolution*. Philadelphia: University of Pennsylvania Press, 1988.

Davidoff, Leonore, and Catherine Hall. *Family Fortunes: Men and Women of the English Middle Class, 1780–1850*. London: Hutchinson, 1987.

Davis, Natalie Zemon. "Religion and Capitalism Once Again? Jewish Merchant Culture in the Seventeenth Century." *Representations* 59 (1997): 56–84.

De Quincey, Thomas. *The Collected Writings of Thomas de Quincey*. Edited by David Masson. 14 vols. Edinburgh: A. and C. Black, 1889–90.

———. *Confessions of an English Opium-Eater and Other Writings*. Edited with an Introduction by Grevel Lindop. Oxford: Oxford University Press, 1985.

———. "The Nation of London." 1828. In *The Collected Writings of Thomas De Quincey*, vol. 1, 178–210. Edited by David Masson. Edinburgh: A. and C. Black, 1889–90.

———. "On Murder Considered as One of the Fine Arts." *Blackwood's Magazine*, February 1827. In *The Collected Writings of Thomas De Quincey*, vol. 13, 9–124. Edited by David Masson. Edinburgh: A. and C. Black, 1889–90.

Dellamora, Richard. *Masculine Desire: The Sexual Politics of Victorian Aestheticism*. Chapel Hill: University of North Carolina Press, 1990.

Desaulniers, Mary. *Carlyle and the Economics of Terror: A Study of Revisionary Gothicism in* The French Revolution. Montreal: McGill-Queens' University Press, 1995.

Dickens, Charles. *Barnaby Rudge*. 1841. New York, Penguin, 1985.

———. *Bleak House*. 1852. London and New York: Penguin, 1996.

———. *Dombey and Son*. 1844–46. London: Penguin, 1984.

———. *Great Expectations*. 1860–61. London: Penguin, 1996.

———. *Hard Times*. 1854. London: Oxford University Press, 1989.

———. *Our Mutual Friend*. 1864–66. London: Penguin, 1971.

———. *A Tale of Two Cities*. 1859. Edited with an introduction by George Woodcock. Harmondsworth, England: Penguin, 1970.

Dietz, Mary. "Feminist Receptions of Hannah Arendt." In Bonnie Honig, ed., *Feminist Interpretations of Hannah Arendt*. University Park: Pennsylvania State University Press, 1995.

Dolin, Tim. "Fictional Territory and a Woman's Place: Regional and Sexual Difference in *Shirley*." *ELH* 62:1 (1995): 197–215.

Donoghue, Denis. *The Old Moderns: Essays on Literature and Theory*. New York: Knopf, 1994.

Dostoyevsky, Fyodor. *The Double: Two Versions*. 1846. Translated by Evelyn Harden. Ann Arbor, Mich.: Ardis, 1985.

Duncan, Ian. "Edinburgh, Capital of the Nineteenth Century." In James Chandler and Kevin Gilmartin, eds., *Romantic Metropolis: Cultural Production of the City, 1770–1850*. Forthcoming.

———. *Modern Romance and the Transformations of the Novel: The Gothic, Scott, and Dickens*. Cambridge: Cambridge University Press, 1992.

Dyos, Harold J. *Victorian Suburb; a Study of the Growth of Camberwell*. With a foreword by Sir John Summerson. Leicester, England: University Press, 1973.

Dyos, Harold J., and Michael Wolff, eds. *The Victorian City; Images and Realities*. London: Routledge & Kegan Paul, 1973.

Eagleton, Terry. *Myths of Power: A Marxist Study of the Brontës*. New York: Barnes and Noble, 1975.

Edgeworth, Frances Anne. *A Memoir of Maria Edgeworth*. 3 vols. London: Privately printed, 1867.

Edgeworth, Maria. *The Absentee*. 1812. In *Castle Rackrent and the Absentee*. London: Dutton, 1934.

———. *Harrington*. In *Harrington and Ormond*. 3 vols. London: R. Hunter, 1817.

———. *Letters for Literary Ladies*. 1795. London: Dent, 1993.

———. *Tales and Novels by Maria Edgeworth in Ten Volumes*. Vol. 9: *Harrington, Thoughts on Bores, and Ormond*. London: Henry Bohn, 1874.

Eley, Geoff. "Nations, Publics and Political Cultures: Placing Habermas in the Nineteenth Century." In Craig Calhoun, ed., *Habermas and the Public Sphere*, 289–339. Cambridge, Mass.: M.I.T. Press, 1992.

Ellis, Kate Ferguson. *The Contested Castle: Gothic Novels and the Subversion of Domestic Ideology*. Urbana: University of Illinois Press, 1989.

Emerson, Ralph Waldo. "Experience." In *Essays: Second Series*. 1844. Reprinted in *Essays and Poems*. New York: Library of America, 1996.

Engels, Friedrich. *The Condition of the Working Class in England*. 1844. Translated by W. O. Henderson and W. H. Chaloner. Oxford: B. Blackwell, 1971.

England, A. B. "Wordsworth's Context for Bartholomew Fair: Intimations of Burke on the Force of Material Objects." *Studies in English Literature, 1500–1900* 30 (1990): 603–16.

Epstein, James. "National Chartist Leadership: Some Perspectives." In Owen Ashton, Robert Fyson, and Stephen Roberts, eds., *The Duty of Discontent: Essays for Dorothy Thompson*, 33–54. London: Mansell, 1995.

———. *Radical Expression: Political Language, Ritual, and Symbol in England, 1790–1850*. New York: Oxford University Press, 1994.

Epstein, James, and Dorothy Thompson, eds. *The Chartist Experience: Studies in Working-Class Radicalism and Culture, 1830–1860*. London: Macmillan, 1982.

Esch, Deborah. "'Things can't go on like this': A Beggar's Itinerary." In Mary Ann Caws, ed., *City Images: Perspectives from Literature, Philosophy, and Film*. New York: Gordon and Breach, 1991.

Esteve, Mary. *Of Being Numerous. Representations of Crowds and Anonymity in Late-Nineteenth- and Early-Twentieth-Century Urban America*. Ph.D. dissertation, University of Washington, 1995.

Falconbridge, Anna Maria. *Narrative of Two Voyages to the River Sierra Leone During the Years 1791–1793, performed by A. M. Falconbridge*. 1794. London: Cass, 1967.

Findlay, J. R. "Thomas De Quincey." In *Encyclopaedia Brittanica*. 9th ed. Edinburgh: Encyclopaedia Brittanica, 1894.

Finn, Margot C. *After Chartism: Class and Nation in English Radical Politics, 1848–1874*. New York: Cambridge University Press, 1993.

———. "Women, Consumption and Coverture in England, c. 1760–1860." *The Historical Journal* 39:3 (1996): 703–22.

Finnegan, Frances. *Poverty and Prostitution: A Study of Victorian Prostitutes in York*. Cambridge: Cambridge University Press, 1979.

Fisher, Carl H. "Crowds, Fictions, and Crowd Fictions." Ph.D. dissertation, University of California, Los Angeles, 1992.

Fishman, Robert. *Bourgeois Utopias: The Rise and Fall of Suburbia.* New York: Basic Books, 1987.

Franklin, Benjamin. *Autobiography and Other Writings.* Edited by L. Jesse Lemisch. New York: New American Library, 1961.

Fraser, Nancy. "Rethinking the Public Sphere: a Contribution to the Critique of Actually Existing Democracy." In Craig Calhoun, ed., *Habermas and the Public Sphere*, 109–42. Cambridge, Mass.: M.I.T. Press, 1992.

———. "What's Critical about Critical Theory? The Case of Habermas and Gender." In Seyla Benhabib and Drucilla Cornell, eds., *Feminism as Critique: Essays on the Politics of Gender in Late-Capitalist Societies*, 31–55. Minneapolis: University of Minnesota Press, 1987.

Freud, Sigmund. *Group Psychology and the Analysis of the Ego.* 1921. Translated and edited by James Strachey. New York: Norton, 1959.

Friedman, Geraldine. "The Letter and the Spirit of the Law: Wordsworth's Restagings of the French Revolution in 'Carrousel Square' and the First 'Spot of Time.'" *Texas Studies in Law and Literature* 34:4 (Winter 1992): 481–508.

Froude, James Anthony. *Thomas Carlyle: a History of his Life in London, 1834–1881.* New York: Scribner, 1884.

———. *Thomas Carlyle; a History of the First Forty Years of his Life, 1795–1835.* London: Longmans, Green, 1882.

Fyson, Robert. "Homage to John Richards." In Ashton et al., *The Duty of Discontent*, 71–96. London: Mansell, 1995.

Gallagher, Catherine. *The Industrial Reformation of English Fiction: Social Discourse and Narrative Form, 1832–1867.* Chicago: University of Chicago Press, 1985.

———. *Nobody's Story: The Vanishing Acts of Women Writers in the Marketplace, 1670–1820.* Berkeley: University of California Press, 1994.

Garnsey, Peter, and Richard Saller. *The Roman Empire: Economy, Society, and Culture.* London: Duckworth, 1987.

Gaskell, Elizabeth. *The Life of Charlotte Brontë.* 1857. New York: Everyman, 1958.

———. *North and South.* 1854–55. London: Penguin, 1970.

Gilbert, Sandra M., and Susan Gubar. *The Madwoman in the Attic: The Woman Writer and the Nineteenth-Century Literary Imagination.* New Haven: Yale University Press, 1984.

Gissing, George. *In the Year of Jubilee.* London: Lawrence and Bullen, 1894.

Goethe, J. W. *Italian Journey.* Translated by Robert R. Heitner. Introduction and notes by Thomas P. Saine. Edited by Thomas P. Saine and Jeffrey L. Sammons. New York: Suhrkamp, 1989.

Goffman, Erving. *Behavior in Public Places: Notes on the Social Organization of Gatherings.* New York: Free Press, 1963.

Gonda, Caroline. *Reading Daughters' Fictions, 1709–1834: From Delarivier Manley to Maria Edgeworth.* Cambridge: Cambridge University Press, 1996.

Goux, Jean-Joseph. *Symbolic Economies*. Translated by Jennifer Curtiss Gage. Ithaca: Cornell University Press, 1990.

Gray, Robert. "The Deconstructing of the English Working Class." *Social History* 11:3 (1986): 363–73.

Greene, Sally. "Apocalypse When? *Shirley*'s Vision and the Politics of Reading." *Studies in the Novel* 26:4 (Winter 1994): 350–71.

Guillory, John. "Bourdieu's Refusal." *MLQ* 58:4 (1997): 367–98.

Habermas, Jurgen. *The Philosophical Discourse of Modernity: Twelve Lectures*. 1985. Translated by Frederick G. Lawrence. Cambridge, Mass.: M.I.T. Press, 1987.

———. "The Public Sphere: An Encyclopedia Article." *New German Critique* 1:3 (1974): 49–55.

———. *The Structural Transformation of the Public Sphere: An Inquiry into a Category of Bourgeois Society*. 1962. Translated by Thomas Burger with Frederick Lawrence. Cambridge, Mass.: M.I.T. Press, 1989.

———. *The Theory of Communicative Action*. Translated by Thomas McCarthy. 2 vols. Boston: Beacon Press, 1984.

Hack, Daniel. "Inter-Nationalism: *Castle Rackrent* and Anglo-Irish Union." *Novel* 29:2 (1996): 145–64.

Hadley, Elaine. *Melodramatic Tactics: Theatricalized Dissent in the English Marketplace, 1800–1885*. Stanford, Calif.: Stanford University Press, 1995.

———. "A Spectacle of Cognition: The Secret Ballot and Mid-Victorian Politics." Unpublished manuscript, 1997.

Haggard, H. Rider. *King Solomon's Mines*. 1885. London: Cassell and Company, 1961.

Hall, Catherine. *White, Male, and Middle Class: Explorations in Feminism and History*. Cambridge, England: Polity Press, 1992.

Hansard's Parliamentary Debates. Third series. London: T. C. Hansard, 1831–1891.

Hanway, Jonas. *The Citizen's Monitor, Showing the Necessity of a Salutary Police*. London, 1780.

Harden, O. Elizabeth McWhorter. *Maria Edgeworth's Art of Prose Fiction*. The Hague: Mouton, 1971.

Hardy, Thomas. *Far from the Madding Crowd*. 1874. Introduction by John Bayley. Notes by Christine Winfield. London: Macmillan, 1974.

———. *Jude the Obscure*. 1895. Edited and with an introduction by Dennis Taylor. London: Penguin, 1998.

Harman, Barbara Leah. "In Promiscuous Company: Female Public Appearance in Elizabeth Gaskell's *North and South*." *Victorian Studies* 31: 3 (1988): 351–74.

Harrison, Mark. *Crowds and History: Mass Phenomena in English Towns, 1790–1835*. Cambridge: Cambridge University Press, 1988.

———. "The Ordering of the Urban Environment: Time, Work, and the Occurrence of Crowds, 1790–1835." *Past and Present* 110 (1986): 134–68.

Hartman, Geoffrey H. *Wordsworth's Poetry, 1787–1814*. New Haven: Yale University Press, 1964.

Harvey, David. *The Urban Experience*. Baltimore: Johns Hopkins University Press, 1989.

Haywood, Ian. *The Literature of Struggle: An Anthology of Chartist Fiction*. Aldershot, Hants, England: Scolar Press, 1995.

Hazlitt, William. "On Going a Journey." 1821. In *Selected Writings*. Edited by Ronald Blythe. Harmondsworth, England: Penguin, 1970.

Heffer, Simon. *Moral Desperado: A Life of Thomas Carlyle*. London: Weidenfeld and Nicolson, 1995.

Heine, Heinrich. *Rabbi of Bacherach: A Fragment*. 1825, 1840. Translated by E. B. Ashton. New York: Schocken Books, 1947.

Henkin, David M. *City Reading: Written Words and Public Spaces in Antebellum New York*. New York: Columbia University Press, 1998.

Herf, Jeffrey. *Reactionary Modernism: Technology, Culture, and Politics in Weimar and the Third Reich*. Cambridge: Cambridge University Press, 1984.

Hertz, Neil. *The End of the Line: Essays on Psychoanalysis and the Sublime*. New York: Columbia University Press, 1985.

Hibbert, Christopher. *King Mob: The Story of Lord George Gordon and the London Riots of 1780*. Cleveland: World Publishing Company, 1958.

Hirschman, Albert O. *The Rhetoric of Reaction: Perversity, Futility, Jeopardy*. Cambridge, Mass.: Belknap Press, 1991.

Hobsbawm, Eric. *The Age of Capital, 1848–1875*. New York: Scribner, 1975.

———. *The Age of Revolution: 1789–1848*. London: Weidenfeld and Nicholson, 1962.

———. *Industry and Empire: An Economic History of Britain since 1750*. London: Weidenfeld and Nicholson, 1968.

———. *Labouring Men; Studies in the History of Labour*. London: Weidenfeld and Nicholson, 1964.

Hobsbawm, Eric, and Terence O. Ranger, eds. *The Invention of Tradition*. Cambridge: Cambridge University Press, 1983.

Hodgson, John. "Tidings: Revolution in *The Prelude*." *Studies in Romanticism* 31 (1992): 45–70.

Hogg, James. *De Quincey and His Friends*. London: S. Low, 1895.

———. *The Private Memoirs and Confessions of a Justified Sinner, Written by Himself, with a Detail of Curious Facts and Other Evidence by the Editor*. 1824. Edited and with an introduction by John Carey. London: Oxford University Press, 1969.

Hoggart, Richard. *The Uses of Literacy*. Introduction by Andrew Goodwin; with a new postscript by John Corner. New Brunswick, N.J.: Transaction Publishers, 1992.

Holcroft, Thomas. *A Plain and Succinct Narrative of the Late Riots and Disturbances in the Cities of London and Westminster and Borough of Southwark with an account of the commitment of Lord George Gordon to the Tower, and anecdotes of his life, to which is prefixed an abstract of the act lately passed in favour of the Roman Catholics*. London: Fielding and Walker, 1780.

Holmes, Richard. *Footsteps: Adventures of a Romantic Biographer*. New York: Viking, 1985.

Honig, Bonnie, ed. *Feminist Interpretations of Hannah Arendt*. University Park: Pennsylvania State University Press, 1995.

Hovell, Mark. *The Chartist Movement*. Manchester: University Press, 1918.

Huish, Robert. *Memoirs of Her Late Royal Highness Charlotte Augusta*. London: T. Kelley, 1818.

Hunt, Lynn. *Politics, Culture, and Class in the French Revolution*. Berkeley: University of California Press, 1984.

Hunter, Ian. *Culture and Government: The Emergence of Literary Education*. Houndsmills, England: Macmillan Press, 1988.

Huysmans, J. K. *The Crowds at Lourdes*. 1906. Translated by W. H. Mitchell. London: Burns, Oates, and Washburne, 1927.

Jacobus, Mary. *Romanticism, Writing and Sexual Difference: Essays on* The Prelude. Oxford: Clarendon Press, 1989.

Jaffe, Audrey. "Detecting the Beggar: Arthur Conan Doyle, Henry Mayhew, and 'The Man with the Twisted Lip.'" In John Hodgson, ed., *Arthur Conan Doyle*. Boston: St. Martin's, 1994.

James, C. L. R. *The Black Jacobins: Toussaint L'Ouverture and the San Domingo Revolution*. London: Allison and Busby, 1980.

Jameson, Frederic. "On Negt and Kluge." In Bruce Robbins, ed., *The Phantom Public Sphere*, 42–74. Minneapolis: University of Minnesota Press, 1993.

Jevons, William Stanley. *Money and the Mechanisms of Exchange*. New York: D. Appleton, 1919.

Johnson, Paul. *A Shopkeeper's Millennium: Society and Revivals in Rochester, New York, 1815–1837*. New York: Hill and Wang, 1978.

Jones, Ernest. *De Brassier: A Democratic Romance*. Serialized in *Notes to the People* (1851–52). Excerpted in Ian Haywood, ed., *The Literature of Struggle: An Anthology of Chartist Fiction*. Aldershot, Hants, England: Scolar Press, 1995.

Jones, Gareth Stedman. *Languages of Class: Studies in English Working Class History, 1832–1982*. Cambridge: Cambridge University Press, 1983.

Joyce, Patrick. *Democratic Subjects: The Self and the Social in Nineteenth-Century England*. Cambridge: Cambridge University Press, 1994.

———. *Visions of the People: Industrial England and the Question of Class, 1848–1914*. Cambridge: Cambridge University Press, 1991.

Kaplan, Fred. *Sacred Tears: Sentimentality in Victorian Literature*. Princeton, N.J.: Princeton University Press, 1987.

———. *Thomas Carlyle: a Biography*. Ithaca, N.Y.: Cornell University Press, 1983.

Keegan, John. *The Face of Battle*. New York: Viking, 1976.

Keen, Suzanne. "Narrative Annexes in Charlotte Brontë's *Shirley*." *Journal of Narrative Technique* 20:2 (Spring 1990): 107–19.

———. "Passionate Reserve and Reserved Passion in the Works of Charlotte Brontë." *ELH* 52:4 (Winter 1985): 913–37.

Kelly, Michael, ed. *Critique and Power: Recasting the Foucault/Habermas Debate*. Cambridge, Mass.: M.I.T. Press, 1994.

Kemnitz, Thomas Milton. "Approaches to the Chartist Movement: Feargus O'Connor and Chartist Strategy." *Albion* 5 (1973): 66–73.

Kittler, Friedrich A. *Discourse Networks 1800/1900.* Translated by Michael Metteer with Chris Cullens. Foreword by David E. Wellbery. Stanford, Calif.: Stanford University Press, 1990.

Klancher, Jon P. *The Making of English Reading Audiences, 1790–1832.* Madison: University of Wisconsin Press, 1987.

Kleist, Heinrich. *Abyss Deep Enough.* Translated by Philip B. Miller. New York: E. P. Dutton, 1982.

Kowaleski-Wallace, Elizabeth. *Their Fathers' Daughters: Hannah More, Maria Edgeworth, and Patriarchal Complicity.* New York: Oxford University Press, 1991.

Kucich, John. *The Power of Lies: Transgression in Victorian Fiction.* Ithaca, N.Y.: Cornell University Press, 1994.

Lamb, Charles. *The Complete Works and Letters of Charles Lamb.* New York: Random House, 1935.

Lamb, John. "Carlyle's 'Chartism,' the Rhetoric of Revolution and the Dream of Empire." *Victorians Institute Journal* 23 (1995): 129–50.

Laqueur, Thomas. "Bodies, Details, and the Humanitarian Narrative." In Lynn Avery Hunt, ed., *The New Cultural History,* 176–204. Berkeley: University of California Press, 1989.

Lazarus, Rachel Mordecai. *Education of the Heart: the Correspondence of Rachel Mordecai Lazarus and Maria Edgeworth.* Edited by Edgar E. MacDonald. Chapel Hill: University of North Carolina Press, 1977.

Le Bon, Gustave. *The Crowd* [*Psychologie des Foules*]. 1895. Introduction by Robert A. Nye. New Brunswick, N.J.: Transaction Publishers, 1995.

Leask, Nigel. *British Romantic Writers and the East: Anxieties of Empire.* Cambridge: Cambridge University Press, 1992.

Lee, Yoon Sun. "Carlyle's Fetishism." *Victorian Literature and Culture,* forthcoming.

———. "Stoicism in Smith and Burke." Unpublished paper, 1998.

Leeds Intelligencer. Leeds, England: Edward and Frederick Barnes, 1807–1901.

Leeds Mercury. Leeds, England: John Hernaman and Robert Perring, 1800–1866.

Lefebvre, Georges. "Foules Revolutionaires" [Revolutionary Crowds]. In *La Grande Peur de 1789; suivi de, Les Foules Revolutionnaires.* Paris: A. Colin, 1988.

———. *The Great Fear of 1789: Rural Panic in Revolutionary France.* Translated by Joan White. New York: Vintage Books, 1973.

Levin, Susan M. *The Romantic Art of Confession: De Quincey, Musset, Sand, Lamb, Hogg, Frémy, Soulié, Janin.* Columbia, S.C.: Camden House, 1998.

Levine, George. *The Boundaries of Fiction: Carlyle, Macaulay, Newman.* Princeton, N.J.: Princeton University Press, 1968.

Lindop, Grevel. *The Opium-Eater: A Life of Thomas De Quincey.* London: Dent, 1981.

Liu, Alan. *Wordsworth: The Sense of History*. Stanford, Calif.: Stanford University Press, 1989.

Logan, Peter. *Nerves and Narratives. A Cultural History of Hysteria in Nineteenth-Century British Prose*. University of California: Berkeley, 1997.

Lukacs, Georg. *The Historical Novel*. Translated by Hannah and Stanley Mitchell. Penguin: London, 1962.

MacFarland, Thomas. *Romantic Cruxes*. Oxford: Clarendon Press, 1987.

MacKay, Charles. *Extraordinary Popular Delusions and the Madness of Crowds*. 1841 and 1852. Foreword by Bernard M. Baruch. Boston: L. C. Page, 1932.

Maier, Pauline. *From Resistance to Revolution; Colonial Radicals and the Development of American Opposition to Britain, 1765–1776*. New York: Knopf, 1972.

Marcus, Sharon. *Apartment Stories: City and Home in Nineteenth-Century Paris and London*. Berkeley: University of California Press, 1999.

———. "The Profession of the Author: Abstraction, Advertising and *Jane Eyre*." *PMLA* 110:2 (1995): 206–19.

Marcus, Steven. *Engels, Manchester, and the Working Class*. New York: Random House, 1974.

Marshall, David. *The Surprising Effects of Sympathy: Marivaux, Diderot, Rousseau, and Mary Shelley*. Chicago: University of Chicago Press, 1988.

Martineau, Harriet. *The Rioters*. Wellington, Salop, England: Houlston and Son, 1827.

Maslan, Susan. "Recreating Representation: Theater and Democracy in Revolutionary France." *Representations* 52 (Fall 1995): 27–51.

Maxwell, Richard. *The Mysteries of Paris and London*. Charlottesville: University Press of Virginia, 1992.

McCalman, Iain. *Radical Underworld: Prophets, Revolutionaries and Pornographers in London, 1795–1840*. Cambridge: Cambridge University Press, 1988.

McClelland, J. S. *The Crowd and the Mob: from Plato to Canetti*. London: Unwin Hyman, 1989.

McDonagh, Josephine. *De Quincey's Disciplines*. Oxford: Clarendon Press, 1994.

McLaughlin, Kevin. "The Financial Imp: Ethics and Finance in Nineteenth-Century Fiction." *Novel* 29:2 (Winter 1996): 165–83.

McPhail, Clark. *The Myth of the Madding Crowd*. New York: A. de Gruyter, 1991.

Michaels, Walter Benn. *The Gold Standard and the Logic of Naturalism: American Literature at the Turn of the Century*. Berkeley: University of California Press, 1987.

Michals, Teresa. "Commerce and Character in Maria Edgeworth." *Nineteenth Century Literature* 49:1 (1994): 1–20.

Mill, John Stuart. *Considerations on Representative Government*. 1861. South Bend, Ind.: Gateway, 1982.

Miller, David A. *The Novel and the Police*. Berkeley: University of California Press, 1988.

Miller, J. Hillis. *The Disappearance of God: Five Nineteenth-Century Writers.* Cambridge, Mass.: Belknap Press, 1963.

Mills, Nicolaus. *The Crowd in American Literature.* Baton Rouge: Louisiana State University Press, 1986.

Mitchell, Brian R., ed. *International Historical Statistics: Europe 1750–1988.* New York: Stockton Press, 1992.

More, Hannah. *Coelebs in Search of a Wife: Comprehending Observations on Domestic Habits and Manner, Religion and Morals.* 1805. Bristol, England: Thoemmes Press, 1995.

Moretti, Franco. *Signs Taken for Wonders: Essays in the Sociology of Literary Forms.* Translated by Susan Fischer, David Forgacs, and David Miller. London: Verso Editions, 1983.

Moritz, Carl Philip. *Journeys of a German in England in 1782.* 1783. Translated and edited by Reginald Nettel. London: Cape, 1965.

Morrison, Arthur. *A Child of the Jago.* Chicago: H. S. Stone & Co., 1896.

———. *Tales of Mean Streets.* Leipzig: B. Tauchnitz, 1895.

Moscovici, Serge. *The Age of the Crowd: A Historical Treatise on Mass Psychology.* Translated by J. C. Whitehouse. Cambridge: Cambridge University Press, 1985.

Mussolini, Benito. *The Doctrine of Fascism.* 1933. Translated by E. Cope. Firenze, Italy: Vallecchi, 1938.

Myers, Mitzi. "The Dilemmas of Gender as Double-Voiced Narrative." In Robert W. Uphaus, ed., *The Idea of the Novel in the Eighteenth Century.* East Lansing, Mich.: Colleagues Press, 1988.

Needham, Lawrence. "De Quincey's Rhetoric of Display and *Confessions of an English Opium-Eater.*" In Don H. Bialostosky and Lawrence D. Needham, eds., *Rhetorical Traditions and British Romantic Literature,* 48–64. Bloomington: Indiana University Press, 1995.

Negt, Oskar, and Alexander Kluge. *Public Sphere and Experience: Toward an Analysis of the Bourgeois and Proletarian Public Sphere.* Translated by Peter Labanyi et al. Foreword by Miriam Hansen. Minneapolis: University of Minnesota Press, 1993.

Nield, Keith., ed. *Prostitution in the Victorian Age: Debates on the Issue from 19th Century Critical Journals.* Farnborough, England: Gregg, 1973.

Nord, Deborah Epstein. *Walking the Victorian Streets: Women, Representation, and the City.* Ithaca, N.Y.: Cornell University Press, 1995.

North, Julian. *De Quincey Reviewed: Thomas De Quincey's Critical Reception, 1821–1994.* Columbia, S.C.: Camden House, 1997.

The Northern Star, and Leeds General Advertiser. Leeds, England: J. Hobson for F. O'Conner, 1837–1844, vols. 1–8.

The Northern Star, and National Trades Journal. London: W. Hewitt for F. O'Conner, 1844–1852, vols. 8–15.

Nussbaum, Martha C. *Poetic Justice: The Literary Imagination and Public Life.* Boston: Beacon Press, 1995.

Nye, Robert A. *The Origins of Crowd Psychology: Gustave Le Bon and the Crisis of Mass Democracy in the Third Republic.* London: Sage Publications, 1975.

O'Farrell, Mary Ann. "Austen's Blush." *Novel* 27:2 (Winter 1994): 125–39.
———. *Telling Complexions: The Nineteenth-Century English Novel and the Blush*. Durham, N.C.: Duke University Press, 1997.
Okri, Ben. *The Joys of Storytelling*. London: Penguin, 1995.
Olsen, Donald J. *The City as a Work of Art: London, Paris, Vienna*. New Haven: Yale University Press, 1986.
Ozouf, Mona. *Festivals and the French Revolution*. 1976. Translated by Alan Sheridan. Cambridge, Mass.: Harvard University Press, 1988.
Papy, Twila Yates. "A Near-Miss on the Psychological Novel: Maria Edgeworth's *Harrington*." In Mary Anne Schofield and Cecilia Macheski, eds., *Fetter'd or Free? British Women Novelists, 1670–1815*. Athens: Ohio University Press, 1986.
Park, Robert. *The Crowd and the Public and Other Essays*. 1904. Edited by Henry Elsner. Chicago: University of Chicago Press, 1972.
Pater, Walter. "Leonardo Da Vinci." 1869. In *The Renaissance: Studies in Art and Poetry*. 1873. Edited and with an introduction by Adam Phillips. Oxford: Oxford University Press, 1986.
Peel, Frank. *The Risings of the Luddites, Chartists, and Plug-Drawers*. [1888]. London: Frank Cass, 1968.
Pickering, Paul. "Class without Words: Symbolic Communication in the Chartist Movement." *Past and Present* 112 (1986): 144–63.
Pinch, Adela. *Strange Fits of Passion: Epistemologies of Emotion, Hume to Austen*. Stanford, Calif.: Stanford University Press, 1996.
Pitkin, Hanna. *The Attack of the Blob: Hannah Arendt's Concept of the Social*. Chicago: University of Chicago Press, 1998.
———. *The Concept of Representation*. Berkeley: University of California Press, 1967.
Plotz, John. "*Coriolanus* and the Failure of Performatives." *ELH* 63 (1996), 809–32.
Poovey, Mary. "Exploring Masculinities." *Victorian Studies* 36:2 (Winter 1993): 223–26.
Poovey, Mary. *Making a Social Body: British Cultural Formation, 1830–1864*. Chicago: University of Chicago Press, 1995.
———. *Uneven Developments: The Ideological Work of Gender in Mid-Victorian England*. Chicago: University of Chicago Press, 1988.
Porter, Jane. *Thaddeus of Warsaw*. 1805. Philadelphia: J. B. Lippincott and Co., 1882.
Porter, Roy. *London: A Social History*. Cambridge: Harvard University Press, 1995.
Prothero, Iorwerth. *Artisans and Politics in Early Nineteenth-Century London: John Gast and His Times*. Baton Rouge: Louisiana State University Press, 1979.
Punter, David. "1789: The Sex of Revolution." *Criticism* 24 (1982): 201–17.
Ragussis, Michael. *Figures of Conversion: "The Jewish Question" and English National Identity*. Durham, N.C.: Duke University Press, 1995.
Reinert, Thomas. *Regulating Confusion: Samuel Johnson and the Crowd*. Durham, N.C.: Duke University Press, 1996.

Reynolds, G. W. M. *Mysteries of London*. 1846. Edited and with an introduction by Trefor Thomas. Keele, Staffordshire, England: Keele University Press, 1996.

Richardson, Thomas C. "Carlyle's *Chartism* and the *Quarterly Review*." *The Carlyle Annual* 10 (1989): 50–55.

Rilke, Rainer M. *Notebook of Malte Laurids Brigge*. Translated by Stephen Mitchell. New York: Vintage, 1985.

Riot, The. 1913. Film.

Robbe-Grillet, Alain. *Jealousy, a Novel*. Translated by Richard Howard. London: Calder, 1959.

Robbins, Bruce. *The Servant's Hand: English Fiction from Below*. New York: Columbia University Press, 1986.

———, ed. *The Phantom Public Sphere*. Minneapolis: University of Minnesota Press, 1993.

Roberts, Stephen. "Who Wrote to the Northern Star?" In Ashton et al., *The Duty of Discontent*, 55–70. London: Mansell, 1995.

Rogal, Samuel. "The Methodist Connection in Charlotte Brontë's *Shirley*." *Victorians Institute Journal* 10 (1981–82): 1–13.

Rogers, Nicholas. *Crowds, Cultures, and Politics in Georgian Britain*. Oxford: Clarendon Press, 1998.

Rogin, Michael. "Blackface, White Noise: The Jewish Jazz Singer Finds his Voice." *Critical Inquiry* 18 (Spring 1992): 417–53.

Rosenberg, Philip. *The Seventh Hero; Thomas Carlyle and the Theory of Radical Activism*. Cambridge, Mass.: Harvard University Press, 1974.

Rubin, Gayle. "The Traffic In Women: Notes on the 'Political Economy' of Sex." In Rayna R. Reiter, ed., *Toward an Anthropology of Women*. New York: Monthly Review Press, 1975.

Rudé, George. *The Crowd in History; A Study of Popular Disturbances in France and England, 1730–1848*. New York: Wiley, 1964.

———. *The Crowd in the French Revolution*. Oxford: Clarendon Press, 1959.

———. *The Face of the Crowd: Studies in Revolution, Ideology and Popular Protest: Selected Essays of George Rudé*. Edited and introduced by Harvey J. Kaye. New York: Harvester/Wheatsheaf, 1988.

Rushdie, Salman. *Midnight's Children*. London: Jonathan Cape, 1981.

Russett, Margaret. *De Quincey's Romanticism: Canonical Minority and the Forms of Transmission*. Cambridge: Cambridge University Press, 1997.

Ryals, Claude de. "Carlyle's *The French Revolution*: A 'True Fiction.'" *ELH* 54:4 (1987): 925–39.

Ryan, Mary P. "The American Parade: Representations of Nineteenth-Century Social Order." In Lynn Avery Hunt, ed., *The New Cultural History*, 131–53. Berkeley: University of California Press, 1989.

———. *Civic Wars: Democracy and Public Life in America during the Nineteenth Century*. Berkeley: University of California Press, 1997.

Rzepka, Charles J. *Sacramental Commodities: Gift, Text, and the Sublime in De Quincey*. Amherst: University of Massachusetts Press, 1995.

Said, Edward. *Culture and Imperialism*. New York: Knopf, 1993.

Sale, Kirkpatrick. *Rebels against the Future: The Luddites and Their War on the Industrial Revolution: Lessons for the Computer Age.* Reading, Mass.: Addison-Wesley, 1995.

Scarry, Elaine. "On Vivacity: The Difference between Daydreaming and Imagining under Authorial Instruction." *Representations* 52 (Fall 1995): 1–26.

————. *Resisting Representation.* New York: Oxford University Press, 1994.

Schivelbusch, Wolfgang. *The Railway Journey: The Industrialization of Time and Space in the 19th Century.* Berkeley: University of California Press, 1986.

Schmitt, Carl. *The Crisis of Parliamentary Democracy.* Translated by Ellen Kennedy. Cambridge, Mass.: M.I.T. Press, 1985.

Schor, Hilary Margo. *Scheherezade in the Marketplace: Elizabeth Gaskell and the Victorian Novel.* New York: Oxford University Press, 1992.

Schor, Naomi. *Zola's Crowds.* Baltimore: Johns Hopkins University Press, 1978.

Scobey, David. "Anatomy of the Promenade." *Social History* 17:2 (1992): 203–27.

Scott, Joan. *Gender and the Politics of History.* New York: Columbia University Press, 1988.

Sedgwick, Eve Kosofsky. *The Coherence of Gothic Conventions.* New York: Methuen, 1976.

Sennet, Richard. *Flesh and Stone: The Body and the City in Western Civilization.* New York: Norton, 1994.

Shakespeare, William. *Coriolanus.* 1609. Edited by R. B. Parker. Oxford: Clarendon Press, 1994.

Shaw, Philip. "'Mimic Sights': A Note on Panorama and Other Indoor Displays in Book 7 of *The Prelude.*" *Notes and Queries* 40 (1993): 462–64.

Shell, Marc. *Money, Language, and Thought: Literary and Philosophical Economies from the Medieval to the Modern Era.* Berkeley: University of California Press, 1982.

Shuttleworth, Sally. *Charlotte Brontë and Victorian Psychology.* Cambridge: Cambridge University Press, 1996.

Sidis, Boris. *The Psychology of Suggestion: a Research into the Subconscious Nature of Man and Society.* Introduction by William James. New York: D. Appleton and Co, 1898.

Siegel, Jules Paul, comp. *Thomas Carlyle: The Critical Heritage.* London: Routledge and Kegan Paul, 1971.

Simmel, Georg. "The Metropolis and Mental Life." In Donald N. Levine, ed., *On Individuality and Social Forms: Selected Writings.* With an introduction by Donald N. Levine. Chicago: University of Chicago Press, 1971.

————. *The Philosophy of Money.* Translated by Tom Bottomore and David Frisby. London, New York: Routledge, 1990.

Simpson, David. *The Academic Postmodern and the Rule of Literature: A Report on Half-Knowledge.* Chicago: University of Chicago Press, 1995.

Smelser, Neil J. *Theory of Collective Behavior.* New York: Free Press, 1963.

Smith, Adam. *Theory of Moral Sentiments.* 1759. Indianapolis: Liberty Classics, 1982.

Smith, Susan Belasco. "'A Yorkshire Burr': Language in *Shirley*." *SEL 1500–1900* 27:4 (Autumn 1987): 637–45.

Somerville, Alexander. *Autobiography of a Working Man.* 1848. London: Turnstile Press, 1951.

Sorel, Georges. *Reflections on Violence.* 1906. Translated by T. E. Hulme. New York: Peter Smith, 1941.

Spivak, Gayatri. "Sex and History in *The Prelude* (1805): Books Nine to Thirteen." *Texas Studies in Language and Literature* 23:3 (Fall 1981): 324–60.

Steinberg, Marc. "'A Way of Struggle.'" *British Journal of Sociology* 48:3 (1997): 471–95.

Stelzig, Eugene. "'The Shield of Human Nature': Wordsworth's Reflections on the Revolution in France." *Nineteenth-Century Literature* 4:2 (1991): 97–106.

Stewart, Dugald. *Philosophy of the Human Mind.* In *Works*, vol. 3. Cambridge: Hilliard and Brown, 1829.

Stewart, Susan. *On Longing: Narratives of the Miniature, the Gigantic, the Souvenir, the Collection.* Baltimore: Johns Hopkins University Press, 1984.

Stoddard, E. W. "'All Freaks of Nature': The Human Grotesque in Wordsworth's City." *Philological Quarterly* 67:1 (Winter 1988): 37–61.

Strike at the Mines. Film. Edison Studios, 1910.

Sue, Eugene. *Mysteries of Paris.* 1843. New York: H. Fertig, 1987.

Swift, Jonathan. "Description of a City Shower." 1710. In Pat Rogers, ed., *Jonathan Swift: the Complete Poems.* New Haven: Yale University Press, 1983.

Taine, Hippolyte. *The French Revolution.* Translated by John Durand. New York: H. Holt and Company, 1878–85.

Tambiah, Stanley J. *Leveling Crowds: Ethnonationalist Conflicts and Collective Violence in South Asia.* Berkeley: University of California Press, 1996.

Tarde, Gabriel. *Laws of Imitation.* Translated by Elsie Clews Parsons. Gloucester, Mass.: P. Smith, 1962.

———. "The Public and the Crowd." 1901. In Terry N. Clark, ed., *On Communication and Social Influence; Selected Papers.* Chicago: University of Chicago Press, 1969.

Thackeray, William Makepeace. *Rebecca and Rowena. A romance upon romance, by Mr. M. A. Titmarsh.* London: Chapman and Hall, 1850.

Thompson, Dorothy. *The Chartists: Popular Politics in the Industrial Revolution.* New York: Pantheon, 1984.

Thompson, E. P. *The Making of the English Working Class.* London: V. Gollancz, 1963.

———. "The Moral Economy of the English Crowd in the Eighteenth Century" and "The Moral Economy Reviewed." In *Customs in Common.* New York: New Press, 1993.

Thomson, F. M. L., ed. *The Rise of Suburbia.* Leicester, England: Leicester University Press, 1982.

Thomson, James. *The City of Dreadful Night.* 1874. Edinburgh: Canongate, 1993.

Tilly, Charles. *Popular Contention in Great Britain, 1758–1834*. Cambridge, Mass.: Harvard University Press, 1995.

Tocqueville, Alexis de. *Democracy in America*. Edited by J. P. Meyer. Translated by George Lawrence. New York: Harper and Row, 1988.

Tratner, Michael. *Modernism and Mass Politics: Joyce, Woolf, Eliot, Yeats*. Stanford, Calif.: Stanford University Press, 1995.

Trela, D. J., and Rodger L. Tarr. *The Critical Response to Thomas Carlyle's Major Works*. Westport, Conn.: Greenwood Press, 1997.

Trevor-Roper, Hugh R. *The Last Days of Hitler*. 1947. New York: Collier Books, 1962.

Trilling, Lionel. *Sincerity and Authenticity*. Cambridge, Mass.: Harvard University Press, 1972.

Tristan, Flora. *The London Journal of Flora Tristan, 1842, or, The Aristocracy and the Working Class of England*. Translated by Jean Hawkes. London: Virago, 1982.

Trumpener, Katie. *Bardic Nationalism: The Romantic Novel and the British Empire*. Princeton, N.J.: Princeton University Press, 1997.

Twain, Mark. *Adventures of Huckleberry Finn*. Edited by Walter Blair and Victor Fischer. Berkeley: University of California Press, 1988.

Ulrich, John. "The Re-inscription of Labor in Carlyle's *Past and Present*." *Criticism* 37:3 (1995): 443–68.

Vanden Bossche, Chris. *Carlyle and the Search for Authority*. Columbus: Ohio State University Press, 1991.

Vernon, James. *Politics and the People: A Study in English Political Culture, c. 1815–1867*. Cambridge: Cambridge University Press, 1993.

Vicinus, Martha. "'To Live Free or Die': The Relationship between Strategy and Style in Chartist Speeches, 1838–1839." *Style* 10:4 (1976): 481–503.

Vickery, Amanda. "Golden Age to Separate Spheres? A Review of the Categories and Chronology of English Women's History." *The Historical Journal* 36:2 (1993): 383–414.

Virilio, Paul. *Speed and Politics: An Essay on Dromology*. Translated by Mark Polizzotti. New York: Columbia University Press, 1986.

Vrettos, Athena. *Somatic Fictions: Imagining Illness in Victorian Culture*. Stanford, Calif.: Stanford University Press, 1995.

Wahrman, Dror. *Imagining the Middle Class: The Political Representations of Class in Great Britain, c. 1780–1840*. Cambridge: Cambridge University Press, 1995.

Walkowitz, Judith. "Going Public: Shopping, Street Harrassment and Streetwalking in Late Victorian London." *Representations* 62 (Spring 1998): 1–30.

———. *Prostitution and Victorian Society: Women, Class, and the State*. Cambridge: Cambridge University Press, 1980.

Warner, Michael. "The Mass Public and the Mass Subject." In Craig Calhoun, ed., *Habermas and the Public Sphere*, 377–401. Cambridge, Mass.: M.I.T. Press, 1992.

Watson, Robert. *The Life of Lord George Gordon with a Philosophical Review of his Political Conduct*. London: H. D. Symonds, 1795.

Welsh, Alexander. *George Eliot and Blackmail*. Cambridge, Mass.: Harvard University Press, 1985.

Whale, John C. *Thomas De Quincey's Reluctant Autobiography*. London: Croon Helm, 1984.

White, Gilbert. *The Natural History and Antiquities of Selborne, 1813 edition: facsimile with an introduction by P. G. M. Foster*. London: Ray Society, 1993.

Williams, Raymond. *The Country and the City*. London: Chatto and Windus, 1973.

———. *Culture and Society: 1780–1950*. London: Chatto and Windus, 1958.

———. *Keywords: A Vocabulary of Culture and Society*. New York: Oxford University Press, 1976.

Wittgenstein, Ludwig. *Culture and Value*. Edited by G. H. von Wright with Heikki Nyman. Translated by Peter Winch. Chicago: University of Chicago Press, 1980.

Wordsworth, William. *The Collected Poetry of William Wordsworth*. Edited by A. Selincourt. Oxford: Clarendon, 1947.

———. *The Prelude*. 1805. In *The Prelude: 1799, 1805, 1850: Authoritative Texts, Context and Reception, Recent Critical Essays*. Edited by Jonathan Wordsworth, M. H. Abrams, and Stephen Gill. New York: Norton, 1979.

———. *The Prelude: A Parallel Text*. Edited by J. C. Maxwell. Harmondsworth, England: Penguin, 1971.

Wrigley, Edward Anthony, and R. S. Schofield. *The Population History of England, 1541–1871: A Reconstruction*. Cambridge, Mass.: Harvard University Press, 1981.

Yeats, William Butler. *The Poems*. Edited by Richard J. Finneran. New York: Macmillan, 1983.

Yeo, Eileen. "Some Practices and Problems of Chartist Democracy." In Epstein and Thompson, *The Chartist Experience*, 345–80. London: Macmillan, 1982.

Zelizer, Viviene. *The Social Meaning of Money*. New York: Basic Books, 1994.

Zola, Emile. *Germinal*. 1885. Translated by Leonard Tancock. New York: Penguin, 1978.

SUPPLEMENTAL BIBLIOGRAPHY

A selection of works consulted but not cited elsewhere.

PRIMARY SOURCES

(This section includes some relevant works from outside the period, but omits contemporary literary criticism, history, and crowd theory.)

Arnold, Matthew. *Culture and Anarchy*. 1868. London: Cambridge University Press, 1970.

Broch, Hermann. *The Spell*. 1935/1976. Translated by H. F. Brach de Rothermann. New York: Farrar, Straus and Giroux, 1987.

Burke, Edmund. *Further Reflections on the Revolution in France.* 1789–1796. Edited by Daniel E. Ritchie. Indianapolis: Liberty Fund, 1992.

———. *Reflections on the Revolution in France.* 1790. Garden City, N.J.: Anchor Press/Doubleday, 1973.

Canetti, Elias. *The Conscience of Words.* Translated by Joachim Neugroschel. New York: Seabury Press, 1979.

Chesnutt, Charles W. *The Marrow of Tradition.* 1901. Edited and with an introduction by Eric J. Sundquist. New York: Penguin, 1993.

Conrad, Joseph. *Lord Jim.* 1900. London: Penguin, 1965.

———. *The Nigger of the "Narcissus."* 1897. Edited by Robert Kimbrough. New York: Norton, 1974.

Cox, Marian. *Crowds and the Veiled Woman.* London: Funk and Wagnalls, 1910.

Crane, Stephen. "When Man Falls, a Crowd Gathers." *New York Press,* December 2, 1894.

DeLillo, Don. *Mao II.* New York: Viking, 1991.

Disraeli, Benjamin. *Sybil; or, The Two Nations.* 1845. London: Oxford University Press, 1968.

Eisenstein, Sergei (Director). *The Battleship Potemkin.* Film. 1925.

Eliot, George. *Felix Holt.* 1866. Harmondsworth, England: Penguin, 1972.

Emerson, Ralph Waldo, *Representative Men.* 1850. Edited by Pamela Schirmeister. New York: Marsilio, 1995.

Gance, Abel (Director). *Napoleon.* Film. 1927.

Gaskell, Elizabeth. *Mary Barton.* 1848. New York: Norton, 1958.

Hecker, J. F. C. *The Dancing Mania of the Middle Ages.* 1832. Translated by B. G. Babington. New York: B. Franklin, 1970.

Hitler, Adolf. *Mein Kampf.* 1924–26. Translated by Ralph Manheim. Boston: Houghton Mifflin, 1943.

Lang, Fritz (Director). *Metropolis.* Film. 1926.

Lawrence, D. H. *Women in Love.* 1920. Edited by David Farmer, Lindeth Vasey, and John Worthen. Cambridge: Cambridge University Press, 1987.

Lederer, Emil. *State of the Masses; The Threat of a Classless Society.* 1940. New York: H. Fertig, 1967.

Lewis, Matthew. *The Monk, A Romance.* 1796. New York: Oxford University Press, 1979.

McKay, Charles. *Voices from the Crowd: And Other Poems.* 2d ed. London: Orr, 1846.

Moravia, Alberto. *The Conformist.* 1951. Translated anonymously. New York: Ace Publishing, 1970.

Oretga y Gasset, José. *Revolt of the Masses.* 1930. Translated anonymously. New York: W. W. Norton and Co., 1932.

Poe, Edgar Allen. "The Man of the Crowd." In Arthur Hobson Quinn and Edward H. O'Neil, eds., *The Complete Poems and Stories of Edgar Allan Poe: with Selections from His Critical Writings.* New York: Knopf, 1958.

Riefenstahl, Leni (Director). *Triumph of the Will.* Film. 1934.

Scott, Walter. *Heart of Midlothian.* 1818. London: Dent, 1956.

Shakespeare, William. *Julius Caesar.* 1599.

Simmel, Georg. "Metropolis and Mental Life" and "Fashion." In Donald N. Levine, ed., *On Individuality and Social Forms; Selected Writings*. Chicago: University of Chicago Press, 1971.

Streiktag. Film. 1906.

Trotter, Wilfred. *Instincts of the Herd in Peace and War*. London: T. F. Unwin, 1917.

Zola, Emile. *Germinal*. 1885. Translated by Peter Collier. New York: Oxford University Press, 1993.

SECONDARY SOURCES

Bush, Gregory W. "Like 'A Drop of Water in the Stream of Life': Moving Images of Mass Man from Griffith to Vidor." *Journal of American Studies* 25:2 (August 1991): 213–34.

Carey, John. *The Intellectuals and the Masses: Pride and Prejudice among the Literary Intelligentsia, 1880–1939*. London: Faber and Faber, 1992.

Case, Alison. "Against Scott: The Antihistory of Dickens's *Barnaby Rudge*." *Clio* 19:2 (1990): 127–45.

Craig, David. "The Crowd in Dickens." In Robert Giddings, ed., *The Changing World of Charles Dickens*. Totowa, N.J.: Barnes and Noble, 1983.

Graumann, Carl F., and Serge Moscovici. *Changing Conceptions of Crowd Mind and Behavior*. New York: Springer-Verlag, 1986.

Kindleberger, Charles P. *Manias, Panics, and Crashes: A History of Financial Crises*. New York: Basic Books, 1978.

Kindleberger, Charles, and Jean Pierre Laffargue, eds. *Financial Crises, Theory, History, and Policy*. Cambridge: Cambridge University Press, 1982.

Marcus, Steven. "Sons and Fathers." In *Dickens, from Pickwick to Dombey*. London: Chatto and Windus, 1965.

Rogers, Nicholas. *Crowds, Culture and Politics*. New York: Oxford University Press, 1996.

———. *Whigs and Cities: Popular Politics in the Age of Walpole and Pitt*. New York: Oxford University Press, 1989.

Index

Compositor: Binghamton Valley Composition
Text: 10/13 Sabon
Display: Sabon
Printer and binder: Maple-Vail